ILTS 111 English Language Arts

Teacher Certification Exam

By: Sharon Wynne, M.S.

XAMonline, INC.
Boston

Copyright © 2013 XAMonline, Inc.
All rights reserved. No part of the material protected by this copyright notice may be reproduced or utilized in any form or by any means, electronic or mechanical, including photocopying, recording or by any information storage and retrievable system, without written permission from the copyright holder.

To obtain permission(s) to use the material from this work for any purpose including workshops or seminars, please submit a written request to:

XAMonline, Inc.
25 First Street, Suite 106
Cambridge, MA 02141
Toll Free 1-800-301-4647
Email: info@xamonline.com
Web www.xamonline.com
Fax: 1-617-583-5552

Library of Congress Cataloging-in-Publication Data

Wynne, Sharon A.
    English language Arts 111: Teacher Certification / Sharon A. Wynne. -2nd Ed.
    ISBN 978-1-58197-722-6
    1. English Language Arts 111.   2. Study Guides.   3. ILTS
    4. Teachers' Certification & Licensure.   5. Careers

Disclaimer:

The opinions expressed in this publication are the sole works of XAMonline and were created independently from the Pearson Corporation, National Education Association, Educational Testing Service, or any State Department of Education, National Evaluation Systems or other testing affiliates.

Between the time of publication and printing, state specific standards as well as testing formats and website information may change that is not included in part or in whole within this product. Sample test questions are developed by XAMonline and reflect similar content as on real tests; however, they are not former tests. XAMonline assembles content that aligns with state standards but makes no claims nor guarantees teacher candidates a passing score. Numerical scores are determined by testing companies such as NES or ETS and then are compared with individual state standards. A passing score varies from state to state.

Printed in the United States of America   œ-1

ILTS: English Language Arts 111
ISBN: 978-1-58197-9817

TEACHER CERTIFICATION STUDY GUIDE

If you have any questions about tests in the ILTS program, you may wish to consult the current version of the ILTS Registration Bulletin. You may obtain an ILTS Registration Bulletin from education departments at Illinois colleges and universities, regional offices of education, or National Evaluation Systems, Inc. (NES®), as listed below. The ILTS Registration Bulletin is also available on the Internet at www.il.nesinc.com. If after reviewing the registration bulletin you have further questions, please contact the offices listed below.

If you have questions about program policies or about which test(s) to take or at what point in your preparation program you should take the test(s), contact:
- your program advisor;
- your certification officer;
- a regional office of education; or
- the Illinois State Board of Education Web site: www.isbe.net/teachers.

If you have questions regarding test registration, administration procedures, or your receipt of registration, admission ticket, or score report, contact:
National Evaluation Systems, Inc.
P.O. Box 226
Amherst, MA 01004-9000
Telephone: (800) 239-8107 or (413) 256-2870, 8:00 A.M.–5:00 P.M. central time
Automated Information System available 24 hours daily
Phone for the Hearing Impaired: (413) 256-8032
Web site: www.il.nesinc.com

About the ILTS English Language Arts 111 Exam

The ILTS English Language Arts 111 exam is offered on all test dates, during both the morning and afternoon sessions.

The exam is criterion referenced, meaning that they grade the candidate's performance against an established standard rather than comparing it to other test-takers' performances.

The exam consists of 125 multiple-choice questions. It is scored on a scale from 100 to 300. Minimum passing score is 240. There is no penalty for guessing. Scores are based on number of questions answered correctly.

There are four domains covered:

- **Reading**
- **Writing and Research**
- **Speaking and Listening**
- **Literature**

TEACHER CERTIFICATION STUDY GUIDE

Table of Contents

DOMAIN I.   **READING**

COMPETENCY 1.0 UNDERSTAND THE NATURE, DEVELOPMENT, AND IMPORTANCE OF READING IN ALL CONTENT AREAS 1

Skill 1.1   Recognize that literacy is a lifelong activity that promotes personal fulfillment and successful functioning in society, including participation as a citizen 1

Skill 1.2   Recognize reading as a process of constructing meaning through the interaction of the reader's existing knowledge and experiences, the information suggested by the written language, and the context of the reading situation 2

Skill 1.3   Recognize language development, cognition, and learning as applied to reading development 3

Skill 1.4   Recognize the roles of motivation and interest in reading 9

Skill 1.5   Recognize the cultural, linguistic, and ethnic diversity and their relationships to reading development 10

Skill 1.6   Recognize the roles that various language components play in reading development, including knowing about the phonemic (sounds of language), morphemic (words and meaningful parts of language), semantic (meaning), syntactic (sentience structure), and pragmatic (how language works in a social context) components of language 11

Skill 1.7   Recognize the relationships of reading to writing, listening, and speaking and know strategies for integrating these through instruction 12

Skill 1.8   Recognize the strategies for using reading in all content areas 14

Skill 1.9   Recognize the home and school experiences that impact literacy development 16

COMPENTENCY 2.0 DEMONSTRATE KNOWLEDGE OF SELECTION AND USE OF VARIOUS MATERIALS TO PLAN READING INSTRUCTION APPROPRIATE TO STUDENTS' KNOWLEDGE AND ABILITIES 17

Skill 2.1   Demonstrate knowledge of a variety of both fiction and nonfiction materials that can be used for teaching reading 17

ENGLISH LANGUAGE ARTS

Skill 2.2 Demonstrate knowledge of how to create, organize, and use a classroom library 17

Skill 2.3 Demonstrate knowledge of strategies for analyzing and evaluating the quality and appropriateness of instructional materials in terms of readability, content, length, format, illustrations, and other pertinent factors 18

Skill 2.4 Demonstrate of strategies for selecting materials (including technological tools) based on students' interests, knowledge and experiences, cultural backgrounds, and developmental levels 19

Skill 2.5 Recognize the use of standardized and informal reading assessments (including ongoing observations) and understand the implications of cultural, linguistic, and ethnic differences for interpretation of assessments 19

Skill 2.6 Demonstrate knowledge of strategies for planning, organizing, and managing reading instruction to create a positive environment that encourages independent reading 21

Skill 2.7 Demonstrate knowledge of strategies for engaging parents in the educational process and for communicating with them about their children's reading progress 21

Skill 2.8 Recognize when a student's reading problems justify referral to appropriate special services 22

COMPETENCY 3.0 DEMONSTRATE KNOWLEDGE OF STRATEGIES FOR TEACHING AND ASSESSING STUDENT KNOWLEDGE OF WORD IDENTIFICATION AND VOCABULARY 24

Skill 3.1 Demonstrate knowledge of strategies for teaching English spelling and word patterns 24

Skill 3.2 Demonstrate knowledge of strategies for assessing students' reading abilities 26

Skill 3.3 Recognize the role of vocabulary in reading comprehension and learning from text in various areas 27

Skill 3.4 Demonstrate knowledge of strategies for teaching vocabulary effectively 27

Skill 3.5 Demonstrate knowledge of how to use technology to enhance and encourage vocabulary skills 29

TEACHER CERTIFICATION STUDY GUIDE

COMPETENCY 4.0 DEMONSTRATE KNOWLEDGE OF IDENTIFYING AND IMPLEMENTING APPROPRIATE STRATEGIES USING ORAL LANGUAGE TO HELP STUDENTS DEVELOP READING SKILLS 30

Skill 4.1 Recognize the implications of differences in students' dialects and language when reading... 30

Skill 4.2 Demonstrate knowledge that oral reading requires accuracy, speed, and expression and understand its role in reading development 30

Skill 4.3 Recognize similarities and differences in oral and written language learning and know how to effectively use oral language activities to teach reading 30

Skill 4.4 Recognize the relationship between oral and silent reading 30

Skill 4.5 Demonstrate knowledge of how to use predictable books, poetry, and songs as the basis for fluency development 31

Skill 4.6 Demonstrate knowledge of how to assess students' reading fluency 32

COMPETENCY 5.0 DEMONSTRATE KNOWLEDGE OF STRATEGIES FOR TEACHING AND ASSESSING STUDENT READING COMPREHENSION 34

Skill 5.1 Recognize the relationship between listening comprehension and reading comprehension 34

Skill 5.2 Demonstrate knowledge of how types of questions affect reading comprehension and how they can be used to promote comprehension and learning expected in different subject areas 35

Skill 5.3 Demonstrate knowledge of strategies for encouraging students to respond personally in a variety of formats to literary and informational materials 35

Skill 5.4 Demonstrate knowledge of strategies for previewing and preparing to read a text effectively 36

Skill 5.5 Demonstrate knowledge of strategies for monitoring comprehension and for correcting confusion and misunderstanding that arises during and after reading 36

Skill 5.6 Demonstrate knowledge of strategies for helping students identify organizational patterns common to information texts to improve understanding and recall of text 36

DOMAIN II. WRITING AND RESEARCH

COMPETENCY 6.0 RECOGNIZE AND UNDERSTAND VARIOUS RHETORICAL STRATEGIES WITHIN WRITING PROCESSES 38

Skill 6.1 Recognize that varying purposes and audiences call for different form, prewriting strategies, organizational strategies, styles, formats, rules of evidence, and composing processes 38

Skill 6.2 Demonstrate knowledge of writing processes for a variety of writing genres 39

Skill 6.3 Recognize write-to-discover strategies such as journaling, log writing, sixty-second writing, and free writing 45

Skill 6.4 Recognize a variety of prewriting strategies for generating and organizing ideas 46

Skill 6.5 Recognize how to write clear and effective prompts that challenge students to practice a variety of prewriting and writing strategies for different rhetorical situations 47

Skill 6.6 Recognize various response strategies for helping student revise texts for appropriateness in a variety of rhetorical situations 49

COMPETENCY 7.0 DEMONSTRATE KNOWLEDGE OF COMPOSITION, INCLUDING DRAFTING STRATEGIES NECESSARY FOR WRITING IN VARIOUS RHETORICAL SITUATIONS 50

Skill 7.1 Recognize the elements of composition in a variety of rhetorical situations 50

Skill 7.2 Recognize how to compose writing prompts that provide opportunities to practice drafting documents 51

Skill 7.3 Recognize that drafting is an important recursive component in the writing process 52

Skill 7.4 Demonstrate knowledge of the conventions of spelling, sentence construction, and usage 53

Skill 7.5 Demonstrate knowledge of how to use modifiers to expand ideas, transitions to produce an effective control of language and ideas, and effective paragraph organization 68

Skill 7.6 Recognize teacher/peer conference techniques that assist students with the drafting of documents 69

Skill 7.7 Demonstrate knowledge of strategies for using technology to facilitate recursive drafting of composition 70

COMPETENCY 8.0 DEMONSTRATE KNOWLEDGE OF STRATEGIES FOR REVISING, EDITING, AND PROOFREADING DOCUMENTS THAT ADDRESS VARIOUS RHETORICAL SITUATIONS AND KNOW HOW TO PREPARE VARIOUS DOCUMENTS FOR PUBLICATION 71

Skill 8.1 Recognize the importance and value of revising and editing as recursive components of the writing process 71

Skill 8.2 Recognize that English conventions, style, diction, voice, and rhetorical situation drive the revision component of the writing process 72

Skill 8.3 Demonstrate knowledge of revision strategies appropriate to a variety of writing genres and rhetorical situations and understand how to provide practice of revising and editing techniques 72

Skill 8.4 Recognize and demonstrate English conventions including usage, semantics, syntax, morphology, and phonology and the application of language structure and conventions in the critiquing and editing of written documents..72

Skill 8.5 Recognize the value of self-editing and peer response as strategies within the writing process...72

Skill 8.6 Recognize the importance and value of publishing as an integral component of the writing process and know specific formats required for publishing a variety of written documents of different rhetorical situations 73

Skill 8.7 Demonstrate knowledge of how to use technology to produce written documents suitable for submission or publication..................................74

COMPETENCY 9.0 DEMONSTRATE KNOWLEDGE OF STRATEGIES FOR LOCATING, ANALYZING, EVALUATING AND ORGANIZING INFORMATION FROM PRINT AND ELECTRONIC RESOURCES THAT EXPRESS VARIOUS PERSPECTIVES 75

Skill 9.1 Recognize methods of information acquisition from a variety of sources 75

Skill 9.2 Recognize criteria and methods for evaluating primary and secondary research sources 75

Skill 9.3 Recognize diversity issues within reference materials and distinguish among them to address diverse student needs 77

Skill 9.4 Recognize the power and potential of print and non-print media to facilitate understanding and critical analysis of contemporary culture 77

Skill 9.5 Recognize planning and organizational strategies in both print and electronic formats for a variety of research projects 78

COMPETENCY 10.0 DEMONSTRATE KNOWLEDGE OF HOW TO SYNTHESIZE AND APPLY ACQUIRED INFORMATION, CONCEPTS, AND IDEAS TO COMMUNICATE IN A VARIETY OF FORMATS FOR A VARIETY OF PURPOSES 80

Skill 10.1 Demonstrate knowledge of how to synthesize and logically sequence information from a variety of sources 80

Skill 10.2 Demonstrate knowledge of how to support and defend a thesis statement through effective communication of documented information 81

Skill 10.3 Recognize and evaluate the critical attributes of effective oral, visual, and written communication for a variety of purposes 82

Skill 10.4 Recognize proficiency expectations for a variety of technology skills 83

Skill 10.5 Recognize the ethical attributes of responsible research and reporting 84

Skill 10.6 Demonstrate knowledge of resources providing citation formats and understand the importance of ethical standards when preparing a research product within any concept, genre, or situation 85

DOMAIN III.   **SPEAKING AND LISTENING**

COMPETENCY 11.0 DEMONSTRATE KNOWLEDGE OF ORAL COMMUNICATION COMPONENTS AND STRATEGIES FOR CONSTRUCTING ORAL PRESENTATIONS 86

Skill 11.1 Identify the communication process as nonlinear, including communicators, verbal and nonverbal messages, feedback, and noise/interference 86

Skill 11.2 Demonstrate knowledge of purposes and functions of communication and oral presentations 87

Skill 11.3 Recognize criteria for selecting content and support for a given communication situation and know the various types and strengths of supporting materials 88

Skill 11.4 Recognize the importance of using and citing accurate and relevant material when communicating 88

Skill 11.5 Demonstrate knowledge of a variety of organizational formats appropriate for different speaking situations and understand the importance of adapting communication to the situation, setting, and context 88

Skill 11.6 Demonstrate knowledge of types of delivery and their uses and effects 89

Skill 11.7 Demonstrate knowledge of how to use electronic media for effective communication 89

Skill 11.8 Recognize strategies for analyzing and communicating with diverse audiences 91

Skill 11.9 Recognize that communication choices should be made with sensitivity to listeners' backgrounds 91

Skill 11.10 Recognize the difference between supportive and non-supportive audiences and appropriate strategies for addressing those audiences 92

Skill 11.11 Demonstrate knowledge of strategies for recognizing when a message is not understood and for making adjustments to presentations to clarify and promote understanding 93

Skill 11.12 Understand the differences among the purposes for speaking and appropriate strategies for each purpose 94

COMPETENCY 12.0 DEMONSTRATE KNOWLEDGE OF THE COMMUNICATION PROCESS COMPONENTS FOR EVALUATING ORAL MESSAGES 95

Skill 12.1 Recognize the responsibilities of listeners and the role of feedback in communication 95

Skill 12.2 Demonstrate knowledge of various types and purposes of listening and the skills unique to each type of purpose 96

Skill 12.3 Recognize the roles and responsibilities of the listener and know appropriate and effective listening responses across a variety of communication situations 97

Skill 12.4 Demonstrate knowledge of strategies for analyzing spoken messages (e.g., questions, perception checking, summarizing, paraphrasing) to understand and evaluate stated and implied meanings 97

Skill 12.5 Recognize criteria for evaluating the content, organization, and support of communication strategies and for evaluating oral messages on the basis of their purpose, quality, and appropriateness 98

Skill 12.6 Recognize the effects of physical and physiological conditions on listening 98

Skill 12.7 Demonstrate knowledge of listening barriers such as bias, close-mindedness, preconceived attitudes, indifference, and emotional involvement in communication situations 99

Skill 12.8 Demonstrate knowledge of the effects of listener appreciation 100

Skill 12.9 Demonstrate knowledge of questioning skills for interviewing and gathering firsthand information 100

COMPETENCY 13.0 UNDERSTAND THAT COMMUNICATION MAY INFLUENCE AND BE INFLUENCED BY PEOPLE AND THEIR RELATIONSHIPS WITH ONE ANOTHER AND BY COMMUNICATION ANXIETY AND UNDERSTAND THE IMPORTANCE AND ETHICAL RESPONSIBILITIES OF ADAPTING COMMUNICATION TO AUDIENCE NEEDS, THE SITUATION, AND THE SETTING 102

Skill 13.1 Recognize the influence of context on communication 102

Skill 13.2 Recognize and understand the individual and social factors that may lead to communication anxiety 102

Skill 13.3 Recognize strategies to help minimize and/or manage communication anxiety 103

Skill 13.4 Recognize strategies for appropriate and effective small group communication, including components and group variables 103

Skill 13.5 Demonstrate knowledge of problem-solving strategies that can be used in group situations 105

Skill 13.6 Demonstrate knowledge of the relationship between nonverbal and verbal communication and how vocal qualities and verbal and nonverbal cues can help clarify the meaning, organization, and goals of speaking 105

Skill 13.7 Recognizes the importance of freedom of speech and ethical communication in a democratic society 106

Skill 13.8 Recognize the ethical responsibility to challenge harmful stereotypical or prejudicial communication and to use inclusive language when addressing others 107

Skill 13.9 Demonstrate knowledge of the differences among oral, written, and electronic communication processes 107

Skill 13.10 Recognize the roles of interpersonal skills in maintaining relationships 109

Skill 13.11 Demonstrate knowledge of strategies for appropriately and effectively negotiating and solving problems in various situations and settings 110

DOMAIN IV.   LITERATURE

COMPETENCY 14.0 RECOGNIZE AND ANALYZE THE DISTINCTIVE FEATURES AND HISTORICAL DEVELOPMENT OF VARIOUS GENRES AND RECOGNIZE RECURRENT THEMES IN ALL GENRES 113

Skill 14.1 Identify and analyze the defining characteristics of a variety of literary forms and genres 113

Skill 14.2 Identify, compare, and contrast recurring themes across diverse literary works from a variety of societies, eras, cultures, traditions, and genres 114

Skill 14.3 Analyze the development of form, style, and point of view and their purpose in American, British, and world literature 115

Skill 14.4 Analyze the form, content, purpose, and major themes of American, British, and world literature in their historical perspectives 115

TEACHER CERTIFICATION STUDY GUIDE

COMPETENCY 15.0 RECOGNIZE AND ANALYZE LITERARY ELEMENTS AND TECHNIQUES AND HOW THEY CONVEY MEANING IN CLASSIC AND CONTEMPORARY LITERATURE FROM A VARIETY OF ERAS, CULTURES, TRADITIONS, GENRES, AND MEDIA 129

Skill 15.1 Identify and analyze literary elements and understand their influence on the effectiveness of a literary piece.................................. 129

Skill 15.2 Identify a variety of literary techniques and devices in classic and contemporary literature representing a variety of genres and media   130

Skill 15.3 Identify and analyze the ways in which an author uses language structure, literary form, point of view, word choice, style, and format to convey the author's viewpoint and to elicit an emotional response from the reader 135

COMPETENCY 16.0 UNDERSTAND GENERAL SKILLS, STRATEGIES, AND PURPOSES FOR READING LITERATURE AND KNOW HOW TO SELECT AND USE LITERARY MATERIALS APPROPRIATE TO THE AGE AND DEVELOPMENT LEVEL OF LEARNERS 137

Skill 16.1 Recognize the importance of using a wide variety of print and electronic materials throughout the curriculum, including high-quality children's and young adult literature and diverse expository materials appropriate to the age, developmental level, and interests of the learner.. 137

Skill 16.2 Recognize the value of reading aloud to learners using a variety of genres and the importance of providing time for reading of entire texts for authentic purposes 137

Skill 16.3 Recognize how making inferences; drawing conclusions making comparisons from personal, creative, and critical points of view and sharing responses with peers encourages learners to respond personally to literature.. 137

Skill 16.4 Recognize that learners have a variety of responses to literature 138

Skill 16.5 Recognize that literature can be a means of transmitting moral and cultural values within a community 141

Skill 16.6 Recognize how literary works can be related to people, perspectives, and personal experiences.. 142

ENGLISH LANGUAGE ARTS

Skill 16.7 Recognize how knowledge gained from literature can be used to understand contemporary historical, economic, social, and political issues and events 143

RESOURCES 145

SAMPLE TEST...151

ANSWER KEY..192

RIGOR TABLE 193

RATIONALES WITH SAMPLE QUESTIONS 194

TEACHER CERTIFICATION STUDY GUIDE

Great Study and Testing Tips!

What to study in order to prepare for the subject assessments is the focus of this study guide but equally important is *how* you study.

You can increase your chances of truly mastering the information by taking some simple, but effective steps.

Study Tips:

1. Some foods aid the learning process. Foods such as milk, nuts, seeds, rice, and oats help your study efforts by releasing natural memory enhancers called CCKs (*cholecystokinin*) composed of *tryptophan*, *choline*, and *phenylalanine*. All of these chemicals enhance the neurotransmitters associated with memory. Before studying, try a light, protein-rich meal of eggs, turkey, and fish. All of these foods release the memory enhancing chemicals. The better the connections, the more you comprehend.

Likewise, before you take a test, stick to a light snack of energy boosting and relaxing foods. A glass of milk, a piece of fruit, or some peanuts all release various memory-boosting chemicals and help you to relax and focus on the subject at hand.

2. Learn to take great notes. A by-product of our modern culture is that we have grown accustomed to getting our information in short doses (i.e. TV news sound bites or USA Today style newspaper articles.)

Consequently, we've subconsciously trained ourselves to assimilate information better in neat little packages. If your notes are scrawled all over the paper, it fragments the flow of the information. Strive for clarity. Newspapers use a standard format to achieve clarity. Your notes can be much clearer through use of proper formatting. A very effective format is called the *"Cornell Method."*

Take a sheet of loose-leaf lined notebook paper and draw a line all the way down the paper about 1-2" from the left-hand edge.

Draw another line across the width of the paper about 1-2" up from the bottom. Repeat this process on the reverse side of the page.

Look at the highly effective result. You have ample room for notes, a left hand margin for special emphasis items or inserting supplementary data from the textbook, a large area at the bottom for a brief summary, and a little rectangular space for just about anything you want.

ENGLISH LANGUAGE ARTS

3. Get the concept then the details. Too often we focus on the details and don't gather an understanding of the concept. However, if you simply memorize only dates, places, or names, you may well miss the whole point of the subject. A key way to understand things is to put them in your own words. If you are working from a textbook, automatically summarize each paragraph in your mind. If you are outlining text, don't simply copy the author's words.

Rephrase them in your own words. You remember your own thoughts and words much better than someone else's, and subconsciously tend to associate the important details to the core concepts.

4. Ask Why? Pull apart written material paragraph by paragraph and don't forget the captions under the illustrations.

Example: If the heading is "Stream Erosion," invert it to read, "Why do streams erode?" Then answer the questions.

If you train your mind to think in a series of questions and answers, not only will you learn more, but it also helps to lessen the test anxiety because you are used to answering questions.

5. Read for reinforcement and future needs. Even if you only have 10 minutes, put your notes or a book in your hand. Your mind is similar to a computer; you have to input data in order to have it processed. *By reading, you are creating the neural connections for future retrieval.* The more times you read something, the more you reinforce the learning of ideas.

Even if you don't fully understand something on the first pass, *your mind stores much of the material for later recall.*

6. Relax to learn so go into exile. Our bodies respond to an inner clock called biorhythms. Burning the midnight oil works well for some people, but not everyone.

If possible, set aside a particular place to study that is free of distractions. Turn off the television, cell phone, pager and exile your friends and family during your study period.

If you really are bothered by silence, try background music. Light classical music at a low volume has been shown to aid in concentration over other types.

Music that evokes pleasant emotions without lyrics is highly suggested. Try just about anything by Mozart. It relaxes you.

7. Use arrows not highlighters. At best, it's difficult to read a page full of yellow, pink, blue, and green streaks.

Try staring at a neon sign for a while and you'll soon see my point; the saturated color obscures the message.

A quick note, a brief dash of color, an underline, and an arrow pointing to a particular passage is much clearer than a horde of highlighted words.

8. Budget your study time. Although you shouldn't ignore any of the material, *allocate your available study time in the same ratio that topics may appear on the test.*

TEACHER CERTIFICATION STUDY GUIDE

Testing Tips:

1. Get smart, play dumb. Don't read anything into the question. Don't make an assumption that the test writer is looking for something else than what is asked. Stick to the question as written and don't read extra things into it.

2. Read the question and all the choices *twice* before answering the question. You may miss something by not carefully reading, and then re-reading both the question and the answers.

If you really don't have a clue as to the right answer, leave it blank on the first time through. Go on to the other questions, as they may provide a clue as to how to answer the skipped questions.

If later on, you still can't answer the skipped ones . . . ***Guess.***
The only penalty for guessing is that you *might* get it wrong. Only one thing is certain; if you don't put anything down, you will get it wrong!

3. Turn the question into a statement. Look at the way the questions are worded. The syntax of the question usually provides a clue. Does it seem more familiar as a statement rather than as a question? Does it sound strange?

By turning a question into a statement, you may be able to spot if an answer sounds right, and it may also trigger memories of material you have read.

4. Look for hidden clues. It's actually very difficult to compose multiple-foil (choice) questions without giving away part of the answer in the options presented.

In most multiple-choice questions you can often readily eliminate one or two of the potential answers. This leaves you with only two real possibilities and automatically your odds go to 50-50 for very little work.

5. Trust your instincts. For every fact that you have read, you subconsciously retain something of that knowledge. On questions that you aren't really certain about, go with your basic instincts. **Your first impression on how to answer a question is usually correct.**

6. Mark your answers directly on the test booklet. Don't bother trying to fill in the optical scan sheet on the first pass through the test.

Just be very careful when you transcribe your answers into the scan sheet.

7. Watch the clock! You have a set amount of time to answer the questions. Don't get bogged down trying to answer a single question at the expense of 10 questions you can more readily answer.

ENGLISH LANGUAGE ARTS

TEACHER CERTIFICATION STUDY GUIDE

DOMAIN I.   READING

COMPETENCY 1.0   UNDERSTAND THE NATURE, DEVELOPMENT, AND IMPORTANCE OF READING IN ALL CONTENT AREAS

Skill 1.1   Recognize that literacy is a lifelong activity that promotes personal fulfillment and successful functioning in society, including participation as a citizen.

Reading for enjoyment makes it possible to go to places in the world we will never be able to visit, or perhaps when we learn about the enchantments of a particular place, we will set a goal of going there someday. When *Under the Tuscan Sun* by Frances Mayes was published, it became a bestseller. It also increased tourism to Italy. Many of the readers of that book visited Italy for the first time in their lives.

In fiction, we can live through experiences that we will never encounter. We delve into feelings that are similar to our own or are so far removed from our own that we are filled with wonder and curiosity. In fact, we read because we're curious—curious to visit, experience, and know new and different things. The reader lives with a crowd of people and a vast landscape. Life is constantly being enriched by reading, and the mind is constantly being expanded. To read is to grow. Sometimes the experience of reading a particular book or story is so delicious that we go back and read it again and again, such as the works of Jane Austen. We keep track of what is truly happening in the world when we read current best-sellers because they not only reflect what everyone else is interested in right now, they can influence trends. We can know in-depth what television news cannot cram in by reading publications like *Time* and *Newsweek*.

How do we model this wonderful gift for our students? We can bring those interesting stories into our classrooms and share the excitement we feel when we discover them. We can relate things that make us laugh so students may see the humor and laugh with us. We can vary the established curriculum to include something we are reading that we want to share. The tendency of students nowadays is to receive all of their information from television or the Internet. It's important for the teacher to help students understand that television and the internet are not substitutes for reading. They should be an accessory, an extension, and a springboard for reading.

Another thing teachers can do to inspire students to become readers is to assign a book that you have never read before and read along with them, chapter by chapter. Run a contest and the winner gets to pick a book that you and they will read chapter by chapter. If you are excited about it and are experiencing satisfaction from the reading, that excitement will be contagious.

ENGLISH LANGUAGE ARTS

Be sure that the discussion sessions allow for students to relate what they are thinking and feeling about what they are reading. Lively discussions and the opportunity to express their own feelings will lead to more spontaneous reading.

You can also hand out a reading list of your favorite books and spend some time telling the students what you liked about each. Make sure the list is diverse. It's good to include nonfiction along with fiction. Don't forget that a good biography or autobiography may encourage students to read beyond thrillers and detective stories.

When the class is discussing the latest movie, whether formally as a part of the curriculum or informally and incidentally, if the movie is based on a book, this is a good opportunity to demonstrate how much more can be derived from the reading than from the watching. Or how the two combined make the experience more satisfying and worthwhile.

Share with your students the excitement you have for reading. Successful writers are usually good readers. The two go hand-in-hand.

Skill 1.2   Recognize reading as a process of constructing meaning through the interaction of the reader's existing knowledge and experiences, the information suggested by the written language, and the context of the reading situation.

Children who learn to read on schedule and who are avid readers have been seen to have superior vocabularies compared to other children their age. The reason for this is that in order to understand what they read, they often must determine the meaning for a word based on its context. Children who constantly turn to a dictionary for the meaning of a word they don't know will not have this advantage.

This is an important clue for providing students the kinds of exercises that help them develop their vocabularies. Learning vocabulary lists is useful, of course, but much less efficient than exercises in determining meaning on the basis of context. It requires an entirely different kind of thinking and learning. Poetry is also useful for developing vocabulary exercises for children, especially rhymed poetry, where the pronunciation of a term may be deduced by what the poet intended for it to rhyme with. In some poets of earlier periods, the teacher may need to intervene because some of the words that would have rhymed when the poem was written do not rhyme in today's English. Even so, this is a good opportunity to help children understand some of the important principles about their constantly changing language.

Another good exercise for developing vocabulary is the crossword puzzle. A child's ability to think in terms of analogy is a step upward toward mature language understanding and use.

The teacher may construct crossword puzzles using items from the class such as students' names or the terms from their literature or language lessons.

Skill 1.3 Recognize language development, cognition, and learning as applied to reading development.

Language, though an innate human ability, must be learned. Thus, the acquisition and use of language is subject to many influences on the learner. Linguists agree that language is first a vocal system of word symbols that enable a human to communicate his feelings, thoughts, and desires to other human beings. Language was instrumental in the development of all cultures and is influenced by the changes in these societies.

Historical influences

English is an Indo-European language that evolved through several periods. The origin of English dates to the settlement of the British Isles in the fifth and sixth centuries by Germanic tribes called the Angles, Saxons, and Jutes. The original Britons spoke a Celtic tongue while the Angles spoke a Germanic dialect. Modern English derives from the speech of the Anglo-Saxons who imposed not only their language but also their social customs and laws on their new land. From the fifth to the tenth century, Britain's language was the tongue we now refer to as Old English. During the next four centuries, the many French attempts at English conquest introduced many French words to English. However, the grammar and syntax of the language remained Germanic.

Middle English, most evident in the writings of Geoffrey Chaucer, dates loosely from 1066 to 1509. William Caxton brought the printing press to England in 1474 and increased literacy. Old English words required numerous inflections to indicate noun cases and plurals as well as verb conjugations. Middle English continued the use of many inflections and pronunciations that treated these inflections as separately pronounced syllables. English in 1300 would have been written "Olde Anglishe" with the *e*'s at the ends of the words pronounced as our short *a* vowel. Even adjectives had plural inflections: "long dai" became "longe daies" pronounced "long-a day-as." Spelling was phonetic, thus every vowel had multiple pronunciations, a fact that continues to affect the language.

Modern English dates from the introduction of The Great Vowels Shift because it created guidelines for spelling and pronunciation. Before the printing press, books were copied laboriously by hand; the language was subject to the individual interpretation of the scribes. Printers and subsequently lexicographers like Samuel Johnson and America's Noah Webster influenced the guidelines. As reading matter was mass produced, the reading public was forced to adopt the speech and writing habits developed by those who wrote and printed books. Despite many students' insistence to the contrary, Shakespeare's writings are in Modern English.

It is important to stress to students that language, like customs, morals, and other social factors, is constantly subject to change. Immigration, inventions, and cataclysmic events change language as much as any other facet of life affected by these changes. The domination of one race or nation over others can change a language significantly. Beginning with the colonization of the New World, English and Spanish became dominant languages in the Western hemisphere. American English today is somewhat different in pronunciation and sometimes vocabulary from British English. The British call a truck a "lorry;" baby carriages a "pram," short for "perambulator;" and an elevator a "lift." There are very few syntactical differences, and even the tonal qualities that were once so clearly different are converging.

Though Modern English is less complex than Middle English, having lost many unnecessary inflections, it is still considered difficult to learn because of its many exceptions to the rules. It has, however, become the world's dominant language by reason of the great political, military, and social power of England from the fifteenth to the nineteenth century and of America in the twentieth century.

Modern inventions - the telephone, phonograph, radio, television, and motion pictures - have especially affected English pronunciation. Regional dialects, once a hindrance to clear understanding, have fewer distinct characteristics. The speakers from different parts of the United States of America can be identified by their accents, but more and more as educators and media personalities stress uniform pronunciations and proper grammar, the differences are diminishing.

The English language has a more extensive vocabulary than any other language. Ours is a language of synonyms, words borrowed from other languages, and coined words - many of them introduced by the rapid expansion of technology.

It is important for students to understand that language is in constant flux. Emphasis should be placed on learning and using language for specific purposes and audiences. Negative criticism of a student's errors in word choice or sentence structures will inhibit creativity. Positive criticism that suggests ways to enhance communication skills will encourage exploration.

Geographical influences

Dialect differences are basically in pronunciation. Bostonians say "pahty" for "party" and Southerners blend words like "you all" into "y'all." Besides the dialect differences already mentioned, the biggest geographical factors in American English stem from minor word choice variances. Depending on the region where you live, when you order a carbonated, syrupy beverage most generically called a soft drink, you might ask for a "soda" in the South, or a "pop" in the Midwest. If you order a soda in New York, then you will get a scoop of ice cream in your soft drink, while in other areas you would have to ask for a "float."

Social influences

Social influences are mostly those imposed by family, peer groups, and mass media. The economic and educational levels of families determine the properness of language use. Exposure to adults who encourage and assist children to speak well enhances readiness for other areas of learning and contributes to a child's ability to communicate his needs. Historically, children learned language, speech patterns, and grammar from members of the extended family just as they learned the rules of conduct within their family unit and community. In modern times, the mother in a nuclear family became the dominant force in influencing the child's development. With increasing social changes, many children are not receiving the proper guidance in all areas of development, especially language.

Those who are fortunate to be in educational day care programs like Head Start or in certified preschools develop better language skills than those whose care is entrusted to untrained care providers. Once a child enters elementary school, he is also greatly influenced by peer language. This peer influence becomes significant in adolescence as the use of teen jargon gives teenagers a sense of identity within his chosen group(s) and independence from the influence of adults. In some lower socio-economic groups, children use Standard English in school and street language outside the school. Some children of immigrant families become bilingual by necessity if no English is spoken in the home.

Research has shown a strong correlation between socio-economic characteristics and all areas of intellectual development. Traditional paper measurement instruments rely on verbal ability to establish intelligence. Research findings and test scores reflect that children reared in nuclear families who provide cultural experiences and individual attention become more language proficient than those who are denied that security and stimulation.

Personal influences

The rate of physical development and identifiable language disabilities also influence language development. Nutritional deficiencies, poor eyesight, and conditions such as stuttering or dyslexia can inhibit a child's ability to master language. Unless diagnosed early they can hamper communication into adulthood. These conditions also stymie the development of self-confidence and, therefore, the willingness to learn or to overcome the handicap. Children should receive proper diagnosis and positive corrective instruction.

In adolescence, the child's choice of role models and his decision about his future determine the growth of identity. Rapid physical and emotional changes and the stress of coping with the pressure of sexual awareness make concentration on any educational pursuits difficult. The easier the transition from childhood to adulthood, the better the competence will be in all learning areas.

Middle school and junior high school teachers are confronted by a student body ranging from fifth graders who are still childish to eighth- or ninth-graders who, at least in their own minds, are young adults. Teachers must approach language instruction as a social development tool with more emphasis on vocabulary acquisition, reading improvement, and speaking/writing skills. High school teachers can deal with the more formalized instruction of grammar, usage, and literature for older adolescents whose social development allows them to pay more attention to studies that will improve their chances for a better adult life.

As a tool, language must have relevance to the student's real environment. Many high schools have developed practical English classes for business/ vocational students whose specific needs are determined by their desire to enter the workforce upon graduation. More emphasis is placed upon accuracy of mechanics and understanding verbal and written directions because these are skills desired by employers. Writing résumés, completing forms, reading policy and operations manuals, and generating reports are some of the desired skills. Emphasis is placed on higher level thinking skills, including inferential thinking and literary interpretation, in literature classes for college-bound students.

Learning approach

Early theories of language development were formulated from learning theory research. The assumption was that language development evolved from learning the rules of language structures and applying them through imitation and reinforcement. This approach also assumed that language, cognitive, and social developments were independent of each other. Thus, children were expected to learn language from patterning after adults who spoke and wrote Standard English. No allowance was made for communication through child jargon, idiomatic expressions, or grammatical and mechanical errors resulting from too strict adherence to the rules of inflection (*Childs* instead of *children*) or conjugation (*runned* instead of *ran*). No association was made between physical and operational development and language mastery.

Linguistic approach

Studies spearheaded by Noam Chomsky in the 1950s formulated the theory that language ability is innate and develops through natural human maturation as environmental stimuli trigger acquisition of syntactical structures appropriate to each exposure level. The assumption of a hierarchy of syntax downplayed the significance of semantics. Because of the complexity of syntax and the relative speed with which children acquire language, linguists attributed language development to biological rather than cognitive or social influences.

Cognitive approach

Researchers in the 1970s proposed that language knowledge derives from both syntactic and semantic structures. Drawing on the studies of Piaget and other cognitive learning theorists, supporters of the cognitive approach maintained that children acquire knowledge of linguistic structures after they have acquired the cognitive structures necessary to process language. For example, joining words for specific meaning necessitates sensory motor intelligence. The child must be able to coordinate movement and recognize objects before she can identify words to name the objects or word groups to describe the actions performed with those objects.

Adolescents must have developed the mental abilities for <u>organizing concepts as well as concrete operations</u>, <u>predicting outcomes</u>, and <u>theorizing</u> before they can assimilate and verbalize complex sentence structures, choose vocabulary for particular nuances of meaning, and examine semantic structures for tone and manipulative effect.

Sociocognitive approach

Other theorists in the 1970s proposed that language development results from sociolinguistic competence. Language, cognitive, and social knowledge are interactive elements of total human development. Emphasis on verbal communication as the medium for language expression resulted in the inclusion of speech activities in most language arts curricula.

Unlike previous approaches, the sociocognitive allowed that determining the appropriateness of language in given situations for specific listeners is as important as understanding semantic and syntactic structures. By engaging in conversation, children at all stages of development have opportunities to test their language skills, receive feedback, and make modifications. As a social activity, conversation is as structured by social order as grammar is structured by the rules of syntax. Conversation satisfies the learner's need to be heard and understood and to influence others. Thus, his choices of vocabulary, tone, and content are dictated by his ability to assess the language knowledge of his listeners. He is constantly applying his cognitive skills to using language in a social interaction. If the capacity to acquire language were inborn, without an environment in which to practice language, a child would not pass beyond grunts and gestures, as did primitive man.

Of course, the varying degrees of environmental stimuli to which children are exposed at all age levels creates a slower or faster development of language.

Some children are prepared to articulate concepts and recognize symbolism by the time they enter fifth grade because they have been exposed to challenging reading and conversations with well-spoken adults at home or in their social groups. Others are still trying to master the sight recognition skills and are not yet ready to combine words in complex patterns.

Concerns for the teacher

Because teachers must, by virtue of tradition and the dictates of the curriculum, teach grammar, usage, and writing as well as reading and eventually literature, the problem becomes when to teach what to whom. The profusion of approaches to teaching grammar alone is mind-boggling. In the universities, we learn about transformational grammar, stratification grammar, sectoral grammar, etc. But in practice, most teachers, supported by presentations in textbooks and by the methods they learned themselves, keep coming back to the same traditional prescriptive approach - read and imitate - or structural approach - learn the parts of speech, the parts of sentence, punctuation rules, sentence patterns. After enough of the terminology and rules are stored in the brain, then we learn to write and speak. For some educators, the best solution is the worst - don't teach grammar at all.

The same problems occur in teaching usage. How much can we demand students communicate in only Standard English? Different schools of thought suggest that a study of dialect and idiom and recognition of various jargons is a vital part of language development. Social pressures, especially on students in middle and junior high schools, to be accepted within their peer groups and to speak the non-standard language spoken outside the school make adolescents resistant to the corrective, remedial approach. In many communities where the immigrant populations are high, new words are entering English from other languages even as words and expressions that were common when we were children have become rare or obsolete.

Regardless of differences of opinion concerning language development, it is safe to say that a language arts teacher will be most effective using the styles and approaches with which she is most comfortable. And, if she subscribes to a student-centered approach, she may find that the students have a lot to teach her and each other. Moffett and Wagner in the Fourth Edition of *Student-centered Language Arts K-12* stress the three I's: individualization, interaction, and integration. Essentially, they are supporting the socio-cognitive approach to language development. By providing an opportunity for the student to select his own activities and resources, his instruction is individualized. By centering on and teaching each other, students are interactive. Finally, by allowing students to synthesize a variety of knowledge structures, they integrate them. The teacher's role becomes that of a facilitator.

Benefits of the socio-cognitive approach

This approach has tended to guide the whole language movement currently in fashion. Most basal readers utilize an integrated, cross-curricular approach to successful grammar, language, and usage. Reinforcement becomes an intradepartmental responsibility. Language incorporates diction and terminology across the curriculum. Standard usage is encouraged and supported by both the core classroom textbooks and current software for technology. Teachers need to acquaint themselves with the computer capabilities in their school district and at their individual school sites. Advances in new technologies require the teacher to familiarize herself with programs that would serve her students' needs. Students respond enthusiastically to technology. Several highly effective programs are available in various formats to assist students with initial instruction or remediation. Grammar texts, such as the Warriner's series, employ various methods to reach individual learning styles. The school library media center should become a focal point for individual exploration.

Skill 1.4   Recognize the roles of motivation and interest in reading.

George G. Spache; H. Alan Robinson; Edward B. Fry; Richard T. Vacca; Strang, McCullough, and Traxlor; and Delores Durkin are a select group of authors who provide the classroom teacher with concrete examples of how to provide insight into a student's reading style, skill development, interest, and other pertinent information regarding the individual student's needs. All this information will serve the classroom teacher in providing a challenging reading program for all.

These texts will assist the teacher with the following:

- Provide appropriate material to meet the need of the student for instruction, enrichment, or remediation

- Provide student-directed or teacher-directed activities in reading literature and content area curriculum texts

- Provide resources and lessons that can provide a challenging opportunity for students to seek information from a wide variety of sources, such as television and computers

- Provide suggestions and make recommendations that will foster a lifetime habit of seeking pleasure and knowledge from the printed word into the student

- Provide the teacher an avenue of referral for students who are experiencing reading/learning disabilities and cannot have their needs met in the regular classroom setting.

- The inclusion of guidance counselors, speech pathologists, and school psychologists in a team approach are available in almost every school

Skill 1.5   Recognize cultural, linguistic, and ethnic diversity and their relationship to reading development.

Young children tend to rely heavily on an either "that is me" or a "that is not me" mentality when evaluating literature. A modern, diverse classroom has the potential to break down those rigid barriers and open students' minds to redefine "what COULD be me" or "what I'd LIKE to learn more about." Differences should be seen as valuable assets to the classroom, as well as in the world.

The teacher should be careful, though, when selecting material that emphasizes diversity, not to choose works that perpetuate stereotypes. The following books are great resources for enhancing diversity in the classroom:

- *Indian Winter* by Russell Freeman, illustrated by Karl Bodmer (Holiday House, 1992). In 1833, German Prince Alexander Philipp Maximilian and Karl Bodmer, a Swiss painter, journeyed up the Missouri River and spent the winter among the Mandan Indians. Russell Freeman draws upon the prince's diary and Bodmer's detailed paintings to create an incredible account of their adventure.
- *¡Viva México! The Story of Benito Juárez and Cinco de Mayo* by Argentina Palacios (Steck-Vaughn, 1993). Inspire kids to have faith against all odds with the story of Zapotec Indian Benito Juárez, who became president of Mexico. The author provides information on Cinco de Mayo, a major holiday celebrated by Mexicans and Mexican-Americans.
- *Alvin Ailey* by Andrea Davis Pinkney, illustrated by Brian Pinkney (Hyperion, 1993). This insightful biography about dancer/choreographer Ailey provides children with a model of an important 20th-century African-American.
- *The Devil's Arithmetic* by Jane Yolen (Viking, 1988). In this compelling novel, a young girl is mystically transported from present-day New York to Poland during World War II, where she goes into a gas chamber to save the life of another.
- *Older Brother, Younger Brother* retold by Nina Jaffe, illustrated by Wenhai Ma (Viking, 1995). This traditional Korean folktale explores the universal theme that if good is returned for ill treatment, good will triumph over evil.

Holidays are also a great way to explore diversity. They provide a fun and interesting outlet to learn about other cultures. Choose books that explore Kwanzaa, Chinese New Year, Cinco de Mayo, or Ramadan. Focusing on how other cultures have fun is more likely to foster future interest in them.

TEACHER CERTIFICATION STUDY GUIDE

Skill 1.6 Recognize the roles that various language components play in reading development, including knowing about the phonemic (sounds of language), morphemic (words and meaningful parts of language), semantic (meaning), syntactic (sentence structure), and pragmatic (how language works in a social context) components of language.

Phonological Awareness

Phonological awareness means the ability of the reader to recognize the sound of spoken language. This recognition includes how these sounds can be blended together, segmented (divided up), and manipulated (switched around). This awareness then leads to phonics, a method for teaching students to read. It helps them sound out words.

Instructional methods to teach phonological awareness may include any or all of the following: Auditory games and drills during which students recognize and manipulate the sounds of words, separate or segment the sounds of words, take out sounds, blend sounds, add in new sounds, or take apart sound to recombine them in new formations are good way to foster phonological awareness.

Syntax

Sentence completeness

Avoid fragments and run-on sentences. Recognition of sentence elements necessary to make a complete thought, proper use of independent and dependent clauses (see *Use correct coordination and subordination*), and proper punctuation will correct such errors.

Sentence structure

Recognize simple, compound, complex, and compound-complex sentences. Use dependent (subordinate) and independent clauses correctly to create these sentence structures.

> **Simple** Joyce wrote a letter.
> **Compound** Joyce wrote a letter, and Dot drew a picture.
> **Complex** While Joyce wrote a letter, Dot drew a picture.
> **Compound/Complex** When Mother asked the girls to demonstrate their newfound skills, Joyce wrote a letter, and Dot drew a picture.

Note: Do **not** confuse compound sentence elements with compound sentences.

> Simple sentence with compound subject
> <u>Joyce</u> and <u>Dot</u> wrote letters.
> The <u>girl</u> in row three and the <u>boy</u> next to her were passing notes across the aisle.

Simple sentence with compound predicate
Joyce <u>wrote letters</u> and <u>drew pictures</u>.
The captain of the high school debate team <u>graduated with honors</u> and <u>studied broadcast journalism in college</u>.

Simple sentence with compound object of preposition
Coleen graded the students' essays for <u>style</u> and <u>mechanical accuracy</u>.

Skill 1.7 **Recognize the relationships of reading to writing, listening, and speaking and know strategies for integrating these through instruction.**

The last twenty years have seen great change in instruction in the English classroom. Gone are the days when literature is taught on Monday, Wednesday is grammar day and Friday you assign writing. Integrating reading, writing, speaking, listening and viewing allows students to make connections between each aspect of language development during each class.

Suggestions for Integrating Language Arts

- Use pre-reading activities such as discussion, writing, research, and journals. Use writing to tap into prior knowledge before students read; engage students in class discussions about themes, issues, and ideas explored in journals, predicting the outcome and exploring related information.

- Use prewriting activities such as reading model essays, researching, interviewing others, combining sentences and other prewriting activities. Remember that developing language proficiency is a recursive process and involves practice in reading, writing, thinking, speaking, listening and viewing.

- Create writing activities that are relevant to students by having them write and share with real audiences.

- Connect correctness - including developing skills of conventional usage, spelling, grammar, and punctuation - to the revision and editing stage of writing. Review of mechanics and punctuation can be done with mini-lessons that use sentences from student papers, sentence combining strategies, and modeling passages of skilled writers.

- Connect reading, writing, listening, speaking, and viewing by using literature as a springboard for a variety of activities.

In middle and secondary schools, the emphasis of reading instruction spans the range of comprehension skills - literal, inferential, and critical.

Most instruction in grades five and six is based on the skills delineated in basal readers adopted for those grade levels. Reading instruction in grades seven through nine is usually part of the general language arts class instead of being a distinct subject in the curriculum, unless the instruction is remedial. Reading in tenth through twelfth grades is part of the literature curriculum - World, American, and British.

Reading emphasis in middle school

Reading for comprehension of factual material - content area textbooks, reference books, and newspapers - is closely related to study strategies in middle/junior high. Organized study models, such as the SQ3R method, a technique that makes it possible and feasible to learn the content of even large amounts of text (Survey, Question, Read, Recite, and Review Studying), teach students to locate main ideas and supporting details, to recognize sequential order, to distinguish fact from opinion, and to determine cause/ effect relationships.

Strategies

Teacher-guided activities that require students to organize and to summarize information based on the author's explicit intent are pertinent strategies in middle grades. Evaluation techniques include oral and written responses to standardized or teacher-made worksheets.

Reading of fiction introduces and reinforces skills in inferring meaning from narration and description. Teaching-guided activities in the process of reading for meaning should be followed by cooperative planning of the skills to be studied and of the selection of reading resources. Many printed reading for comprehension instruments as well as individualized computer software programs exist to monitor the progress of acquiring comprehension skills.

Older middle school students should be given opportunities for more student-centered activities - individual and collaborative selection of reading choices based on student interest, small group discussions of selected works, and greater written expression. Evaluation techniques include teacher monitoring and observation of discussions and written work samples.

Certain students may begin some fundamental critical interpretation - recognizing fallacious reasoning in news media, examining the accuracy of news reports and advertising, explaining their reasons for preferring one author's writing to another's. Development of these skills may require a more learning-centered approach in which the teacher identifies a number of objectives and suggested resources from which the student may choose his course of study. Self-evaluation through a reading diary should be stressed. Teacher and peer evaluation of creative projects resulting from such study is encouraged.

Reading aloud before the entire class as a formal means of teacher evaluation should be phased out in favor of one-to-one tutoring or peer-assisted reading. Occasional sharing of favored selections by both teacher and willing students is a good oral interpretation basic.

Reading emphasis in high school

Students in high school literature classes should focus on interpretive and critical reading. Teachers should guide the study of the elements of inferential (interpretive) reading - drawing conclusions, predicting outcomes, and recognizing examples of specific genre characteristics, for example - and critical reading to judge the quality of the writer's work against recognized standards. At this level students should understand the skills of language and reading that they are expected to master and be able to evaluate their own progress.

Strategies

The teacher becomes more facilitator than instructor - helping the student to make a diagnosis of his own strengths and weaknesses, keeping a record of progress, and interacting with other students and the teacher in practicing skills.

Despite the requisites and prerequisites of most literature courses, students should be encouraged to pursue independent study and enrichment reading.

Ample opportunities should be provided for oral interpretation of literature, special projects in creative dramatics, and writing for publication in school literary magazines or newspapers, and speech/debate activities. A student portfolio provides for teacher and peer evaluation.

Skill 1.8   Recognize the strategies for using reading in all content areas.

Content areas such as science, mathematics, history and social studies rely on textbooks and other printed materials that use primarily expository text to introduce, explain, and illustrate new subject matter. From a reading perspective, students face several challenges when approaching these texts, such as deciphering unfamiliar vocabulary, and adapting to new structures of content organization, that directly impact their ability to understand, synthesize, and apply the information contained therein.

Students lacking a solid foundation of reading strategies will likely experience difficulties in developing the competencies needed to master a subject area's academic requirements. At the secondary level, reading and understanding is only the beginning. Students are expected to absorb, evaluate, and form opinions and theories about topics within the subject matter, and then discuss, write about, and apply what they've learned on high level.

Metacognitive reading development strategies can help students engage effectively with their reading materials across the curriculum. The sample strategies below can be employed through structured activities that occur before reading, during reading, and after reading.

Before reading
- Incorporate prior knowledge: Draw a connection between students' previous experiences – both personal and educational – and the topic at hand. A student who has helped out in the family garden, for example, will have a visual and basic vocabulary starting point for the study of plant physiology.
- Make predictions about what will be learned: Encourage students to identify what they think they will learn from the text, based on cues in the material (e.g., book titles, chapter headings, pictures, etc.)
- Prepare questions: Write specific questions to be answered during reading.

During reading
- Use context cues: Utilize other words and concepts in same the sentence or paragraph to determine the meaning of an unfamiliar word.
- Reread challenging texts: Practice rereading a selection of text to check for understanding.
- Use visualizing techniques: Mental pictures formed during the reading of text can aid in comprehension and retention of information. Read aloud, followed by a discussion of how these mental pictures factually reflect the text, provide opportunity for practicing and reinforcing this technique at all grade levels.
- Make inferences: Much of human communication relies on our ability to read between the lines of explicit statements and make logical guesses that fill in the blanks of information not provided. Similarly, for textbooks, making inferences means making connections to information extending beyond the text and subject matter at hand. For example, a geography book making the simple declaration that Brazil has a tropical climate can allow the student to deduce a wealth of information not stated in the text (e.g., tropical climates have warm year-round temperatures and high precipitation levels, therefore certain crops will grow quite successfully and can positively impact the local economy, etc.).
- Check the predictions made before reading: Use the text to confirm earlier predictions about content and answer the questions posed prior to reading.

After reading:
- Summarize information: Students who understand the information they have read should be able to restate what they have learned in an organized manner. This activity can be practiced in both written and oral forms.
- Make critical evaluations: Encourage students to respond to the text with the ideas and opinions they've formed during reading. Facilitate discussions by devising questions that lead students to make qualitative and evaluative judgments about the content they've read.

Skill 1.9   **Recognize the home and school experiences that impact literacy development.**

Parents who are readers and a family that values books generally produce children who read early and well. This is enhanced if parents and others read to the child even before he/she is able to read alone. In a home where learning and books are treated with respect, children go off to school much better prepared than children from homes where the opposite is true. There's no doubt that physical activity, sports, and outdoor experiences contribute to the healthy development of a child, but so do reading and appreciation of books.

There is considerable controversy over how schools should teach reading, so much so that Congress appointed fourteen researchers, educators, and parents to a National Reading Panel to examine the research on the teaching of reading. Its report is an interpretation of "research-based instruction." The panel's findings are now a cornerstone of U.S. federal reading education policy.

The panel found many things that schools could do to teach reading better. They recommend that a small amount of instructional time be devoted to teaching young children to hear the sounds in words (phonemic awareness) and to teaching phonics during the early elementary grades.

Also, certain kinds of oral reading practice improve reading ability markedly as does work on word meanings and instruction in how to understand, figure out, and remember what is read. High-quality professional development opportunities for teachers were also found to have a positive impact on children's learning. The main point the panel makes is that teaching matters. Children can figure out a lot of things on their own and practice is helpful, but the greatest success comes about when teachers offer explicit instruction and guidance in reading skills and strategies. The report reminds teachers, parents, and policymakers that sound reading instruction helps children to figure out the words (pronunciations and meanings), to read fluently, and to think effectively about what they read.

COMPETENCY 2.0 DEMONSTRATE KNOWLEDGE OF SELECTION AND USE OF VARIOUS MATERIALS TO PLAN READING INSTRUCTION APPROPRIATE TO STUDENTS' KNOWLEDGE AND ABILITIES

Skill 2.1 Demonstrate knowledge of a variety of both fiction and nonfiction materials that can be used for teaching reading.

Teachers should select a variety of texts to give students a broad experience in the reading process. Exposure to both narrative and expository texts allows them to build and expand their knowledge base, identify and distinguish genres, learn how different texts are structured, and experience a variety of authors' writing styles, ideas and language usage across eras.

Fiction: Students should read an assortment of fiction works to provide opportunity to learn about character and plot development in the various genres, the role of setting and dialog, themes and narrative story structure, as well as the ability to define and identify elements of fiction (e.g., tone, mood, foreshadowing, irony, symbolism). Types of texts to be included in the reading curriculum are folktales, myths, legends, short stories, mysteries, historical fiction, science fiction, plays and general-interest novels.

Nonfiction: Appropriate selection of nonfiction materials provides the opportunity to practice and reinforce the complex reading comprehension skills necessary to succeed across the curriculum. Topics should contain a high level of detail, covering diverse topics that encourage active discussion, questioning, synthesizing and evaluation of the information presented. Readers should be exposed to complex content structures and be required to apply critical reading skills to evaluate the quality of information. Text selection should include textbooks, autobiographies/biographies, informational books, websites, newspapers, magazines, encyclopedias, and brochures.

Skill 2.2 Demonstrate knowledge of how to create, organize, and use a classroom library.

Several decisions must be made before volumes begin to be collected. The primary decision, of course, is the location of the library. Is there room for shelves and, hopefully, at least one table near the shelves? The second decision has to do with whether this will be a physical, visible library or a virtual one or both? Is a computer with Internet access available? Finally, what kind of supplemental information do students need in order to realize the greatest benefit from the class?

It's a good idea to begin with reference books. In the past, only large libraries were able to shelve the unabridged Merriam Webster's 3rd, a valuable reference work, particularly in the English classroom, even though it is somewhat out of date since it is not revised very frequently.

The good news is that it's online and subscriptions are inexpensive. The better news is that the subscription also includes the collegiate version, which is frequently updated, so both resources are available in one subscription. Also, an English-Spanish dictionary, a medical dictionary, a thesaurus, and Webster's encyclopedia are included for one price.

Question.com is a 50,000-volume online library that is also available by subscription.

The second important reference is *The Encyclopedia Britannica.* Again, the good news is that it's available online. While your budget may not reach far enough to purchase a set, you might be able to afford the subscription price for Merriam-Webster's volumes and the Britannica.

Beyond the reference books, the library in the English classroom should include a range of literature that students can check out: a few English literature volumes up to and including the sixteenth century and some British literature from the sixteenth century forward; American literature up to the Civil War and following the war, with good representation of current best-selling writers.

Most libraries are still using the Library of Congress classification system. This would be a good opportunity to teach your students about how libraries work and how to use them. A trip to a large library might be helpful, especially if students have been assigned a simple research assignment. The objective of having a library is to encourage students to go beyond their textbooks for information but it is also a good opportunity to stimulate their interest in using libraries.

Skill 2.3 **Demonstrate knowledge of strategies for analyzing and evaluating the quality and appropriateness of instructional materials in terms of readability, content, length, format, illustrations, and other pertinent factors.**

Materials selection should take several factors into consideration. Reading curriculum should consist of literary and non-literary texts in a variety of formats and include selections from the science, history, and social sciences areas.

Texts should be grade-level appropriate, where approximately 75% of the words are decodable, with appropriately challenging English words. Illustrations and photographs should enhance and clarify the meaning of the text, and expository materials should use graphical organizers (or provide supplemental materials that do) when content is complex. The length of text should be both grade-appropriate (i.e., manageable by students within the given time frame) and lesson-appropriate (e.g., if reading and discussing a poem in class, make sure the poem is an appropriate length to allow time for clarification, questioning, interpretation, and discussion).

Skill 2.4 **Demonstrate strategies for selecting materials (including technological tools) based on students' interests, knowledge and experiences, cultural backgrounds, and developmental levels.**

Materials and activities that correspond to high levels of student interest will motivate students to immerse themselves in the lesson, thus opening the door for the application and reception of effective teaching strategies. Likewise, connecting a lesson to a student's knowledge base, life experience and cultural history provides a foundation of familiarity that allow the student to explore higher order concepts without feeling alienated from the material.

Technology is, of course, a key factor in modern society – especially adolescent culture – and must be incorporated into students' learning experiences. Email and internet-based activities (such as keyword searches for information) provide students with a variety of communication experiences by connecting them with peers, conveying and interpreting messages, obtaining, evaluating, and processing information from experts, preparing documents, and managing and using information responsibly.

The multimedia nature of technological tools, such as Microsoft Word and PowerPoint, allows for creative and practical dissemination of information that not only sparks student interest, but also covers the spectrum of individual learning styles by smoothly incorporating reading comprehension best practices, such as visual cues and graphic organizers, with the core text. The flexible nature of digital media allows the teacher to customize and share the same lesson material from class to class to reflect different needs of the students.

Skill 2.5 **Recognize the use of standardized and informal reading assessments (including ongoing observations) and understand the implications of cultural, linguistic, and ethnic differences for interpretation of assessments.**

Skills to Evaluate:

- Ability to use syntactic cues when encountering an unknown word. A good reader will expect the word to fit the syntax he is familiar with. A poor reader may substitute a word that does not fit the syntax and will not correct himself.
- Ability to use semantic cues to determine the meaning of an unknown word. A good reader will consider the meanings of all the known words in the sentence. A poor reader may read one word at a time with no regard for the other words.
- Ability to use schematic cues to connect words read with prior knowledge. A good reader will incorporate what she knows with what the text says or implies. A poor reader may think only of the word she is reading without associating it with prior knowledge.

- Ability to use phonics cues to improve ease and efficiency in reading. A good reader will apply letter and sound associations almost subconsciously. A poor reader may have one of two kinds of problems. He may have underdeveloped phonics/skills, and use only an initial clue without analyzing vowel patterns before quickly guessing the word. Or he may use phonics skills in isolation, becoming so absorbed in the word "noises" that he ignores or forgets the message of the text.
- Ability to process information from text. A student should be able to get information from the text, as well as store, retrieve and integrate it for later use.
- Ability to use interpretive thinking to make logical predictions and inferences.
- Ability to use critical thinking to make decisions and insights about the text.
- Ability to use appreciative thinking to respond to the text, whether emotionally, mentally, ideologically, etc.

Methods of Evaluation:

- Assess students at the beginning of each year to determine grouping for instruction.
- Judge whether a student recognizes when a word does not make sense.
- Monitor whether the student corrects herself, if she knows when to ignore and read on or when to reread a sentence.
- Looks for skill such as recognizing cause and effect, finding main ideas, and using comparison and contrast techniques.
- Use oral reading to assess reading skills. Pay attention to word recognition skills rather than the reader's ability to communicate the author's message. Strong oral reading sounds like natural speech, utilizes phrasing and pace that match the meaning of the text, and uses pitch and tone to interpret the text.
- Keep dated records to follow individual progress. Focus on a few students each day. Grade them on a scale of 1-5 according to how well they perform certain reading abilities (e.g., logically predicts coming events). Also include informal observations, such as "Ed was able to determine the meaning of the word 'immigrant' by examining the other words in the sentence."
- Remember that evaluation is important, but enjoyment of reading is the most important thing to emphasize. Keep reading as a pressure-free, fun activity so students do not become intimidated by reading. Even if the student is not meeting excellent standards, if he continues to want to read each day, that is a success!

Skill 2.6 **Demonstrate knowledge of strategies for planning, organizing, and managing reading instruction to create a positive environment that encourages independent reading.**

See Skill 1.1.

Skill 2.7 **Demonstrate knowledge of strategies for engaging parents in the educational process and for communicating with them about their children's reading progress.**

In discussing a student's performance with a parent, it's best to begin with good news, even if there are serious problems that must be talked about. A child is often a visible manifestation of the parent's own ego, and any discussion is sensitive and potentially emotional. Hearing their child praised usually goes a long way to neutralizing parents' natural tendency to be defensive.

Rather than focusing on problems or a negative performance in the student's classes where you are the teacher, it's better to find positive solutions that will involve input both from you and the parents. Treating the parents as partners in the important job of helping their child develop in positive ways will have the most positive yield both for you and for the student. Try to have a plan that has been worked out by both you and the parents before the meeting ends.

Since you are the expert source in academic matters, working out a plan for improving the child's reading should depend heavily on your knowledge of what works and what does not. Depending on the age of the child, the following are some things a parent can do to help the child improve:

- Echo read: The parent reads a small amount of text and the child repeats it.
- Repetition: If the student is still struggling with some of the text, go back through the same text, echoing again.
- Wide reading: Use the echo approach but do not repeat. Go on to the next text.

Once the student begins to build some fluency, the parent can read a page and then the student will read the next page. Make certain that the story is one that interests the child. Most children like Harry Potter books, and they lend themselves very well to this kind of reading. Once a book is finished, parent and child can talk about what they have read and compare it to other things, perhaps even another Harry Potter story.

Have the child read the entire book aloud to the parent, spending a set amount of time reading each evening. Once the child has read the book, discussion is again in order. If parents have trouble knowing what to discuss, the teacher can distribute a list of questions to ask to stimulate discussion.

Both parent and child can read a book separately and discuss it. A deadline should be set for finishing it and for the discussion to take place. Keeping the reading time that has been established in earlier stages is a good idea. Parent and child can sit in the same room and read. Parents can report on progress at the next parent/teacher meeting and get feedback from the teacher on what changes he/she has seen in the student's performance.

A parent-child visit to a library is another way to promote fluency and a love of reading.

Skill 2.8 **Recognize when a student's reading problems justify referral to appropriate special services.**

If students take turns reading aloud in your classroom, those who read word to word and haltingly have probably not developed reading fluency and could use some special help to improve their reading skills. Readers who are not fluent must intentionally decode a majority of the words they encounter in a text. Fluent readers are able to read texts with expression or prosody, the combination that makes oral reading sound like spoken language.

If students don't read aloud in your classroom but have reading assignments that call for written reports, those reports will have clues to reading ability also. If sentences are poorly organized structurally, if words are left out, and if the student is using a vocabulary he or she does not have control of, these are signs that his or her reading level is below par.

There are a number of reliable reading tests that can be administered to provide empirical data to let you know where your students' reading skills lie. Your school or your district can probably recommend one. Some of these can be given at the beginning of the school year and at the end to let you know what impact your teaching is having.

For slow, immature readers, a special section with activities designed to improve reading may be in order, making as certain as possible that it isn't seen as criticism or judgment. Some of the activities that might be useful for that separate section:

- Repeated readings: the group reads short passages several times, trying to improve with each reading.
- Echo reading: Teacher reads a sentence and students read after her. Once a story has been completed, use the same text and do the exercise one more time.
- Wide reading: Teacher reads a sentence and students read after her, but they move on to a new reading once the first one is finished.

- Choosing a story that the students like, such as a Harry Potter story, have each student read a page in turn until the book is completed. Discuss what the story is about, and then give an exam on the content of the story. When the focus of an assignment is on meaning, students tend to make greater gains in comprehension than when the focus is on word analysis and accurate reading.
- Sometimes watching a dramatization of a story played on a television set or a screen will encourage an interest in reading a particular story and provide variety as well as an opportunity to think about language in spoken as well as written form.

Among the causes that make reading a struggle are auditory trauma and ear infections that affect the ability to hear speech. Such a student will need one-on-one support with articulation and perception of different sounds. It might be necessary to consult with a speech therapist or audiologist. As a teacher educator, you need to take time to identify those children who may be struggling due to a hearing difficulty. Some students may also have vision problems that call for treatment. Inquiring about a vision examination is in order if you suspect that a child is not reading well because of a vision impairment.

Students who are using English as a second language may need special consideration. If they are not able to comprehend at a passing level in your class, they should be referred to an ELL class.

If you conclude that a student is not prepared to participate successfully in your classroom, then referral may be the best choice. Guidance counselors, speech pathologists, and school psychologists are available in most schools.

COMPTENCY 3.0 DEMONSTRATE KNOWLEDGE OF STRATEGIES FOR TEACHING AND ASSESSING STUDENT KNOWLEDGE OF WORD IDENTIFICATION AND VOCABULARY

Skill 3.1 Demonstrate knowledge of strategies for teaching English spelling and word patterns.

In the past, the Oxford English Dictionary has been the most reliable source for etymologies. Some of the collegiate dictionaries are also useful. *Merriam-Webster's 3rd Unabridged Dictionary* is useful in tracing the sources of words in American English. *Merriam-Webster's Unabridged Dictionary* may be out of date, so a teacher should also have a *Merriam-Webster's Collegiate Dictionary*, which is updated regularly.

However, there are many up-to-date sources for keeping up and keeping track of the changes that have occurred and are occurring constantly. Google "etymology," for instance, or even the word you're unsure of, and you can find a multitude of sources. Don't trust a single one. The information should be validated by at least three sources. Wikipedia is very useful, but it can be changed by anyone who chooses, so any information you find there should be backed up by other sources.

If you go to http://www.etymonline.com/sources.php, you will find a long list of resources on etymology.

In order to know when to label a usage "jargon" or "colloquial" nowadays, the teacher must be aware of the possibility that it's a word that is now accepted as standard. In order to be on top of this, the teacher must continually keep up with the etymological aids that are available, particularly online.

Spelling in English is complicated by the fact that it is not phonetic—that is, it is not based on the one-sound/one letter formula used by many other languages. The reason for this is that it is based on the Latin alphabet, which originally had twenty letters, consisting of the present English alphabet minus J, K, V, W, Y, and Z. The Romans added K to be used in abbreviations and Y and Z in words that came from the Greek. This 23-letter alphabet was adopted by the English, who developed W as a ligatured doubling of U and later J and V as consonantal variants of I and U. The result was our alphabet of 26 letters with upper case (capital) and lower case forms.

Spelling is based primarily on fifteenth-century English. The problem is that pronunciation has changed drastically since then, especially long vowels and diphthongs. This Great Vowel Shift affected the seven long vowels. For a long time, spelling was erratic—there were no standards. As long as the meaning was clear, spelling was not considered very important. Samuel Johnson tackled this problem and his *Dictionary of the English Language* (1755) brought standards to spelling, so important once printing presses were invented. There have been some changes, of course, over the years, but spelling is still not strictly phonetic. There have been many attempts to nudge the spelling into a more phonetic representation of the sounds, but for the most part, all have failed. A good example is Noah Webster's *Spelling Book* (1783), which was a precursor to the first edition (1828) of his *American Dictionary of the English Language*. While there are rules for spelling and it's important that students learn the rules, there are many exceptions; memorizing exceptions and giving plenty of opportunities for practicing them seems the only solution for the teacher of English.

Identification of common morphemes, prefixes, and suffixes

This aspect of vocabulary development is to help students look for structural elements within words, which they can use independently to help them determine meaning.

The terms listed below are generally recognized as the key structural analysis components.

Root words: A root word is a word from which another word is developed. The second word can be said to have its "root" in the first. This structural component nicely lends itself to a tree with roots illustration that can concretize the meaning for students. Students may also want to literally construct root words using cardboard trees and/or actual roots from plants to create word family models. This is a lovely way to help students own their root words.

Base words: A stand-alone linguistic unit, which cannot be deconstructed or broken down into smaller words. For example, in the word "re-tell," the base word is "tell."

Contractions: These are shortened forms of two words in which a letter or letters have been deleted. These deleted letters have been replaced by an apostrophe.

Prefixes: These are beginning units of meaning which can be added (the vocabulary word for this type of structural adding is "affixed") to a base word or root word. They are also sometimes known as "bound morphemes," meaning that they cannot stand alone as a base word.

Suffixes: These are ending units of meaning, which can be "affixed" or added on to the ends of root or base words. Suffixes transform the original meanings of base and root words. Like prefixes, they are also known as "bound morphemes" because they cannot stand alone as words.

Compound words: Occur when two or more base words are connected to form a new word. The meaning of the new word is in some way connected with that of the base word.

Inflectional endings: Are types are suffixes that impart a new meaning to the base or root word. These endings in particular change the gender, number, tense, or form of the base or root words. Just like other suffixes, these are also termed "bound morphemes."

Skill 3.2   Demonstrate knowledge of strategies for assessing students' reading abilities.

Skills to Evaluate:

- Ability to use syntactic cues when encountering an unknown word. A good reader will expect the word to fit the syntax he/she is familiar with. A poor reader may substitute a word that does not fit the syntax and will not correct herself.
- Ability to use semantic cues to determine the meaning of an unknown word. A good reader will consider the meanings of all the known words in the sentence. A poor reader may read one word at a time with no regard for the other words.
- Ability to use schematic cues to connect words read with prior knowledge. A good reader will incorporate what she knows with what the text says or implies. A poor reader may think only of the word she is reading without associating it with prior knowledge.
- Ability to use phonics cues to improve ease and efficiency in reading. A good reader will apply letter and sound associations almost subconsciously. A poor reader may have one of two kinds of problems. He may have underdeveloped phonics/skills and use only an initial clue without analyzing vowel patterns before quickly guessing the word. Or he may use phonics skills in isolation, becoming so absorbed in the word "noises" that he ignores or forgets the message of the text.
- Ability to process information from text. A student should be able to get information from the text, as well as store, retrieve and integrate it for later use.
- Ability to use interpretive thinking to make logical predictions and inferences.
- Ability to use critical thinking to make decisions and insights about the text.

- Ability to use appreciative thinking to respond to the text, whether emotionally, mentally, ideologically, etc.

Methods of Evaluation:

- Assess students at the beginning of each year to determine grouping for instruction.
- Judge whether a student recognizes when a word does not make sense.
- Monitor whether the student corrects herself, if she knows when to ignore and read on or when to reread a sentence.
- Looks for skill such as recognizing cause and effect, finding main ideas, and using comparison and contrast techniques.
- Use oral reading to assess reading skills. Pay attention to word recognition skills rather than the reader's ability to communicate the author's message. Strong oral reading sounds like natural speech, utilizes phrasing and pace that match the meaning of the text, and uses pitch and tone to interpret the text.
- Keep dated records to follow individual progress. Focus on a few students each day. Grade them on a scale of 1-5 according to how well they perform certain reading abilities (e.g., logically predicts coming events). Also include informal observations, such as "Ed was able to determine the meaning of the word 'immigrant' by examining the other words in the sentence."
- Remember that evaluation is important, but enjoyment of reading is the most important thing to emphasize. Keep reading as a pressure-free, fun activity so students do not become intimidated by reading. Even if the student is not meeting excellent standards, if he continues to want to read each day, that is a success!

Skill 3.3 **Recognize the role of vocabulary in reading comprehension and learning from text in various areas.**

See Skill 3.4.

Skill 3.4 **Demonstrate knowledge of strategies for teaching vocabulary effectively.**

A planned, effective vocabulary program is not an extra but an across-the-curriculum necessity. The four-step process in such a program includes

1. Evaluate to determine what the students know.

2. Devise a plan to teach the students what they must learn as part of a continuum.

3. Determine if students have heard the words to be studied and in what context.

4. Teach vocabulary for MASTERY.

To reach mastery, clear-cut objectives and pacing are important since some students will need more practice than others. Building in time for practice, review, and testing is an integral component of a successful program.

Re-teaching words missed on tests or misused in writing is essential until mastery is achieved.

The learning of vocabulary through visual, auditory, kinesthetic, and tactical experiences in a systematic order will enhance the learning process.

Methods of presentation, for a well-balanced program at all levels, include

1. Recognizing and using words in context.

2. Giving attention to varying definitions of the same word.

3. Studying word families (synonyms, antonyms, and homonyms).

4. Locating etymologies (word origins).

5. Analyzing word parts (roots, prefixes, suffixes).

6. Locating phonetic spellings and identifying correct pronunciation.

7. Spelling words properly.

8. Using words semantically.

Countless enrichment materials are available and include computer software, CD-ROM, board games, flashcards, puzzles, etc. The more varied the experience, the easier and quicker students will commit the words to memory and mastery will be achieved.

The Shostak Vocabulary Series that spans middle school through grade 13, including SAT/ACT preparation, is recommended by the authors for use in grades 9-12.

Within the literature series, vocabulary lists and practices are included. Classroom teachers should also review content area texts to add technical and specialized words to the weekly vocabulary study.

Skill 3.5 **Demonstrate knowledge of how to use technology to enhance and encourage vocabulary skills.**

Many resources are available to the teacher of reading, including technological ones; however, by themselves they will not change reading competency. A planned, effective vocabulary program, preferably across the curriculum, is required if the technological help is to be effective. The four-step process in such a program includes the following:

1. Evaluation to determine what the students know.
2. A plan to teach the students what they must learn as part of a continuum.
3. Determining whether students have heard the words to be studied and in what context.
4. Mastery as the primary objective.

COMPETENCY 4.0 DEMONSTRATE KNOWLEDGE OF IDENTIFYING AND IMPLEMENTING APPROPRIATE STRATEGIES USING ORAL LANGUAGE TO HELP STUDENTS DEVELOP READING SKILLS

Skill 4.1 Recognize the implications of differences in students' dialects and language when reading.

Students who are raised in homes where English is not the first language and/or where standard English is not spoken, may have difficulty with hearing the difference between similar sounding words like "send" and "sent." Any student who is not in an environment where English phonology operates, may have difficulty perceiving and demonstrating the differences between English language phonemes. If students cannot hear the difference between words that sound the same like "grow" and "glow," they will be confused when these words appear in a print context. This confusion will of course, sadly, impact their comprehension.

Considerations for teaching to English Language Learners include recognition by the teacher that what works for the English language speaking student from an English language speaking family, does not necessarily work in other languages.

Research recommends that ELL students learn to read initially in their first language. It has been found that a priority for ELL should be learning to speak English before being taught to read English. Research supports oral language development, since it lays the foundation for phonological awareness.

Skill 4.2 Demonstrate knowledge that oral reading requires accuracy, speed, and expression and understand its role in reading development.

See Skill 4.4.

Skill 4.3 Recognize similarities and differences in oral and written language learning and know how to effectively use oral language activities to teach reading.

See Skill 13.9.

Skill 4.4 Recognize the relationship between oral and silent reading.

When children begin to learn to read, they bring to the task a set of well-developed oral language comprehension skills. These skills, remarkably developed in a short period of time, are relative and important to the task of learning to read. Learning to read is not learning the language but learning to decode *symbols* for the language they already know. A child's language skills continue to develop as he grows and learning to read plays a role in that development.

Previous experience has been in conversations where the child plays both speaker and listener roles. The conversationalists are together and share a space, time, and situation context. Their speech to each other is facilitated by intonation, facial expression, and gestures.

In reading, that is, in visually decoding the written words, aspects of the spoken word play a role: stress, intonation, and other prosodic features. Temporal characteristics of speech such as pauses and changes in speed often provide clues for the chunking of words into larger constituents. Also, pauses and breaths occur at the ends of sentences. Actually, pauses at phrase and clause boundaries increase comprehension. We rely on stress in spoken language to communicate those boundaries and convey the meanings they contribute. A good example is the restrictive versus the nonrestrictive clause: "Dogs that are of mixed breed often make good pets" (nonrestrictive). "Dogs, which are of mixed breed, often make good pets" (restrictive). The difference is clearly understood in speech. Punctuation provides a code for communicating even some of those aspects of spoken language. However, there are many more of those devices available in spoken language than in written.

Even so, written language does have some compensatory aspects. Paragraph demarcations, for example, are an organizational aid not available in oral language. Also, the ability to look back over passages that have been previously read and making corrections the second time around is only available in writing. A major strategy a student must develop is a method for using the permanence of text, for example, keeping some structure of the text in mind to facilitate looking back and checking a fact. In oral language, of course, the listener may just ask for clarification.

For the English teacher, the implication of all of this is that students need to read aloud in order to strengthen the link between their superior understanding of the structure of the language and their decoding skills with regard to written language. They need to be encouraged to use facial expressions, intonation, pauses, etc. as they read aloud to other students, and they need to practice these skills as frequently as possible. They also need to develop skills for using the advantages of written language in their silent reading.

Skill 4.5 Demonstrate knowledge of how to use predictable books, poetry, and songs as the basis for fluency development.

If a student is reading a story he/she is familiar with, attention can be given to developing fluency since it will not be necessary to concentrate on the content so much. The teacher can concentrate on teaching oral reading skills more easily if the story is already known.

Students who have not achieved fluency tend to read word-to-word or by creating unnatural groupings, and their reading is usually monotonous, reflecting their inability to transfer prosodic elements that occur naturally in speech onto written text. A repeated-reading strategy has been demonstrated to be successful in developing fluency. Echo-reading text twice, followed by the students' reading without the echo has been demonstrated to promote fluency. A variation of genres is useful in these exercises because students need to learn to reflect in their oral reading phrasing, pitch, and emphasis, typical of fluent readers. Reading poetry in addition to prose has been shown to be advantageous in these exercises.

Skill 4.6   Demonstrate knowledge of how to assess students' reading fluency.

Academic literacy, which encompasses ways of knowing particular content and refers to strategies for understanding, discussing, organizing, and producing texts, is key to success in school. To be literate in an academic sense, one should be able to understand and to articulate conceptual relationships within, between, and among disciplines. Academic literacy also encompasses critical literacy, that is, the ability to evaluate the credibility and validity of informational sources. In a practical sense, when a student is academically literate, she should be able to read and understand interdisciplinary texts, to articulate comprehension through expository written pieces, and to further knowledge through sustained and focused research.

Developing academic literacy is especially difficult for ESL students who are struggling to acquire and improve the language and critical thinking skills they need to become full members of the academic mainstream community. The needs of these ESL students may be met through the creation of a functional language learning environment that engages them in meaningful and authentic language processing through planned, purposeful, and academically-based activities, teaching them how to extract, question, and evaluate the central points and methodology of a range of material, and construct responses using the conventions of academic/expository writing. Effective academic writing requires that the student be able to choose appropriate patterns of discourse, which in turn involves knowing sociolinguistic conventions relating to audience and purpose. These skills, acquired through students' attempts to process and produce texts, can be refined over time by having students complete a range of assignments of progressive complexity which derive from the sustained and focused study of one or more academic disciplines.

Sustained content area study is more effectively carried out when an extensive body of instructional and informational resources, such as is found on the internet, is available. Through its extensive collection of reading materials and numerous contexts for meaningful written communication and analysis of issues, the internet creates a highly motivating learning environment that encourages ESL students to interact with language in new and varied ways. Used as a resource for focus discipline research, the internet is highly effective in helping these students develop and refine the academic literacy so necessary for a successful educational experience.

Used as a tool for sustained content study, the internet is a powerful resource that offers easier, wider, and more rapid access to interdisciplinary information than do traditional libraries. Using the internet allows ESL students to control the direction of their reading and research, teaches them to think creatively, and increases motivation for learning as students work individually and collaboratively to gather focus discipline information. By allowing easy access to cross-referenced documents and screens, internet hypertext encourages students to read widely on interdisciplinary topics. This type of reading presents cognitively demanding language, a wide range of linguistic forms, and enables ESL students to build a wider range of schemata and a broader base of knowledge, which may help them grasp future texts. Additionally, hypermedia provides the benefit of immediate visual reinforcement through pictures and/or slideshows, facilitating comprehension of the often-abstract concepts presented in academic readings.

Academic research skills are often underdeveloped in the ESL student population making research reports especially frightening and enormously challenging. The research skills students need to complete focus discipline projects are the same skills they need to succeed in classes. Instruction that targets the development of research skills teaches ESL students the rhetorical conventions of term papers, which subsequently leads to better writing and hence improved performance in class. Moreover, the research skills acquired through sustained content study and focus discipline research enable students to manage information more effectively, which serves them throughout their academic years and into the workforce.

COMPETENCY 5.0 DEMONSTRATE KNOWLEDGE OF STRATEGIES FOR TEACHING AND ASSESSING STUDENT READING COMPREHENSION

Skill 5.1 Recognize the relationship between listening comprehension and reading comprehension.

Listening Comprehension Language is both receptive and expressive. Receptive language has to do with how well language is comprehended, and a listening problem can be the root of a receptive language weakness. If information is not being heard as intended, comprehension will not happen. It may be difficult to determine whether a student is having difficulty comprehending what people say because the ears are not processing the sounds correctly or the brain is not processing what the ears are sending or even that there is a physical hearing problem. Some tests are available to help answer the question; even so, it's not always possible to determine whether it's a processing or a comprehension problem. Some children simply have more difficulty than others separating out the important sounds from distracting background sounds and will eventually just give up. The daydreamer or the doodler may need a break from concentrated listening.

Assuming that the students in your classroom do not have a hearing/comprehension deficit, however, effective listening can be taught, and the English classroom is a good place for this instruction. It can go hand-in-hand with instruction on note taking.

Elements of such training:

- Listening for the main idea
- Listening for supporting ideas
- Listening for examples
- Reconstructing the lecture
- Asking constructive questions to improve comprehension
- Teacher-led discussion that gives students an opportunity to demonstrate what they have comprehended and their own thoughts on the topic

Reading Comprehension Many of the same things can be said for reading comprehension. Some children have reading difficulties, and there are tests that can determine what the exact nature of the difficulty is. There are several kinds of reading disabilities, some of which are linked to neurological dysfunction. If the teacher suspects that a student falls into one of these categories, testing and specialized instruction is in order. The student with such a deficit will have difficulty succeeding in a regular classroom and will either need to be in a special program or have professional supplemental out-of-class assistance.

Some special research studies have demonstrated that the student with a reading disability scores lower on comprehension tests than the student with ADHD; they are clearly two different things and that difference needs to be taken into account.

Assuming that the students in your classroom do not have reading disabilities, reading comprehension skills can be taught. This works particularly well if it goes hand-in-hand with teaching writing skills. Students need to practice looking for the *point* of a written discourse just as they need to learn to focus their writing. What was the writer's aim or purpose? Can the writing be said to be persuasive in nature, for instance, or is it simply conveying useful (or not useful) information? Is it purely expressive with the intention of opening up an experience for the reader? These skills will be taught in the writing classroom and can be reinforced in the reading classroom. If the student understands what the possible structures are in a piece of writing, she will be more skilled at comprehending what is being said.

Another tool for comprehension is learning to react to the written information. What does it have to do with me? Do I agree or disagree with this writer? Once a reader gets to that point, the ability to comprehend has matured to a useful level.

Skill 5.2 Demonstrate knowledge of how types of questions affect reading comprehension and how they can be used to promote comprehension and learning expected in different subject areas.

Questioning is a powerful tool for developing reading comprehension skills. Asking questions before, during and after reading gives a goal to the reading process, helps students recognize what they do and do not know, and engages the mind in higher-order thinking about a topic.

Further, different types of questions lead to different points of focus. Questions seeking factual information guide the student to read the text with an eye towards plucking certain facts out of the content. Generalized questions seeking inferential connections encourage students to seek broader meaning from the text than simply what is read.

Other question types include questions that elicit remembering, check for understanding, encourage application of information, and evaluate the quality of text.

Skill 5.3 Demonstrate knowledge of strategies for encouraging students to respond personally in a variety of formats to literary and informational materials.

See Skill 16.4.

Skill 5.4 **Demonstrate knowledge of strategies for previewing and preparing to read a text effectively.**

Just jumping into a reading assignment may be tempting. Most students just want to get the assignment done and are unwilling to add any steps. Persuading them that they will save time in the long run if they will take the time to do some preliminary preparation for reading a piece will be worth the classroom time. Perhaps a quiz on what each student has done before beginning to read would be effective here.

So what can be done ahead of time? Looking at the date of publication is useful. Knowing that a story, for example, was published in 1930 or in 2005 tells a lot about the setting, characters, etc. Knowing what was going on in the world at that time would also be useful, and an encyclopedia can provide a quick overview. Also, knowing something about the author is useful. Where did the author grow up? What is known about the author's background? Most well known authors will have at least a short biography in an appropriate encyclopedia.

A quick overview of the story before beginning to read can also be useful. Are there chapters with headings? If not, a quick survey of the sections, either chapters or paragraphs, will yield clues that will guide the reading and improve comprehension.

If the assignment is an essay, a quick skimming for paragraph topic sentences and a look at the conclusion will provide useful information before beginning the actual reading.

Students should be warned not to make premature judgments based on any of these pre-reading activities but to let the story or essay speak for itself.

Skill 5.5 **Demonstrate knowledge of strategies for monitoring comprehension and for correcting confusion and misunderstanding that arises during and after reading.**

See Skill 1.8.

Skill 5.6 **Demonstrate knowledge of strategies for helping students identify organizational patterns common to information texts to improve understanding and recall of text.**

Organizational Structures

Authors use a particular organization to best present the concepts, which they are writing about. Teaching students to recognize organizational structures helps them to understand authors' literary intentions, and helps them in deciding which structure to use in their own writing.

Cause and Effect: When writing about *why* things happen, as well as *what* happens, authors commonly use the cause and effect structure. For example, when writing about how he became so successful, a CEO might talk about how he excelled in math in high school, moved to New York after college, and stuck to his goals even after multiple failures. These are all *causes* that lead to the *effect*, or result, of him becoming a wealthy and powerful businessman.

Compare and Contrast: When examining the merits of multiple concepts or products, compare and contrast lends itself easily to organization of ideas. For example, a person writing about foreign policy in different countries will put them against each other to point out differences and similarities, easily highlighting the concepts the author wishes to emphasize.

Problem and Solution: This structure is used in a lot of handbooks and manuals. Anything organized around procedure-oriented tasks, such as a computer repair manual, gravitates toward a problem and solution format, because it offers such clear, sequential text organization.

| DOMAIN II. | WRITING AND RESEARCH |

COMPETENCY 6.0 RECOGNIZE AND UNDERSTAND VARIOUS RHETORICAL STRATEGIES WITHIN WRITING PROCESSES

Skill 6.1 Recognize that varying purposes and audiences call for different form, prewriting strategies, organizational strategies, styles, formats, rules of evidence, and composing processes.

In the past teachers have assigned reports, paragraphs and essays that focused on the teacher as the audience with the purpose of explaining information. However, for students to be meaningfully engaged in their writing, they must write for a variety of reasons. Writing for different audiences and aims allows students to be more involved in their writing. If they write for the same audience and purpose, they will continue to see writing as just another assignment. Listed below are suggestions that give students an opportunity to write in more creative and critical ways.

* Write letters to the editor, to a college, to a friend, to another student that would be sent to the intended audience.

* Write stories that would be read aloud to a group (the class, another group of students, to a group of elementary school students) or published in a literary magazine or class anthology.

* Write plays that would be performed.

* Have students discuss the parallels between the different speeches styles we use and writing styles for different readers or audiences.

* Allow students to write a particular piece for different audiences.

* Make sure students consider the following when analyzing the needs of their audience:

• Why is the audience reading my writing? Do they expect to be informed, amused or persuaded?

• What does my audience already know about my topic?

• What does the audience want or need to know? What will interest them?

• What type of language suits my readers?

* As part of the prewriting have students identify the audience.

* Expose students to writing that is on the same topic but with a different audience and have them identify the variations in sentence structure and style.

- Remind your students that it is not necessary to identify all the specifics of the audience in the initial stage of the writing process but that at some point they must make some determinations about audience.

Skill 6.2   Demonstrate knowledge of writing processes for a variety of writing genres.

It seems simplistic, yet it's an often overlooked truism: the first and most important measure of a story is the story itself. *The story's the thing.* However, a good story must have certain characteristics. Without conflict there is no story, so determining what the conflicts are should be a priority for the writer. Once the conflicts are determined, the outcome of the story must be decided. Who wins? Who loses? And what factors go into making one side of the equation win out over the other one? The pattern of the plot is also an important consideration. Where is the climax going to occur? Is denouement necessary? Does the reader need to see the unwinding of all the strands? Many stories fail because a denouement is needed but not supplied.

Characterization, the choice the writer makes about the devices he will use to reveal character, requires an understanding of human nature and the artistic skill to convey a personality to the reader. This is usually accomplished subtly through dialogue, interior monologue, description, and the character's actions and behavior. In some successful stories, the writer comes right out and tells the reader what this character is like. However, sometimes there will be discrepancies between what the narrator tells the reader about the character and what is revealed to be actual, in which case the narrator is unreliable, and that unreliability of the voice the reader must depend on becomes an important and significant device for understanding the story.

Point of view is a powerful tool not only for the writer but also for the enjoyment and understanding of the reader. The writer must choose among several possibilities: first-person narrator objective, first-person narrator omniscient, third-person objective, third-person omniscient, and third-person limited omniscient. The most successful storywriters use point of view very creatively to accomplish their purposes. If a writer wishes to be successful, he must develop point-of-view skills.

Style—the unique way a writer uses language—is often the writer's signature. The reader does not need to be told that William Faulkner wrote a story to know it because his style is so distinctive that it is immediately recognizable. Even the writing of Toni Morrison, which could be said to be Faulknerian, cannot be mistaken for the work of Faulkner himself.

The writer must be cognizant of his own strengths and weaknesses and continually work to hone the way sentences are written, words are chosen, and descriptions are crafted until they are razor-sharp. The best advice to the aspiring writer: read the works of successful writers. If a writer wants to write a bestseller, then that writer needs to be reading bestsellers.

Poetry. Writing poetry in the twenty-first century is quite a different thing from writing it in earlier periods. There was a time when a poem was required to fit a certain pattern or scheme. Poetry was once defined as a piece of writing that was made up of end-rhymes. No more. The rhymed poem makes up only a small percentage of worthwhile and successful poems nowadays.

The first skill to work on for the budding poet is descriptive writing, defined as language that appeals to one or more of the five senses. A good poem makes it possible for the reader to experience an emotional event—seeing a mountain range as the sun dawns, watching small children on a playground, smelling the fragrance of a rose, hearing a carillon peal a religious tune at sunset, feeling fine silk under one's fingers. Creating language that makes that experience available to the readers is only the first step, however, because the ultimate goal is to evoke an emotional response. Feeling the horror of the battleground, weeping with the mother whose child was drowned, exulting with a winning soccer team. It's not enough to tell the reader what it's like. It's the *showing* that is necessary.

The aspiring poet should know the possibilities as well as the limitations of this genre. A poem can tell a story, for instance, but the emotional response is more important than the story itself. Edgar Allen Poe, in an 1842 review of Hawthorne's *Twice-Told Tales* in *Graham's Magazine* had important advice for the writer of poetry: " . . . the unity of effect or impression is a point of the greatest importance." Even though he considered the tale or short story the best way to achieve this, he wrote several memorable poems and much of his prose writing is considered to be as close to poetry as to prose by most critics. He also wrote in 1847, in an expansion of his critique of Hawthorne's works, that " . . . true originality . . . is that which, in bringing out the half-formed, the reluctant, or the unexpressed fancies of mankind, or in exciting the more delicate pulses of the heart's passion, or in giving birth to some universal sentiment or instinct in embryo, thus combines with the pleasurable effect of *apparent* novelty, a real egoistic delight."

Playwriting. Playwriting uses many of the same skills that are necessary to successful story writing. However, in addition to those skills, there are many more required of the writer who wishes her story to be told on stage or on film. The point of view, of course, is always objective unless the writer uses the Shakespearean device of the soliloquy in which a player steps forward and gives information about what's going on. The audience must figure out the meaning of the play on the basis of the actions and speeches of the actors.

A successful playwright is expert in characterization as described above under **Story**. What a character is like is determined by dialogue, appearance (costume, etc.), behavior, and actions. A successful playwright also understands motivation. If a character's behavior cannot be traced to motivating circumstances, the audience will probably find the action incoherent—a major barrier to positive reception of the play.

The writing must be very carefully honed. Absolutely no excess of words can be found in a successful play. It takes very little time to lose an audience; every word counts. The playwright should concentrate on saying the most possible with the fewest words possible.

Setting is an important feature of the play. Most plays have only one because changing settings in the middle is difficult and disrupting. This calls for a very special kind of writing. The entire action of the play must either take place within the setting or be brought forth in that setting by the reporting or recounting of what is going on outside of the setting by one or more of the characters. The writer must determine what the setting will be. The actual building and creation of the set is in the hands of another kind of artist—one who specializes in settings.

The plot of most plays is rising; that is, the conflicts are introduced early in the play and continue to develop and intensify over the life of the play. As a general rule, the climax is the last thing that happens before the final curtain falls, but not necessarily. Plots of plays demonstrate the same breadth of patterns that are true of stories. For example, a play may end with nothing resolved. Denouement is less likely to follow a climax in a play than in a story, but epilogues do sometimes occur.

News reporters generally become excellent writers because they get a lot of practice, which is a principle most writing teachers try to employ with their students. Also, news writing is instructive in skills for writing clearly and coherently. Reporters generally write in two modes: straight reporting and feature writing. In both modes, the writer must be concerned with accuracy and objectivity. The reporter does not write his opinions. He/she does not write persuasive discourse. The topic is typically assigned, although some experienced reporters have the opportunity to seek out and develop their own stories.

Investigative reporting is sometimes seen as a distinct class although, technically, all reporters are "investigative." That is, they research the background of the story they're reporting, using as many means as are available. For example, the wife of a conservative, model minister murders him premeditatively and in cold blood. The reporter reports the murder and the arrest of the wife, but the story is far from complete until some questions are answered, the most obvious one being "why?"

The reporter is obligated to try to answer that question and to do so will interview as many people as will talk to him about the lives of both minister and wife, their parents, members of the church, their neighbors, etc. The reporter will also look at newspaper archives in the town where the murder took place as well as in newspapers in any town the husband and/or wife has lived in previously. High-school yearbooks are sources that are often explored in these cases.

When Bob Woodward and Carl Bernstein, reporters for *The Washington Post*, began to break the Watergate story in 1972 and 1973, they set new standards for investigative reporting and had a strong influence on journalistic writing. Most reporters wanted to be Woodward and Bernstein and became more aggressive than reporters had been in the past. Even so, the basic techniques and principles still apply. The reporting of these two talented journalists demonstrated that while newspapers keep communities aware of what's going on, they also have the power to influence it.

A good news story is written in the inverted pyramid style. That is, the reasoning is deductive. The thesis or point is stated first and is supported with details. It reasons from general to specific. The lead sentence might be, "The body of John Smith was found in the street in front of his home with a bullet wound through his skull." The headline will be a trimmed-down version of that sentence and shaped to grab attention. It might read: "Murdered man found on Spruce Street." The news article might fill several columns, the first details having to do with the finding of the body, the next the role of the police; the third will spread out and include details about the victim's life, then the scope will broaden to details about his family, friends, neighbors, etc. If he held a position of prominence in the community, those details will broaden further and include information about his relationships to co-workers and his day-to-day contacts in the community. The successful reporter's skills include the ability to do thorough research, to maintain an objective stance (not to become involved personally in the story), and to write an effective inverted pyramid.

Feature writing is more like an informative essay although it may also follow the inverted pyramid model. This form of reporting focuses on a topic designed to be interesting to at least one segment of the readership—possible sports enthusiasts, travelers, vacationers, families, women, food lovers, etc. The article will focus on one aspect of the area of interest such as a particular experience for the vacationing family. The first sentence might read something like this: "Lake

Lure offers a close-to-home relaxing weekend getaway for families in East Tennessee." The development can be an ever-widening pyramid of details focused particularly on what the family can experience at Lake Lure but also directions for how to get there.

While the headline is intended to contain in capsule form the point that an article makes, the reporter rarely writes it. This can sometimes result in a disconnection between headline and article.

Well-written headlines will provide a guide for the reader as to what is in the article; they will also be attention-grabbers. This requires a special kind of writing; quite different from the inverted pyramid that distinguishes these writers from the investigative or feature reporter.

It may seem sometimes that the **business letter** is a thing of the past. Although much business-letter writing has been relegated to email communications, letters are still a valuable and potentially valuable form of communication. A carefully written letter can be powerful. It can alienate, convince, persuade, entice, motivate, and/or create goodwill.

As with any other communication, it's worthwhile to learn as much as possible about the receiver. This may be complicated if there will be more than one receiver of the message; in these cases, it's best to aim for the lowest common denominator if that can be achieved without condescending to any of those who will read and be affected or influenced by the letter. It may be better to send more than one form of the letter to the various receivers in some cases.

Purpose is the most powerful factor in writing a business letter. What is the letter expected to accomplish? Is it intended to get the receiver to act or to act in a specific manner? Are you hoping to see some action take place as the result of the letter? If so, you should clearly define for yourself what the purpose is before you craft the letter, and it's good to include a time deadline for the response.

Reasons for choosing the letter as the channel of communication include the following:
- It's easy to keep a record of the transaction.
- The message can be edited and perfected before it is transmitted.
- It facilitates the handling of details.
- It's ideal for communicating complex information.
- It's a good way to disseminate mass messages at a relatively low cost.

The parts of a business letter are as follows: date line, inside address, salutation, subject line, body, complimentary close, company name, signature block, reference initials, enclosure notation, copy notation, and postscript.

Business letters typically use formal language. They should be straightforward and courteous. The writing should be concise and special care should be taken to avoid omitting important information out. Clarity is very important; otherwise, it may take more than one exchange of letters or phone calls to get the message across.

A complaint is a different kind of business letter. It can come under the classification of a "bad news" business letter, and there are some guidelines that are helpful when writing this kind of letter. A positive writing style can overcome much of the inherent negativity of a letter of complaint.

No matter how much in the right you may be, maintaining self-control and courtesy and avoiding demeaning or blaming language is more likely to be effective. Abruptness, condescension, or harshness of tone will not help achieve your purpose, particularly if you are requesting a positive response such as reimbursement for a bad product or some help in righting a wrong that may have been done to you. It's important to remember that you want to solve the specific problem and to retain the good will of the receiver if possible.

Induction is better than deduction for this type of communication. Beginning with the details and building to the statement of the problem generally has the effect of softening the bad news. It's also useful to begin with an opening that will serve as a buffer. The same is true for the closing. It's a good idea to leave the reader with a favorable impression by writing a closing paragraph that will generate goodwill rather than bad.

News articles are written in the inverted pyramid format—they are deductive in nature: the opening statement is the point of the article; everything else is detail. "Who, what, why, when, and where" are usually the questions to be answered in a news article.

A formal essay, on the other hand, may be persuasive, informative, descriptive, or narrative in nature. The purpose should be clearly defined, and development must be coherent and easy to follow.

Email has revolutionized business communications. It has most of the advantages of business letters and the added ones of immediacy, lower costs, and convenience. Even very long reports can be attached to an email. On the other hand, a two-line message can be sent and a response received immediately bringing together the features of a postal system and the telephone. Instant messaging goes even one step further. It can do all of the above—send messages, attach reports, etc.—and still have many of the advantages of a telephone conversation. Email has an unwritten code of behavior that includes restrictions on how informal the writing can be. The level of accepted business conversation is usually also acceptable in emails. Capital letters and bolding are considered shouting and are usually frowned on.

Freedom of the press is essential to democracy. In this form of government, representatives are elected by the people, are responsible to them, and they are entitled to know what those representatives are doing. The only way that can happen is if the press is free to report the news in an unbiased manner. If the mayor of a city has a conflict of interest that is profiting him, the people need to know. If an elected representative is arrested for driving under the influence, that representative's constituency has a right to know. It's the only way unbiased management of the public interest can occur.

For these reasons, news media have an obligation to keep themselves unencumbered and unbiased. Most newspeople pride themselves on their objectivity.

News stories are always assumed to be unbiased. It can be argued, of course, that no one can be entirely unbiased and that it's the nature of the written word that those biases may creep into the reporting of news. Even so, the professional reporter and/or editor will exercise the strength necessary to keep his or her own biases out of the reporting as much as possible.

Editorializing is an entirely different thing. Most newspapers, for instance, have an editorial position, which will often correspond to political parties. A newspaper may, for instance, declare itself to be Republican. This does not mean that the newspaper will favor the party of choice in news reporting. It does, however, mean that editorial materials will probably be slanted in that direction. In a time of election, a newspaper will often come out for one candidate over another and try to influence its readership to follow suit. A newspaper will often take a side when an *issue* is on the docket at time of election or even at other times. An editorial will frequently state an opinion about a matter that concerns the newspaper's readership.

Skill 6.3 Recognize write-to-discover strategies such as journaling, log writing, sixty-second writing, and free writing.

Student writers tend to feel that they have nothing worthwhile to write about. If they read significant writers and identify with them, this can be a way to get them to open up and record their own uniqueness in their writing. If they understand that a writer lived a life that was unique just as their own lives are unique and the only difference is that the writer found a way to turn that uniqueness into something that others would enjoy reading and would benefit from, perhaps they will be more willing to probe their inner selves and write meaningfully—not just the standard "What I Did on My Vacation Last Summer" but "How the Birth of My Baby Brother Changed My Life." If they can accept that their own unique experiences, observations, and cogitations are worthwhile, then they will be able to use write-to-discover strategies successfully.

Using the journaling of a successful writer whose work they have read, enjoyed, and discussed would be a good way to start with a journaling assignment. Make the distinction between keeping a journal and keeping a diary. The journal entries should be made with the conscious thought that they might become a resource for a written piece.

Sixty-second writing adds the element of pressure to the prewriting activity, and sometimes this pressure will increase its productivity. If writers know that they must get everything down in sixty seconds, the results may be very surprising. It's a quite different activity than the open-ended free writing that is often so useful in the first stage of composing.

Free writing is just writing what comes to mind, page after page. If some research or some thinking has already been done about a topic, this is particularly useful. From such a prewriting can come enough material to structure a successful essay, story, or even poem. Deriving a thesis statement, a purpose, or a point for the composition is usually facilitated in this way.

Students sometimes just want to cut to the chase and get the essay written and are unwilling to spin their wheels on prewriting. Once they understand how helpful it is in getting started, they will be more willing to participate. Sometimes students find they enjoy the opportunity to put their ideas, feelings, etc., on paper, especially if no one else is going to look at them. It's recommended that the teacher respect the privacy of the student and only discuss what has gone on the paper during prewriting if the student requests help moving to the next stage and is comfortable sharing the prewriting.

Remember that you are teaching writing as it actually occurs for successful writers—a process. If students understand that everyone who writes goes through some stage of prewriting, they will be more willing to learn the skill. It's an important skill. Even more, it's an important understanding for the student whose future as a student and as an adult will probably depend on the development of the techniques that lead to effective presentation of their own thoughts and ideas.

Skill 6.4   Recognize a variety of prewriting strategies for generating and organizing ideas.

Remind students that as they prewrite they need to consider their audience. Prewriting strategies assist students in a variety of ways. Listed below are the most common prewriting strategies students can use to explore, plan and write on a topic. It is important to remember when teaching these strategies that not all prewriting must eventually produce a finished piece of writing. In fact, in the initial lesson of teaching prewriting strategies, it might be more effective to have students practice prewriting strategies without the pressure of having to write a finished product.

* Keep an idea book so that they can jot down ideas that come to mind.

* Write in a daily journal.

* Write down whatever comes to mind; this is called free writing. Students do not stop to make corrections or interrupt the flow of ideas. A variation of this technique is focused free writing - writing on a specific topic - to prepare for an essay.

* Make a list of all ideas connected with their topic; this is called brainstorming. Make sure students know that this technique works best when they let their mind work freely. After completing the list, students should analyze the list to see if a pattern or way to group the ideas.

* Ask the questions Who? What? When? Where? When? and How? Help the writer approach a topic from several perspectives.

* Create a visual map on paper to gather ideas. Cluster circles and lines to show connections between ideas. Students should try to identify the relationship that exists between their ideas. If they cannot see the relationships, have them pair up, exchange papers and have their partners look for some related ideas.

* Observe details of sight, hearing, taste, touch, and taste.

* Visualize by making mental images of something and write down the details in a list.

After students have practiced with each of these prewriting strategies, ask them to choose the ones they prefer and discuss how they might use the techniques to help them with future writing assignments. It is important to remember that they can use more than one prewriting strategy at a time. Also they may find that different writing situations may suggest certain techniques.

Skill 6.5 **Recognize how to write clear and effective prompts that challenge students to practice a variety of prewriting and writing strategies for different rhetorical situations.**

Most teachers have the experience of carefully preparing writing assignments that seem to miss the mark. What seemed clear and straightforward in preparation didn't turn out to be so for the students. Because students learn the most about writing by writing, the ability to create effective assignments that lead students to creatively use and practice the strategies you're teaching them is crucial if they are to experience the growth we look forward to seeing when the course is over. Fortunately, there are some guidelines for writing such assignments.

From the time students enter middle school, the goals of the English curriculum must include the production of the kind of writing that will be required when they enter college, which will include writing for a variety of audiences such as faculty in various departments, the general public, and the work place. Objectives, on the other hand, will include the ability to write in several genres and for different audiences.

The goals and objectives must be realizable. The effective writing teacher will perfect the ability to write achievable, worthwhile goals and objectives. No class should begin without the teacher's having a clear concept of what will be true in terms of student understanding and performance once the class has ended. The same thing can be said of the various stages the course will go through. Many teachers write their assignments before the class ever begins, and then make adjustments in those assignments to fit the progress of a particular group of students. Whatever approach the teacher takes, the class should be envisioned as a complete entity, and outcomes should be anticipated before it ever begins.

Sequencing the assignments The rhetorical mode that students have the most experience with is persuasion. They have become quite expert at persuading their parents to give them what they want or to let them do what they want to do. They begin practicing these skills almost as soon as they can speak, so this is a good place to start and a good place to end. Remember that critical-thinking skills can and should be taught, and they apply most directly to this mode. This is not to say that other modes should be neglected; however, they do need to be set in the structure of the persuasive mode. Certainly comparison/analysis is one way of making a point clear. Descriptive writing is often used to move an audience emotionally, and this is a good time to help students understand the ethical aspects of persuasion, that emotion as a persuader is only one tool, not the only tool, as many religious and political speakers and writers seem to believe. Establishing credibility is important for any writer/speaker, and students can be led to understand its use in the persuasion process. Exposition, of course, the explaining, informative mode, is vital to effective persuasion as is definition.

Persuasive writing provides an excellent opportunity to teach thesis, support, critical thinking, and use of examples. The skeleton of an argument is a good way for students to see how the thinking and writing process works. An analysis of a poem or a story or an essay is persuasive in nature: it states an opinion about the work and then uses examples from the work itself as support.

Assignments should never be made orally, and they should be straightforward. It's good to give students the outline as soon as the class begins to meet. This doesn't mean that it is set in stone forever. No two classes progress exactly the same, and the teacher needs the freedom and flexibility to make adjustments as the class moves through the semester. Even so, giving students some insight on what is to come can be helpful for some and is likely to lead them to be more cooperative. Also, creating an outline that they will have in their own hands will help the teacher to think more critically about outcomes and goals.

Some teachers who are very good writers of prompts will link all the essays in a writing class together, perhaps beginning with observation that will make no attempt to make a point. Using that observation, the sequence can move forward, teaching each of the skills and tools that are available in writing to make a statement, writing that someone will want to read.

The final essay, then, can take the assignments and work of the semester and demonstrate their use in a worthwhile piece of writing that will display what has been learned.

Some guidelines for effective prompts:
- Fit into a sequence that is understood and seen by the students as one step toward a final goal.
- Make clear what the student is expected to do, and the mode being worked on in this assignment is clear.
- Be specific about how the assignment is to be completed and presented. If an informal tone is expected, then the assignment should say so. If outside sources are to be used, details should be specified. Such things as whether it's to be typed; sent electronically, what the due date is; required length; etc.
- Give guidelines about purpose—what the paper is supposed to do and who the audience is.
- Criteria to be used in assessing the paper.

Writing is a very complex skill. There is no way to make it simple. Trying to teach and test everything at once will inevitably lead to failure on the teacher's part as well as on the students'. Teaching the complexities in stages and then linking them together has the best chance of changing the writing behaviors of students in a positive way—the best objective a writing class can achieve.

Skill 6.6   Recognize various response strategies for helping students revise texts for appropriateness in a variety of rhetorical situations.

See Skills 7.2, 7.3, and 7.7.

COMPETENCY 7.0 DEMONSTRATE KNOWLEDGE OF COMPOSITION, INCLUDING DRAFTING STRATEGIES NECESSARY FOR WRITING IN VARIOUS RHETORICAL SITUATIONS

Skill 7.1   Recognize the elements of composition in a variety of rhetorical situations.

Once a topic is assigned or chosen, the next step is to begin to gather supporting materials. Those materials may come from the writer's own experience, and the best way to collect them is in prewriting—simply putting on paper whatever is there by way of past experience relevant to the topic; observations concerning it; newspaper articles or books that have been read on the topic; and television or radio presentations that have to do with the topic. The writer needs to keep in mind the importance of making a statement about the topic—to declare something about it. Very often, once the writer has gone through this exercise, getting his own ideas and thoughts down on paper, a thesis or several theses may emerge. If not, then it is time to do active research on the topic.

If possible, it's better to write more than one thesis statement before research begins. However, a successful writer will set a point when a single one must be chosen so the development of the paper may proceed. Once that decision has been made, the narrowing process begins. The writer should be asking such questions as "Is the scope too broad to cover in a 500-word paper?" For example, if the thesis statement is "Democracy is the best form of government," it will take a book or even several books to develop. However, if the thesis statement is "Democracy is the best form of government for Iraq," then it begins to become more doable. Even so, some narrowing of the predicate may still be in order. "The development of a democratic government will solve the problems of cultural and religious divisions in Iraq" may be a thesis that could be developed in one classroom assignment.

Remembering that the introduction and conclusion should be written after the paper is developed so the writer will know what is being introduced and concluded. A decision should be made as to whether the reasoning will be inductive, from particular to general or deductive, general to particular. Will the pattern be inductive—evidence presented first and the thesis stated at the end? Will the thesis—the generalization—be presented first and then the proofs and evidence?

Will the introduction offer background information or be an anecdote or other device that will help lead the reader into the thesis and proofs? Or will it simply be designed to grab the reader's interest? It can also be used to establish the credibility of the writer. In the conclusion, will the reasoning be restated briefly with emphasis on the point of the paper, or will it also be anecdotal in nature? Whatever form it takes, it should reinforce the point the paper makes and leave the reader with a favorable impression.

Skill 7.2 Recognize how to compose writing prompts that provide opportunities to practice drafting documents.

Students must write to improve writing skills, and students must learn and practice editing techniques to become effective writers. The prompts the teacher writes should include not only opportunities for doing this but also requirements for it. The best teaching that happens in the writing class happens here. In the first place, assignments should be sequenced (see Skill 6.5) so that the student begins dealing with a part of a final production piece with the very first essay. Once this essay has been graded—that is, edited by the teacher with queries and recommendations—the student will respond with an edited version, which will again be read by the teacher/editor and returned with, possibly, more queries and recommendations.

Some do's for responding:
- Always find something to praise and do that first.
- Help students understand what it means to edit a piece of writing and how this stage fits in the process. Sometimes, it's helpful to show students how the editing process works even with professional writers.
- Set inflexible dates for return of a response from the student and ensure that you make quick responses yourself. Be reasonable about your own schedule and allow enough time to return the papers as promptly as possible. The whole process breaks down if the exchanges are not timely.
- Heavy doses of encouragement are important for fledgling writers. Remember that the very nature of putting one's own words on paper is sensitive, and the student's words should be treated respectfully and with the intent to encourage.

Some don'ts for responding:
- Making it personal. A student may be arrogant and troublesome, but responding to that on a paper instead of the paper itself is counterproductive. Find other ways to deal with class behavior.
- Responding with too little information.
- Responding with too much information. Get to the point.
- Lack of clarity. Make sure the student understands how to move forward.
- Seeming too busy to give student the time needed to help with the writing. One-on-one help is difficult in a busy schedule. Try to work out the time needed to work with each student, even if you need to take class time to do it.

Some recommendations:
- Use something other than a red pencil if you are responding on a hard copy.

- Use Word's tracking feature to communicate with students regarding their papers.
- Always find some time in a semester to talk with a student one-on-one regarding his or her writing.
- Help students see writing not as a classroom activity but as a real part of their futures.

Skill 7.3 **Recognize that drafting is an important recursive component in the writing process.**

Writing is a recursive process. As students engage in the various stages of writing, they develop and improve not only their writing skills, but their thinking skills as well. The stages of the writing process are as follows:

PREWRITING

Students gather ideas before writing. Prewriting may include clustering, listing, brainstorming, mapping, free writing, and charting. Providing many ways for a student to develop ideas on a topic will increase his/her chances for success.

WRITING

Students compose the first draft.

REVISING

Students examine their work and make changes in sentences, wording, details and ideas. "Revise" comes from the Latin word *revidere*, meaning, "to see again."

EDITING

Students proofread the draft for punctuation and mechanical errors.

PUBLISHING

Students may have their work displayed on a bulletin board, read aloud in class, or printed in a literary magazine or school anthology.

It is important to realize that these steps are recursive; as a student engages in each aspect of the writing process, he or she may begin with prewriting, write, revise, write, revise, edit, and publish. They do not engage in this process in a lockstep manner; it is more circular.

TEACHING THE COMPOSING PROCESS

Prewriting Activities

1. Class discussion of the topic.
2. Map out ideas, questions, and graphic organizers on the chalkboard.
3. Break into small groups to discuss different ways of approaching the topic and develop an organizational plan and create a thesis statement.
4. Research the topic if necessary.

Drafting/Revising

1. Students write first draft in class or at home.
2. Students engage in peer response and class discussion.
3. Using checklists or a rubric, students critique each other's writing and make suggestions for revising the writing.
4. Students revise.

Editing and Proofreading

1. Students, working in pairs, analyze sentences for variety.
2. Students work in groups to read papers for punctuation and mechanics.
3. Students perform final edit.

Skill 7.4 Demonstrate knowledge of the conventions of spelling, sentence construction, and usage.

It is assumed that any candidate for a certificate to teach language arts will have a thorough understanding of English grammar.

Test Format

Most teacher tests of professional knowledge of grammar will consist of either multiple-choice questions that require selecting an example of correct sentence structure, grammar, punctuation, capitalization, spelling, or usage from four or five options and/or an essay question that requires application of all grammatical skills. These questions may also require knowledge of traditional and non-traditional approaches to the study of grammar. Familiarity with terms such as prescriptive/ traditional, transformational/ generative, and structural grammars and recognition of their differences in the approaches to learning grammar is to be expected.

Areas of Review

To review rules of grammar in more depth, use any high school/college grammar textbook. (Warriner's books or Strunk and White's *Elements of Style* are highly recommended.)

SYNTAX

Sentence completeness

Avoid fragments and run-on sentences. Recognition of sentence elements necessary to make a complete thought, proper use of independent and dependent clauses (see *Use correct coordination and subordination*), and proper punctuation will correct such errors.

Sentence structure

See Skill 1.6.

Parallelism

Recognize parallel structures using phrases (prepositional, gerund, participial, and infinitive) and omissions from sentences that create the lack of parallelism.

Prepositional phrase/single modifier

Incorrect: Coleen ate the ice cream with enthusiasm and hurriedly.

Correct: Coleen ate the ice cream with enthusiasm and in a hurry.

Correct: Coleen ate the ice cream enthusiastically and hurriedly.

Participial phrase/infinitive phrase

Incorrect: After hiking for hours and to sweat profusely, Joe sat down to rest and drinking water.

Correct: After hiking for hours and sweating profusely, Joe sat down to rest and drink water.

Recognition of dangling modifiers

Dangling phrases are attached to sentence parts in such a way they create ambiguity and incorrectness of meaning.

Participial phrase

Incorrect: Hanging from her skirt, Dot tugged at a loose thread.

Correct: Dot tugged at a loose thread hanging from her skirt.

Incorrect: Relaxing in the bathtub, the telephone rang.

Correct: While I was relaxing in the bathtub, the telephone rang.

Infinitive phrase

Incorrect: To improve his behavior, the dean warned Fred.

Correct: The dean warned Fred to improve his behavior.

Prepositional phrase

Incorrect: On the floor, Father saw the dog eating table scraps.

Correct: Father saw the dog eating table scraps on the floor.

Recognition of syntactical redundancy or omission

These errors occur when superfluous words have been added to a sentence or key words have been omitted from a sentence.

Redundancy

Incorrect: Joyce made sure that when her plane arrived that she retrieved all of her luggage.

Correct: Joyce made sure that when her plane arrived she retrieved all of her luggage.

Incorrect: He was a mere skeleton of his former self.

Correct: He was a skeleton of his former self.

Omission

Incorrect: Dot opened her book, recited her textbook, and answered the teacher's subsequent question.

Correct: Dot opened her book, recited from the textbook, and answered the teacher's subsequent question.

Avoidance of double negatives

This error occurs from positioning two negatives that in fact cancel each other in meaning.

Incorrect: Harold couldn't care less whether he passes this class.

Correct: Harold could care less whether he passes this class.

Incorrect: Dot didn't have no double negatives in her paper.

Correct: Dot didn't have any double negatives in her paper.

Correct use of coordination and subordination

Connect independent clauses with the coordinating conjunctions - *and*, *but*, *or*, *for*, or *nor* - when their content is of equal importance. Use subordinating conjunctions - *although, because, before, if, since, though, until, when, whenever, where* - and relative pronouns - *that, who, whom, which* - to introduce clauses that express ideas that are subordinate to main ideas expressed in independent clauses. (See *Sentence Structure* above.) Be sure to place the conjunctions so that they express the proper relationship between ideas (cause/effect, condition, time, space).

Incorrect: Because mother scolded me, I was late.

Correct: Mother scolded me because I was late.

Incorrect: The sun rose after the fog lifted.

Correct: The fog lifted after the sun rose.

Notice that placement of the conjunction can completely change the meaning of the sentence. Main emphasis is shifted by the change.

Although Jenny was pleased, the teacher was disappointed.
Although the teacher was disappointed, Jenny was pleased.

The boys who had written the essay won the contest.

The boys who won the contest had written the essay.

Note: *While not syntactically incorrect, the second sentence makes it appear that the boys won the contest for something else before they wrote the essay.*

GRAMMAR

Subject-verb agreement

A verb agrees in number with its subject. Making them agree relies on the ability to properly identify the subject.

One of the boys *was playing* too rough.

No one in the class, not the teacher nor the students, was listening to the message from the intercom.

The candidates, including a grandmother and a teenager, are debating some controversial issues.

If two singular subjects are connected by *and* the verb must be plural.

A *man* and his *dog* were jogging on the beach.

If two singular subjects are connected by *or* or *nor*, a singular verb is required.

Neither Dot nor Joyce has missed a day of school this year.

Either Fran or Paul is missing.

If one singular subject and one plural subject are connected by *or* or *nor*, the verb agrees with the subject nearest to the verb.

Neither the coach nor the players were able to sleep on the bus.

If the subject is a collective noun, its sense of number in the sentence determines the verb: singular if the noun represents a group or unit and plural if the noun represents individuals.

The House of Representatives has adjourned for the holidays.

The House of Representatives has failed to reach agreement on the subject of adjournment.

Use of verbs (tense)

Present tense is used to express that which is currently happening or is always true.

Randy is playing the piano.

Randy plays the piano like a pro.

Past tense is used to express action that occurred in a past time.

Randy learned to play the piano when he was six years old.

Future tense is used to express action or a condition of future time.

Randy will probably earn a music scholarship.

Present perfect tense is used to express action or a condition that started in the past and is continued to or completed in the present.

Randy has practiced piano every day for the last ten years.

Randy has never been bored with practice.

Past perfect tense expresses action or a condition that occurred as a precedent to some other past action or condition.

Randy had considered playing clarinet before he discovered the piano.

Future perfect tense expresses action that started in the past or the present and will conclude at some time in the future.

By the time he goes to college, Randy will have been an accomplished pianist for more than half of his life.

Use of verbs (mood)

Indicative mood is used to make unconditional statements; subjunctive mood is used for conditional clauses or wish statements that pose conditions that are untrue. Verbs in subjunctive mood are plural with both singular and plural subjects.

If I were a bird, I would fly.

I wish I were as rich as Donald Trump.

Verb conjugation

The conjugation of verbs follows the patterns used in the discussion of tense above. However, the most frequent problems in verb use stem from the improper formation of past and past participial forms.

Regular verb: believe, believed, (have) + believed

Irregular verbs: run, ran, run; sit, sat, sat; teach, taught, taught

Other problems stem from the use of verbs that are the same in some tense but have different forms and different meanings in other tenses.

I lie on the ground. I lay on the ground yesterday. I have lain down.

I lay the blanket on the bed. I laid the blanket there yesterday. I have laid the blanket every night.

The sun rises. The sun rose. The sun has risen.

He raises the flag. He raised the flag. He had raised the flag.

I sit on the porch. I sat on the porch. I have sat in the porch swing.

I set the plate on the table. I set the plate there yesterday. I had set the table before dinner.

Two other verb problems stem from misusing the preposition *of* for the verb auxiliary *has* and misusing the verb *ought* (now rare).

Incorrect: I should of gone to bed.

Correct: I should have gone to bed.

Incorrect: He hadn't ought to get so angry.

Correct: He ought not to get so angry.

Use of pronouns

A pronoun used as a subject of predicate nominative is in nominative case.

She was the drum majorette. The lead trombonists were Joe and he.

The band director accepted whoever could march in step.

A pronoun used as a direct object, indirect object or object of a preposition is in objective case.

The teacher praised him. She gave him an A on the test. Her praise of him was appreciated. The students whom she did not praise will work harder next time.

Common pronoun errors occur from misuse of reflexive pronouns:

Singular: *myself, yourself, herself, himself, itself*

Plural: *ourselves, yourselves, themselves.*

Incorrect: Jack cut hisself shaving.

Correct: Jack cut himself shaving.

Incorrect: They backed theirselves into a corner.

Correct: They backed themselves into a corner.

Use of adjectives

An adjective should agree with its antecedent in number.

Those apples are rotten. This one is ripe. These peaches are hard.

Comparative adjectives end in -er and superlatives in -est, with some exceptions like *worse* and *worst*. Some adjectives that cannot easily make comparative inflections are preceded by *more* and *most*.

Mrs. Carmichael is the better of the two basketball coaches.

That is the hastiest excuse you have ever contrived.

Candy is the most beautiful baby.

Avoid double superlatives.

Incorrect: This is the worstest headache I ever had.

Correct: This is the worst headache I ever had.

When comparing one thing to others in a group, exclude the thing under comparison from the rest of the group.

Incorrect: Joey is larger than any baby I have ever seen. (Since you have seen him, he cannot be larger than himself.)

Correct: Joey is larger than any other baby I have ever seen.

Include all necessary words to make a comparison clear in meaning.

I am as tall as my mother. I am as tall as she (is).

My cats are better behaved than those of my neighbor.

MECHANICS

The candidate should be cognizant of proper rules and conventions of punctuation, capitalization, and spelling. Competency exams will generally test the ability to apply the more advanced skills; thus, a limited number of more frustrating rules are presented here. Rules should be applied according to the American style of English, e.g., spelling *theater* instead of *theatre* and placing terminal marks of punctuation almost exclusively within other marks of punctuation.

Punctuation

Using terminal punctuation in relation to quotation marks

In a quoted statement that is either declarative or imperative, place the period inside the closing quotation marks.

"The airplane crashed on the runway during takeoff."

If the quotation is followed by other words in the sentence, place a comma inside the closing quotations marks and a period at the end of the sentence.

"The airplane crashed on the runway during takeoff," said the announcer.

In most instances in which a quoted title or expression occurs at the end of a sentence, the period is placed before either the single or double quotation marks.

"The middle school readers were unprepared to understand Bryant's poem 'Thanatopsis.'"

Early book-length adventure stories like *Don Quixote* and *The Three Musketeers* were known as "picaresque novels."

There is an instance in which the final quotation mark would precede the period - if the content of the sentence were about a speech or quote so that the understanding of the meaning would be confused by the placement of the period.

The first thing out of his mouth was "Hi, I'm home." *but* The first line of his speech began "I arrived home to an empty house".

In sentences that are interrogatory or exclamatory, the question mark or exclamation point should be positioned outside the closing quotation marks if the quote itself is a statement or command or cited title.

Who decided to lead us in the recitation of the "Pledge of Allegiance"?

Why was Tillie shaking as she began her recitation, "Once upon a midnight dreary..."?

I was embarrassed when Mrs. White said, "Your slip is showing"!

In sentences that are declarative but the quotation is a question or an exclamation, place the question mark or exclamation point inside the quotation marks.

The hall monitor yelled, "Fire! Fire!"

"Fire! Fire!" yelled the hall monitor.

Cory shrieked, "Is there a mouse in the room?" (In this instance, the question supersedes the exclamation.)

Using periods with parentheses or brackets

Place the period inside the parentheses or brackets if they enclose a complete sentence, independent of the other sentences around it.

Stephen Crane was a confirmed alcohol and drug addict. (He admitted as much to other journalists in Cuba.)

If the parenthetical expression is a statement inserted within another statement, the period in the enclosure is omitted.

Mark Twain used the character Indian Joe (He also appeared in *The Adventures of Tom Sawyer*) as a foil for Jim in *The Adventures of Huckleberry Finn*.

When enclosed matter comes at the end of a sentence requiring quotation marks, place the period outside the parentheses or brackets.

"The secretary of state consulted with the ambassador [Albright]."

Using commas

Separate two or more coordinate adjectives, modifying the same word and three or more nouns, phrases, or clauses in a list.

Maggie's hair was dull, dirty, and lice-ridden.

Dickens portrayed the Artful Dodger as skillful pickpocket, loyal follower of Fagin, and defendant of Oliver Twist.

Ellen daydreamed about getting out of the rain, taking a shower, and eating a hot dinner.

In Elizabethan England, Ben Jonson wrote comedy, Christopher Marlowe wrote tragedies, and William Shakespeare composed both.

Use commas to separate antithetical or complimentary expressions from the rest of the sentence.

The veterinarian, not his assistant, would perform the delicate surgery.

The more he knew about her, the less he wished he had known.

Randy hopes to, and probably will, get an appointment to the Naval Academy.

His thorough, though esoteric, scientific research could not easily be understood by high school students.

Using double quotation marks with other punctuation

Quotations - whether words, phrases, or clauses - should be punctuated according to the rules of the grammatical function they serve in the sentence.

The works of Shakespeare, "the bard of Avon," have been contested as originating with other authors.

"You'll get my money," the old man warned, "when 'Hell freezes over'."

Sheila cited the passage that began "Four score and seven years ago...." (Note the ellipsis followed by an enclosed period.)

"Old Ironsides" inspired the preservation of the U.S.S. Constitution.

Use quotation marks to enclose the titles of shorter works: songs, short poems, short stories, essays, and chapters of books. (See "Using Italics" for punctuating longer titles.)

"The Tell-Tale Heart"   "Casey at the Bat"   "America the Beautiful"

Using semicolons

Use semicolons to separate independent clauses when the second clause is introduced by a transitional adverb. (These clauses may also be written as separate sentences, preferably by placing the adverb within the second sentence.)

The Elizabethans modified the rhyme scheme of the sonnet; thus, it was called the English sonnet.

or

The Elizabethans modified the rhyme scheme of the sonnet. It thus was called the English sonnet.

Use semicolons to separate items in a series that are long and complex or have internal punctuation.

The Italian Renaissance produced masters in the fine arts: Dante Alighieri, author of the *Divine Comedy;* Leonardo da Vinci, painter of *The Last Supper;* and Donatello, sculptor of the *Quattro Coronati*, the four saints.

The leading scorers in the WNBA were Haizhaw Zheng, averaging 23.9 points per game; Lisa Leslie, 22; and Cynthia Cooper, 19.5.

Using colons

Place a colon at the beginning of a list of items. (Note its use in the sentence about Renaissance Italians on this page.)

The teacher directed us to compare Faulkner's three symbolic novels: *Absalom, Absalom; As I Lay Dying;* and *Light in August*.

Do **not** use a comma if the list is preceded by a verb.

Three of Faulkner's symbolic novels are *Absalom, Absalom; As I Lay Dying,* and *Light in August*.

Using dashes

Place dashes to denote sudden breaks in thought.

Some periods in literature - the Romantic Age, for example - spanned different time periods in different countries.

Use dashes instead of commas if commas are already used elsewhere in the sentence for amplification or explanation.
The Fireside Poets included three Brahmans - James Russell Lowell, Henry David Wadsworth, Oliver Wendell Holmes and John Greenleaf Whittier.

Use italics to punctuate the titles of long works of literature, names of periodical publications, musical scores, works of art and motion picture television, and radio programs. (When unable to write in italics, students should be instructed to underline in their own writing where italics would be appropriate.)

The Idylls of the King   *Hiawatha*   *The Sound and the Fury*
Mary Poppins   *Newsweek*   *The Nutcracker Suite*

Capitalization

Capitalize all proper names of persons (including specific organizations or agencies of government); places (countries, states, cities, parks, and specific geographical areas); and things (political parties, structures, historical and cultural terms, and calendar and time designations); and religious terms (any deity, revered person or group, sacred writings).

Percy Bysshe Shelley, Argentina, Mount Rainier National Park, Grand Canyon, League of Nations, the Sears Tower, Birmingham, Lyric Theater, Americans, Midwesterners, Democrats, Renaissance, Boy Scouts of America, Easter, God, Bible, Dead Sea Scrolls, Koran

Capitalize proper adjectives and titles used with proper names.

California gold rush, President John Adams, French fries, Homeric epic, Romanesque architecture, Senator John Glenn

Note: *Some words that represent titles and offices are not capitalized unless used with a proper name.*

Capitalized	Not Capitalized
Congressman McKay	the congressman from Florida
Commander Alger	commander of the Pacific Fleet
Queen Elizabeth	the queen of England

Capitalize all main words in titles of works of literature, art, and music. (See "Using Italics" in the Punctuation section.)

Spelling

Concentration in this section will be on spelling plurals and possessives. The multiplicity and complexity of spelling rules based on phonics, letter doubling, and exceptions to rules - not mastered by adulthood - should be replaced by a good dictionary. As spelling mastery is also difficult for adolescents, our recommendation is the same. Learning the use of a dictionary and thesaurus will be a more rewarding use of time.

Most plurals of nouns that end in hard consonants or hard consonant sounds followed by a silent *e* are made by adding *s*. Some words ending in vowels only add *s*.

fingers, numerals, banks, bugs, riots, homes, gates, radios, bananas

Nouns that end in soft consonant sounds *s, j, x, z, ch,* and *sh,* add *es.* Some nouns ending in *o* add es.

dresses, waxes, churches, brushes, tomatoes, potatoes

Nouns ending in *y* preceded by a vowel just add *s*.

boys, alleys

Nouns ending in *y* preceded by a consonant change the *y* to *i* and add *es.*

babies, corollaries, frugalities, poppies

Some nouns plurals are formed irregularly or remain the same.

sheep, deer, children, leaves, oxen

Some nouns derived from foreign words, especially Latin, may make their plurals in two different ways - one of them Anglicized. Sometimes, the meanings are the same; other times, the two plurals are used in slightly different contexts. It is always wise to consult the dictionary.

appendices, appendixes   criterion, criteria
indexes, indices   crisis, crises

Make the plurals of closed (solid) compound words in the usual way except for words ending in *ful* which make their plurals on the root word.

timelines, hairpins, cupsful

ENGLISH LANGUAGE ARTS

Make the plurals of open or hyphenated compounds by adding the change in inflection to the word that changes in number.

fathers-in-law, courts-martial, masters of art, doctors of medicine

Make the plurals of letters, numbers, and abbreviations by adding s.

fives and tens, IBMs, 1990s, *p*s and *q*s (Note that letters are italicized.)

Possessives

Make the possessives of singular nouns by adding an apostrophe followed by the letter *s* ('s).

baby's bottle, father's job, elephant's eye, teacher's desk, sympathizer's protests, week's postponement

Make the possessive of singular nouns ending in *s* by adding either an apostrophe or a ('s) depending upon common usage or sound. When making the possessive causes difficulty, use a prepositional phrase instead. Even with the sibilant ending, with a few exceptions, it is advisable to use the ('s) construction.

dress's color, species' characteristics or characteristics of the species, James' hat or James's hat, Delores's shirt

Make the possessive of plural nouns ending in *s* by adding the apostrophe after the *s*.

horses' coats, jockeys' times, four days' time

Make possessives of plural nouns that do not end in *s* the same as singular nouns by adding 's.

children's shoes, deer's antlers, cattle's horns

Make possessives of compound nouns by adding the inflection at the end of the word or phrase.

the mayor of Los Angeles' campaign, the mailman's new truck, the mailmen's new trucks, my father-in-law's first wife, the keepsakes' values, several daughters-in-law's husbands

Note: Because a gerund functions as a noun, any noun preceding it and operating as a possessive adjective must reflect the necessary inflection. However, if the gerundive following the noun is a participle, no inflection is added.

The general was perturbed by the private's sleeping on duty. (The word *sleeping* is a gerund, the object of the preposition *by*.)

but

The general was perturbed to see the private sleeping on duty. (The word *sleeping* is a participle modifying "private.")

Skill 7.5   Demonstrate knowledge of how to use modifiers to expand ideas, transitions to produce an effective control of language and ideas, and effective paragraph organization.

A mark of maturity in writing is the effective use of transitional devices at all levels. For example, a topic sentence can be used to establish continuity, especially if it is positioned at the beginning of a paragraph. The most common use would be to refer to what has preceded, repeat it, or summarize it and then go on to introduce a new topic. An essay by W. H. Hudson uses this device: "Although the potato was very much to me in those early years, it grew to be more when I heard its history." It summarizes what has preceded, makes a comment on the author's interest, and introduces a new topic: the history of the potato.

Another example of a transitional sentence could be, "Not all matters end so happily." This refers to the previous information and prepares for the next paragraph, which will be about matters that do not end happily. This transitional sentence is a little more forthright: "The increase in drug use in our community leads us to another general question."

Another fairly simple and straightforward transitional device is the use of numbers or their approximation: "First, I want to talk about the dangers of immigration; second, I will discuss the enormity of the problem; third, I will propose a reasonable solution."

An entire paragraph may be transitional in purpose and form. In "Darwiniana," Thomas Huxley used a transitional paragraph:

> So much, then, by way of proof that the method of establishing laws in science is exactly the same as that pursued in common life. Let us now turn to another matter (though really it is but another phase of the same question), and that is, the method by which, from the relations of certain phenomena, we prove that some stand in the position of causes toward the others.

The most common transitional device is a single word. Some examples: *and, furthermore, next, moreover, in addition, again, also, likewise, similarly, finally, second*, etc. There are many.

In marking student papers, a teacher can encourage a student to think in terms of moving coherently from one idea to the next by making transitions between the two. If the shift from one thought to another is too abrupt, the student can be asked to provide a transitional paragraph. Lists of possible transitions can be put on a handout and students can be encouraged to have the list at hand when composing essays. These are good tools for nudging students to more mature writing styles.

Techniques to Maintain Focus:
- **Focus on a main point.** The point should be clear to readers, and all sentences in the paragraph should relate to it.
- **Start the paragraph with a topic sentence.** This should be a general, one-sentence summary of the paragraph's main point, relating both back towards the thesis and toward the content of the paragraph. (A topic sentence is sometimes unnecessary if the paragraph continues a developing idea clearly introduced in a preceding paragraph, or if the paragraph appears in a narrative of events where generalizations might interrupt the flow of the story.)
- **Stick to the point.** Eliminate sentences that do not support the topic sentence.
- **Be flexible.** If there is not enough evidence to support the claim your topic sentence is making, do not fall into the trap of wandering or introducing new ideas within the paragraph. Either find more evidence, or adjust the topic sentence to collaborate with the evidence that is available.

Skill 7.6 **Recognize teacher/peer conference techniques that assist students with the drafting of documents.**

An effective teacher/peer conference can be best defined as creative listening. Some characteristics of student writers that affect the conference with the teacher:
- Has little confidence that he/she has anything worth writing.
- Doesn't know where to start.
- Is sensitive to criticism.
- Wants to get the assignment done with as little effort as possible and as quickly as possible and still get an A.

Trust-building is important in teaching writing. Putting words on a page for someone else to see is an act of faith. "Touching" those words is like touching the writer's most sensitive spots. Students must believe that they will be taken seriously—that their teacher is a friend and confidant, not an enemy, and that the outcome of a writing exercise will be a pleasant experience. The teacher/student conference with writing students is very important. More will be accomplished here than in class sessions if the conference is carefully structured and carried out. The teacher listens to what the student has come up with thus far. If the student has not managed to write anything at all, then the teacher needs to help her develop a strategy for moving forward. Questioning is very helpful here, remembering that the student must begin to probe her own thoughts and experiences in order to be successful in the class. There must come a time when she doesn't need the teacher's inquiring mind to get themes started, so the purpose of the conference is to help the student develop strategies for whatever stage of the writing process she is in.

If the student is clearly off on the wrong track or has not narrowed the topic sufficiently or has created a thesis that will be difficult, if not impossible, to develop, then the purpose of the conference is to help get her back on track and do the work on the thesis that is required, again remembering that the purpose is to help the student develop strategies for doing these things for herself the next time around.

Students need as much writing practice as possible. The more times through the process, the more comfortable and accomplished they become in producing successful compositions, so as time goes on, teacher conferences should only be necessary when a student is stuck and needs some help getting past the block. In these cases, the same rules apply: creative questioning usually helps the writer move forward.

Skill 7.7 Demonstrate knowledge of strategies for using technology to facilitate recursive drafting or composition.

In learning to write and in improving one's writing, the most useful exercise is editing/revising. Extensive revision is the hallmark of most successful writers. In the past, writers, student writers in particular, have been reluctant to revise because it meant starting over to prepare the document for final presentation. However, that time is long gone. The writing of graduate dissertations took on a whole new dimension after the creation of the word processor and before long, classroom writing teachers were able to use this function to help students improve their writing. Requiring extensive revision in writing classrooms nowadays is not unreasonable and can be an important stage in the production of papers. Microsoft Word has had a "tracking" capability in its last several upgrades, which carries revision a step further. Now the teacher and student can carry on a dialogue on the paper itself. The teacher's deletions and additions can be tracked, the student can respond, and the tracking will be facilitated by automatically putting the changes in a different color. The "comment" function makes it possible for both teacher and student to write notes at the exact relevant point in the manuscript.

COMPETENCY 8.0 DEMONSTRATE KNOWLEDGE OF STRATEGIES FOR REVISING, EDITING, AND PROOFREADING DOCUMENTS THAT ADDRESS VARIOUS RHETORICAL SITUATIONS AND KNOW HOW TO PREPARE VARIOUS DOCUMENTS FOR PUBLICATION

Skill 8.1 Recognize the importance and value of revising and editing as recursive components of the writing process.

Sometimes this exercise is seen by students as simply catching errors in spelling or word use. Students need to reframe their thinking about revising and editing. Some questions that need to be asked:

- Is the reasoning coherent?
- Is the point established?
- Does the introduction make the reader want to read this discourse?
- What is the thesis? Is it proven?
- What is the purpose? Is it clear? Is it useful, valuable, and interesting?
- Is the style of writing so wordy that it exhausts the reader and interferes with engagement?
- Is the writing so spare that it is boring?
- Are the sentences too uniform in structure?
- Are there too many simple sentences?
- Are too many of the complex sentences the same structure?
- Are the compounds truly compounds or are they unbalanced?
- Are parallel structures truly parallel?
- If there are characters, are they believable?
- If there is dialogue, is it natural or stilted?
- Is the title appropriate?
- Does the writing show creativity or is it boring?
- Is the language appropriate? Is it too formal? Too informal? If jargon is used, is it appropriate?

Studies have clearly demonstrated that the most fertile area in teaching writing is this one. If students can learn to revise their own work effectively, they are well on their way to becoming effective, mature writers. Word processing is an important tool for teaching this stage in the writing process. Microsoft Word has tracking features that make the revision exchanges between teachers and students more effective than ever before.

Skill 8.2   **Recognize that English conventions, style, diction, voice, and rhetorical situation drive the revision component of the writing process.**

The process of revision is often confused with editing and proofreading, and students frequently declare an assignment finished when the grammar and spelling corrections have been performed, running from the task as though it were punishment for their perceived poor writing skills. Revision, however, serves a much more important purpose: It's the opportunity to draw the finished piece together into a cohesive, consistent whole.

Revision strategies that can be expected to be practiced at the secondary level include:

- Evaluating and improving the logic and coherence of the organization of information.
- Refining word choice to match and reflect the voice of the writer.
- Reviewing overall grammatical style to ensure sentence variety.
- Tightening and smoothing transitions from one point to the next.
- Enhancing meaning and tone for consistency, always keeping in mind the audience, purpose, formality level, and genre.

Skill 8.3   **Demonstrate knowledge of revision strategies appropriate to a variety of writing genres and rhetorical situation and understand how to provide practice of revising and editing techniques.**

See Skills 7.2, 7.3, and 7.7.

Skill 8.4   **Recognize and demonstrate English conventions including usage, semantics, syntax, morphology, and phonology and the application of language structure and conventions in the critiquing and editing of written documents.**

See Skills 1.6, 3.1, and 7.4.

Skill 8.5   **Recognize the value of self-editing and peer response as strategies within the writing process.**

Viewing writing as a process allows teachers and students to see the writing classroom as a cooperative workshop where students and teachers encourage and support each other in each writing endeavor. Listed below are some techniques that help teachers to facilitate and create a supportive classroom environment.

1. Create peer response/support groups that are working on similar writing assignments. The members help each other in all stages of the writing process, from prewriting, writing, revising, editing, and publishing.

2. Provide several prompts to give students the freedom to write on a topic of their own. Writing should be generated out of personal experience and students should be introduced to in-class journals. One effective way to get into writing is to let them write often and freely about their own lives, without having to worry about grades or evaluation.

3. Respond in the form of a question whenever possible. Teacher/facilitator should respond non-critically and use positive, supportive language.

4. Respond to formal writing acknowledging the student's strengths and focusing on the composition skills demonstrated by the writing. A response should encourage the student by offering praise for what the student has done well. Give the student a focus for revision and demonstrate that the process of revision has applications in many other writing situations.

5. Provide students with readers' checklists so they can write observational critiques of others' drafts, and then they can revise their own papers at home using the checklists as a guide.

6. Pair students so that they can give and receive responses. Pairing students keeps them aware of the role of an audience in the composing process and in evaluating stylistic effects.

7. Focus critical comments on aspects of the writing that can be observed in the writing. Comments like "I noticed you use the word 'is' frequently" will be more helpful than "Your introduction is dull" and will not demoralize the writer.

8. Provide the group with a series of questions to guide them through the group writing sessions.

Skill 8.6 **Recognize the importance and value of publishing as an integral component of the writing process and know specific formats required for publishing a variety of written documents of different rhetorical situations.**

There are many factors that play a role in improving writing skills, but perhaps none is more powerful than writing for an audience. Once that dimension is introduced, everything changes. It's always a good exercise to require students to declare who the audience is for a particular writing assignment, but it's much more effective to give them the opportunity to experience writing for an audience, especially if there is opportunity for feedback.

Most of the writing students do in a writing class is for their writing teacher, who is typically the only one to give feedback.

Peer exchange is sometimes helpful in this regard but can do more harm than good if the student providing feedback uses the opportunity to accomplish some goal of his own such as retaliation or criticizing for the purpose of making himself look superior.

Publishing student papers can occur in many ways. A bulletin board at the school is useful for this. It gives the writer the experience of a specific audience that is likely to give feedback. The writing should conform to the requirements for display; that is, the title should be in bold and the type size should be large enough to be easily read on a bulletin board.

Another good way to give students publishing/feedback experience is in the school paper. The editor of the paper should furnish guidelines for how the article should be presented. If it is to be submitted electronically, the format (Microsoft Word, Word Perfect, etc.) will be specified as well as the channel (disk, email, FTP, etc.) Also, type size, length, type characteristics (italics and bold accepted or not accepted, for instance), photos or other illustrations, etc., should be specified. If it's to be submitted in hard copy, the editor should issue guidelines for many of the same matters.

In many cities, local newspapers give students an opportunity to publish articles. In those cases, the newspaper will have a style sheet that will specify such things as length, format, and the other matters mentioned above.

Skill 8.7   Demonstrate knowledge of how to use technology to produce written documents suitable for submission or publication.

See 7.7

COMPETENCY 9.0 DEMONSTRATE KNOWLEDGE OF STRATEGIES FOR LOCATING, ANALYZING, EVALUATING AND ORGANIZING INFORMATION FROM PRINT AND ELECTRONIC RESOURCES THAT EXPRESS VARIOUS PERSPECTIVES

Skill 9.1 Recognize methods of information acquisition from a variety of sources.

The best place to start research is usually at your local library. Not only does it have numerous books, videos, and periodicals to use for references, the librarian is always a valuable resource for information or where to get that information.

"Those who declared librarians obsolete when the internet rage first appeared are now red-faced. We need them more than ever. The internet is full of 'stuff' but its value and readability is often questionable. 'Stuff' doesn't give you a competitive edge, high-quality related information does."

-Patricia Schroeder, President of the Association of American Publishers

The internet is a multifaceted goldmine of information, but you must be careful to discriminate between reliable and unreliable sources. Stick to sites that are associated with an academic institution, whether it be a college or university or a scholarly organization.

Keep **content** and **context** in mind when researching. Don't be so wrapped up in how you are going to apply your resource to your project that you miss the author's entire purpose or message. Remember that there are multiple ways to get the information you need. Read an encyclopedia article about your topic to get a general overview, and then focus in from there. Note important names of people associated with your subject, time periods, and geographic areas. Make a list of key words and their synonyms to use while searching for information. And finally, don't forget about articles in magazines and newspapers, or even personal interviews with experts related to your field of interest.

Skill 9.2 Recognize criteria and methods for evaluating primary and secondary research sources.

Before accepting as gospel anything that is printed in a newspaper or advertising or presented on radio, television, or the Internet, it is wise first of all to consider the source. Even though news reporters and editors claim to be unbiased in the presentation of news, they usually take an editorial point of view. A newspaper may avow that it is Republican or conservative and may even make recommendations at election time, but it will still claim to present the news without bias. Sometimes this is true, and sometimes it is not. For example, Fox News declares itself to be conservative and to support the Republican Party. Its presentation of news often reveals that bias.

When Vice-President Cheney made a statement about his shooting of a friend in a duck-hunting accident, it was only made available to Fox News.

On the other hand, CBS has tended to favor more liberal politicians although it avows that it is even-handed in its coverage. Dan Rather presented a story critical of President Bush's military service that was based on a document that could not be validated. His failure to play by the rules of certification of evidence cost him his job and his career. Even with authentication, such a story would not have gotten past the editors of a conservative-leaning news system.

Even politicians usually play by the rules of fairness in the choices they make about going public. They usually try to be even-handed. However, some channels and networks will show deference to one politician over another.

Advertising, whether in print or electronic media is another thing. Will using a certain tooth paste improve a person's love life? Is a satellite dish better than cable? The best recourse a reader/viewer has is to ask around and find someone who has experience that is relevant or conduct research and conduct interviews of users of both.

When evaluating sources, first go through this checklist to make sure the source is even worth reading:
- Title (How relevant is it to your topic?)
- Date (How current is the source?)
- Organization (What institution is this source coming from?)
- Length (How in depth does it go?)

Check for signs of bias:
- Does the author or publisher have political ties or religious views that could affect their objectivity?
- Is the author or publisher associated with any special-interest groups that might only see one side of an issue, such as Greenpeace or the National Rifle Association?
- How fairly does the author treat opposing views?
- Does the language of the piece show signs of bias?

Keep an open mind while reading, and don't let opposing viewpoints prevent you from absorbing the text. Remember that you are not judging the author's work, you are examining its assumptions, assessing its evidence and weighing its conclusions.

Skill 9.3 Recognize diversity issues within reference materials and distinguish among them to address diverse student needs.

Adaptations to meet diverse students' needs should be incorporated into the curriculum so that students at all levels can successfully master the lesson without modifying the goal of instruction. Reference materials come in many formats, and understanding the needs of the individual student is essential to selecting appropriate materials.

Tips for addressing diverse needs in this area:

- Use large-print or Braille texts
- Use audio or videotaped materials (books on tape, captioned videos, etc.)
- Use visual imagery to explain concepts
- Use supplemental graphic organizers or choose texts that incorporate appropriate use of graphic organizers
- Allow students to perform computer-based research
- Prepare study sheets or outlines of material ahead of time

Skill 9.4 Recognize the power and potential of print and non-print media to facilitate understanding and critical analysis of contemporary culture.

Media's impact on today's society is immense and ever increasing. As children, we watch programs on television that are amazingly fast-paced and visually rich. Parent's roles as verbal and moral teachers are diminishing in response to the much more stimulating guidance of the television set. Adolescence, which used to be the time for going out and exploring the world firsthand, is now consumed by the allure of MTV, popular music, and video games. Young adults are exposed to uncensored sex and violence.

But media's effect on society is beneficial and progressive at the same time. Its affect on education in particular provides special challenges and opportunities for teachers and students.

Thanks to satellite technology, urban classrooms and rural villages can receive instructional radio and television programs. CD-ROMs can allow students to learn information through a virtual reality experience. The internet allows instant access to unlimited data and connects people across all cultures through shared interests. Educational media, when used in a productive way, enriches instruction and makes it more individualized, accessible, and economical.

Skill 9.5   **Recognize planning and organizational strategies in both print and electronic formats for a variety of research projects.**

Seeing writing as a process is very helpful in saving preparation time, particularly in taking notes and developing drafts. Once a decision is made about the topic to be developed, some preliminary review of literature is helpful in thinking about the next step, which is to determine what the purpose of the written document will be. For example, if the topic is immigration, a cursory review of the various points of view in the debate going on in the country will help the writer decide what this particular written piece will try to accomplish. The purpose could just be a review of the various points of view, which would be an informative purpose. On the other hand, the writer might want to take a point of view and provide proof and support with the purpose of changing the reader's mind. The writer might even want the reader to take some action as the result of reading. Another possible purpose might be simply to write a description of a family of immigrants.

Once that cursory review has been completed, it's time to begin research in earnest and to prepare to take notes. If the thesis has been clearly defined, and some thought has been given to what will be used to prove or support it, a tentative outline can be developed. A thesis plus three points is typical. Decisions about introduction and conclusion should be deferred until the body of the paper is written. Note-taking is much more effective if the notes are being taken to provide information for an outline. There is much less danger that the writer will go off on time-consuming tangents.

Formal outlines inhibit effective writing. However, a loosely constructed outline can be an effective device for note taking that will yield the information for a worthwhile statement about a topic. Sentence outlines are better than topic outlines because they require the writer to do some thinking about the direction a subtopic will take.

Once this preliminary note-taking phase is over, the first draft can be developed. The writing at this stage is likely to be highly individualistic. However, successful writers tend to just write, keeping in mind the purpose of the paper, the point that is going to be made in it, and the information that has been turned up in the research. Student writers need to understand that this first draft is just that—the first one. It takes more than one draft to write a worthwhile statement about a topic. This is what successful writers do. It's sometimes helpful to have students read the various drafts of a story by a well-known writer.

Once the draft is on paper, a stage that is sometimes called editing occurs. With word processors, this is much more easily achieved than in the past. Sections can be deleted, words can be changed, and additions can be made without doing the entire project over a second time.

What to look for: mechanics, of course, spelling, punctuation, etc., but it's important that student writers don't confuse proofreading and editing. Editing is rereading objectively, testing the effectiveness on a reader of the arrangement and the line of reasoning. Several kinds of changes may be required: rearranging the parts, adding necessary information that has been omitted, and deleting information that doesn't fit or contribute to the accomplishment of the purpose.

Once the body of the paper has been shaped to the writer's satisfaction, the introduction and conclusion should be fashioned. An introduction should grab the reader's interest and, perhaps, announce the purpose and thesis of the paper, unless the reasoning is inductive, in which case, purpose and thesis may come later in the paper. The conclusion should reaffirm the purpose in some way.

COMPETENCY 10.0 DEMONSTRATE KNOWLEDGE OF HOW TO SYNTHESIZE AND APPLY ACQUIRED INFORMATION, CONCEPTS, AND IDEAS TO COMMUNICATE IN A VARIETY OF FORMATS FOR A VARIETY OF PURPOSES

Skill 10.1 Demonstrate knowledge of how to synthesize and logically sequence information from a variety of sources.

Once a topic has been selected then the search for resources begins. Say the topic is immigration. Like so many subjects, so much information is available that a review of titles will suggest ways to narrow it, the next step in the process. If the topic is narrowed to "protecting our southern border," then some of the better, more interesting ones can be selected. Some sources may be hard copy—newspapers, journals, etc.,—and some will be electronic, found on the Internet.

Everything that will be used in the synthesis must be documented. Don't fail to gather and organize bibliographic information at the very outset. To fail to do this leads to frustration and lost time. Also, it's vital to read thoroughly and to underline, highlight, or take notes. On hard copy, if you don't own the copy and are unable to underline or highlight, you might consider copying it so you can do so. Otherwise, you'll need to settle for note taking. This can be done with note pad and pencil or it can be done in a word-processed document as you go. Be sure to identify all the notes as you go. If you are taking notes from an electronic document, you can copy it into Word and use the highlighter or simply take notes, again being sure to put in identifiers as you go.

Now you are ready to organize your paper. Just as with any other piece of writing, this paper should have a thesis. What idea are you going to support with the information you've found? If you've decided, for instance, on "Putting up a high fence is the best way to deal with the immigrant problem," you will use the information taken from your sources to support that.

Some of the information may be used to show the arguments against your thesis, so you can borrow from the documents that support it to refute the opposing point of view. Remember, you will probably need to discard some of the material, even though you may have spent time on it. You don't want irrelevancies in your final document.

The ideas taken from sources must be identified. It can be as simple as "John Jones, a Texas legislator feels . . ." or it can be footnoted or end noted. The role of the transitional paragraph is important in a synthesis of what others are saying. In the editing stage of this paper, you will want to ask yourself whether enough has been done to move from one point to the next, whether there are abrupt shifts that are confusing, and whether you may need to insert some transitional paragraphs in certain places.

The synthesis will end with a concluding paragraph that will draw everything together and restate the thesis.

Skill 10.2   Demonstrate knowledge of how to support and defend a thesis statement through effective communication of documented information.

Once a thesis is put forth, there are various ways to support it. The most obvious one is reasoning. Usually a reason will answer the question why. Another technique is to give examples or provide details.

The presentation of a prosecutor in a court trial is a good example of an argument that uses all of these.

The **thesis** of the prosecutor may be: John O'Hara stole construction materials from a house being built at 223 Hudson Ave. by the Jones Construction Company. As a **reason**, he might cite the following: He is building his own home on Green Street and needs materials and tools. This will answer the question why. He might give **examples**: 20 bags of concrete disappeared the night before Mr. O'Hara poured the basement for his house on Green Street. The electronic nail-setter disappeared from the building site on Hudson Ave. the day before Mr. O'Hara began to erect the frame of his house on Green Street. He might fill in the **details**: Mr. O'Hara's truck was observed by a witness on Hudson Ave. in the vicinity of the Jones Construction Company site the night the concrete disappeared. A witness observed Mr. O'Hara's truck again on that street the night the nail-setter disappeared.

Another example of a trial might be: **Thesis**, Adam Andrews murdered Joan Rogers in cold blood on the night of December 20. **Reason #1**: She was about to reveal their affair to his wife. **Reason #2**: Andrews' wife would inherit half of his sizeable estate in case of a divorce since there is no prenuptial agreement. **Example #1**: Rogers has demonstrated that he is capable of violence in an incident with a partner in his firm.

Example #2: Rogers has had previous affairs in which he was accused of violence. **Detail #1**: Andrews' wife once called the police and signed a warrant. **Detail #2**: A previous lover sought police protection from Andrews.

An **opinion** is a thesis and requires support. A writer should also use reasons, examples, and details.

For example:

Opinion: Our borders must be protected.

Reason #1: Terrorists can get into the country undetected. **Example #1**: An Iranian national was able to cross the Mexican border and live in this country for years before being detected. **Detail**: The Iranian national came up through Central America to Mexico then followed the route that Mexican illegal immigrants regularly took. **Example #2**: A group of Middle Eastern terrorists were arrested in Oregon after they had crossed the Canadian border. **Detail**: There was no screening at that border.

Reason #2: Illegal aliens are an enormous drain on resources such as health care. **Example**: The states of California and Texas bear enormous burdens for health care and education for illegal immigrants. **Detail**: Legal citizens are often denied care in those states because resources are stretched so thin.

Skill 10.3 **Recognize and evaluate the critical attributes of effective oral, visual, and written communication for a variety of purposes.**

Different from the basic writing forms of discourse is the art of debating, discussion, and conversation. The ability to use language and logic to convince the audience to accept your reasoning and to side with you is an art. This form of writing/speaking is extremely confined and structured, logically sequenced, with supporting reasons and evidence. At its best, it is the highest form of propaganda. A position statement, evidence, reason, evaluation and refutation are integral parts of this writing schema.

Interviewing provides opportunities for students to apply expository and informative communication. It teaches them how to structure questions to evoke fact-filled responses. Compiling the information from an interview into a biographical essay or speech helps students to list, sort, and arrange details in an orderly fashion.

Speeches that encourage them to describe persons, places, or events in their own lives or oral interpretations of literature help them sense the creativity and effort used by professional writers.

Useful resources

Price, Brent - *Basic Composition Activities Kit* - provides practical suggestions and student guide sheets for use in the development of student writing.

Simmons, John S., R.E. Shafer, and Gail B. West. (1976). *Decisions About The Teaching of English - "Advertising, or Buy It, You'll Like It."* Allyn & Bacon.

Additional resources may be found in the library, social studies, economic, debate and journalism textbooks and locally published newspapers.

Skill 10.4   Recognize proficiency expectations for a variety of technology skills.

Let's face it. The day of the handwritten essay is past. We have been suddenly projected into a world where many of the activities of the writing classroom of the past have vanished. It's important to remember that the students sitting in your writing class are going to be required to have the skills to write clearly and succinctly and to think critically in the world they will soon be entering. Even those who will not be going on to college will be required to use technological tools to deal with their worlds. They will be filling out forms on a computer and communicating with many people via website and e-mail that they have dealt with face-to-face or via telephone in the past. The demands on the writing teacher are no longer simply teaching thinking/writing skills, but also teaching students skills that will connect them to the technological world of the twenty-first century.

Students need to know how to get on the Internet, where to find e-mail (there is more than one mail program, Microsoft Outlook, for example; how to compose an e-mail in order to be understood; and some of the etiquette required for effective e-mail communications. Job applications are often filled out on a website. Students need to know how to interact on Acrobat, which includes finding the icon that permits text insertion. They also need to know how to conduct searches, so they need to be aware of what "search" means, what Boolean terms are, what the major search engines are, and how to use them.

In most colleges nowadays, themes are exchanged on a website set up specifically for the school. The students need to be prepared to present their themes electronically and exchange messages with their teachers in this way, so they need to understand Microsoft Word well enough to be able to read and respond to comments on Word's tracking function and to create a clean version of a paper while retaining the one from the teacher with edits and comments.

Skill 10.5 Recognize the ethical attributes of responsible research and reporting.

Plagiarism, whether intentional or accidental, has ethical implications, and anyone who writes needs to have a clear understanding of what it is. Basically, it means passing off the words or ideas of another person as one's own without giving proper credit to the source.

It's acceptable to paraphrase someone else's words just as long as you provide a citation—that is, announce where and whom it came from. Remember, though, that any exact words or phrases that come from the original work must be set off in quotation marks and the point in the original where it came from indicated. These rules apply to all words and ideas whether they are written, are from a speech, from a television or radio program, from e-mail messages, from interviews, or from conversations. It's even more important to be careful about lifting any such information from a website because nowadays there are very powerful search engines that identify plagiarism, and many people who provide information on the Internet use them to make sure their words and information are not being stolen. Potential fines for plagiarism are very steep.

Lifting another person's words or ideas and presenting them as one's own is no different from thievery. Many people who wouldn't think of committing a theft of material or property think nothing of presenting the words and ideas of others as their own.

A second kind of unethical misuse of information is falsely reporting or attributing words or ideas. This can be putting words in another's mouth or bending what was said to create a false impression. Sometimes, simply failing to report the context in which something was said becomes false reporting. So many misuses of the printed and spoken word have taken place in a world that is constantly flooded with communications from all directions that students sometimes feel that it is acceptable to commit these misuses themselves. The writing classroom is an ideal forum for teaching and discussing what is ethical and moral in the use of language from a source and what is not.

Skill 10.6 Demonstrate knowledge of resources providing citation formats and understand the importance of ethical standards when preparing a research product within any concept, genre, or situation.

- Keep a record of any sources consulted during the research process.
- As you take notes, avoid unintentional plagiarism.
- Summarize and paraphrase in your own words without the source in front of you.
- Cite anything that is not common knowledge. This includes direct quotes as well as ideas or statistics.

Blueprint for Standard Attribution:

1. Begin the sentence with, "According to _____,"
2. Proceed with the material being cited, followed by the page number in parentheses.
3. Include the source information in a bibliography or works cited page.
(Last name, first name. *Book Title*. Location: Publisher, year.)

Example:

In-Text Citation

According to Steve Mandel, "our average conversational rate of speech is about 125 words per minute" (78).

Works Cited Entry

Mandel, Steve. *Effective Presentation Skills*. Menlo Park, California: Crisp Publications, 1993.

DOMAIN III. SPEAKING AND LISTENING

COMPETENCY 11.0 DEMONSTRATE KNOWLEDGE OF ORAL COMMUNICATION COMPONENTS AND STRATEGIES FOR CONSTRUCTING ORAL PRESENTATIONS

Skill 11.1 Identify the communication process as nonlinear, including communicators, verbal and nonverbal messages, feedback, and noise/interference.

Life would be simpler if communication were like mathematics: two plus two equals four. Unfortunately, language users are human beings, and language is very human; therefore, it is not always organized, it is often messy, and it's very difficult to organize. In preparing to make a speech, for instance, we know that we must write a thesis statement, develop several lines of proof for it, and give examples—all very straightforward and simple. However, when we begin to write our thesis, narrow it, come up with something that says what we want to say and that can be developed, it's wobbly. More than one thesis will slip and slide out of the original one. Once we have settled on one and try to use the research we have done, we keep finding holes in the research and have to go back to the drawing board. Even once the speech is written, we may find ourselves having to go back to the early stages—do more research, rewrite the thesis, throw out some of what we have already put in, and fill holes we didn't see the first time around. Messy!

Students are often unwilling to go through all of this, or they become frustrated and just decide that they can't do it.

We need to help them understand that first of all, language is not linear—it doesn't necessarily move in a straightforward march toward a goal until we work with it. They need to understand before they start their research and try to posit a thesis that, while they must establish a time limit on how long they will spend on these stages, they are not set in concrete. They can be changed even after the speech is written. Recursive is a good term to use in helping students understand how this process works. It is also useful if they can understand that people who do this for a living and make a great deal of money doing it go through the same processes. There's no way to avoid this nonlinear nature of language and communication.

Sometimes in listening to a speaker, we feel a disconnection between what he is saying and what the body language conveys. The gestures may be discordant with the tone or even the language of the speech. An aspiring speaker should be very careful in preparing the message that there are not lingering doubts about the veracity, the value, even the advisability of the contents. They will probably be apparent to those who will be listening. The speech itself needs to be adjusted to fit what the speaker feels confident and comfortable with.

Only lawyers are very good at presenting points of view that are not necessarily in line with their own viewpoints. A defense lawyer, for example, may suspect that his client is guilty of a crime, but he has a professional duty to keep that conviction out of his presentation to the judge and jury. Most speakers are not willing or trained to do that. Even politicians sometimes tip their hands because they are saying things only for the purpose of influencing votes, and their body language reveals their duplicity.

Feedback comes in many varieties. For example, an audience may give feedback with applause or a lack of it. Those listening also usually give feedback with their facial expressions. A successful speaker becomes very good at reading that feedback from an audience. A good way to obtain useful feedback is with a well-designed feedback questionnaire that will be collected following the speech. Not everyone will fill these out, and those who do may be those who are most pleased with what they've heard, and those who are most displeased with what they've heard; nevertheless, this form of feedback is often helpful. Another way to obtain feedback is to take a poll. It has been statistically proven that a small number of people randomly chosen out of a possibly large population can be reasonably accurate in recording what people are thinking and believing. Polls are continually being conducted, particularly regarding political issues but also on other issues as well. These have become very powerful in influencing what people believe and even how people behave sometimes.

It's annoying to try to listen to a vocal broadcast and have it obscured by static, usually brought about by some kind of interference on the line. This is a good metaphor for interference in the communications process.

We may hear a speaker who has convinced us that something is true or that we should do something, but there are many other voices that are interfering with our once clear thinking on this topic so we end up either changing our minds or not knowing what we should believe or do. Nowadays, there are so many information sources that we find ourselves often in this situation. On the Internet, for instance, we can find a wide range of viewpoints about immigration. It's very difficult to know what is good or right because there is so much interference.

Skill 11.2   Demonstrate knowledge of purposes and functions of communication and oral presentations.

See Skill 10.3.

Skill 11.3 Recognize criteria for selecting content and support for a given communication situation and know the various types and strengths of supporting materials.

See Skill 10.2.

Skill 11.4 Recognize the importance of using and citing accurate and relevant material when communicating.

See Skill 10.6.

Skill 11.5 Demonstrate knowledge of a variety of organizational formats appropriate for different speaking situations and understand the importance of adapting communication to the situation, setting, and context.

Listening to students sitting on the steps that lead into the building that houses their classrooms, teachers will hear dialogue that may not even be understandable to them. The student who is writing to his peers will need to know and understand the peculiarities of that discourse in order to be very effective with them. This is a good example for students of what it means to tailor language for a particular audience and for a particular person.

This is a good time to teach the concept of jargon. Writing to be read by a lawyer is a different thing from writing to be read by a medical doctor. Writing to be read by parents is different from writing to be read by the administrator of the school. Not only are the vocabularies different, but also the formality/informality of the discourse will need to be adjusted.

The things to be aware of in determining what the language should be for a particular audience, then, hinge on two things: vocabulary and formality/informality. The most formal language does not use contractions or slang. The most informal language will certainly use contractions and the slang that is appropriate for the particular audience. Formal language will use longer sentences and will not sound like a conversation.

The most informal language will use shorter sentences—not necessarily simple sentences—but shorter constructions and will sound like a conversation.

Novels use formal language only when it is in the mouth of a character that would speak that way, such as a lawyer or a school superintendent. It's jarring to read a novel that has a construction worker using formal language.

Using examples of various characters and their dialogues from fiction is useful in helping students understand this crucial aspect of writing.

Skill 11.6 Demonstrate knowledge of types of delivery and their uses and effects.

Types of Persuasive Speech

Fact: Similar to an informative speech, a persuasive speech on a question of fact seeks to find an answer where there isn't a clear one. The speaker evaluates evidence and attempts to convince the audience that their conclusion is correct. The challenge is to accept a certain carefully crafted view of the facts presented.

Value: This kind of persuasion tries to convince the audience that a certain thing is good or bad, moral or immoral, valuable or worthless. It focuses less on knowledge and more on beliefs and values.

Policy: This speech is a call to action, arguing that something should be done, improved or changed. Its goal is action from the audience, but it also seeks passive agreement with the proposition proposed. It appeals to both reason and emotion, and tells listeners what they can do and how to do it.

Skill 11.7 Demonstrate knowledge of how to use electronic media for effective communication.

The Internet has transformed all kinds of communications all over the world. Very few people write letters in the twenty-first century that will be delivered physically to an individual's mailbox. However, there are still important reasons for writing letters. For one thing, they are more personal and convey a quite different message from an e-mail, especially if they are handwritten. For another, not everybody has and uses e-mail regularly.

An electronic mailbox will retain what has been sent and received, sometimes to the writer's regret; even so, those messages and exchanges will not endure in the way that paper letters sometimes do over long periods. A husband and wife who married in 1954 always corresponded with his parents by mail approximately once a week in the first thirty years of their marriage. The three children often included a note of their own. It was before the long-distance call became routine and affordable.

After the grandmother and grandfather had died, the family discovered that they had kept all of those letters. It's a priceless record of a period in the family's life. If that correspondence had occurred via e-mail, it would be lost to history.

Sometimes there's a business reason for a paper letter. It may contain a receipt or legal information that needs to be retained. For those people who do not yet have a computer or access to e-mail, paper letters are necessary. Sometimes a company or organization wishes to advertise a product or even issue invitations to an event when not all e-mail addresses are known. Mass-mailings can be sent quite easily to make sure that everyone on the list can be reached. Advertisers, of course, use mass-mail more than anyone else because they do not even need to know the addresses to get their literature into all the mailboxes in a zip code.

Sometimes courtesy requires a personally written letter either typed or handwritten. If a person in high office has taken the time to do something for an individual, certainly a handwritten letter of thanks would be in order. In the U.S., the form of the letter can be full block (all lines blocked at the left margin); modified block (all lines blocked at the left margin except the date and closing lines, which begin at the center point); and semi-block (same as modified block except that the first lines of paragraphs are indented by five points). Microsoft Word's letter wizard will automatically format a business letter according to these three styles.

Social notes should be handwritten on notepaper, which varies in size but is smaller than letter-sized paper. They should be courteous and brief and should be specific about what is intended. For example, if the note is to say thank you, then the gift or favor should be specifically acknowledged in the note. If the note is an invitation, the same rule applies: the language should be courteous, the place and time specified, and any useful information such as "casual dress" or parking recommendations should be included.

A high percentage of communications between individuals, groups, and businesses is conducted nowadays over the Internet. It has even replaced many telephone calls. Internet language should be courteous, free of words that might be offensive, and clear. In the early days of e-mail, a writer was censured for using bold or capital letters. That has relaxed somewhat. Nowadays, almost anything goes although it's generally accepted that restrained language is assumed for business people and personal communications. The blog, where a person has his/her own website and uses it to send messages, is a new wrinkle. Chat is available on most blogs as well as other Internet sites. The language and the messages tend to be unrestrained there.

Some people use the same styles for letters via e-mail that are recommended for paper letters; however, the formatting has tended to become less and less formal. It is not uncommon for thank-you letters and invitations to be sent via e-mail.

One important feature of the Internet that makes it so valuable is that it reaches everywhere—to small communities, all the way across the country, and overseas.

It's possible to dash off an e-mail note to a person or business or several persons or businesses in Europe as quickly as to a person in the next office, and it costs no extra money beyond the cost of equipment and Internet services.

The fax machine is yet another dimension of electronic communications. At first, it was used primarily by businesses, but it has become so affordable that many people have them in their homes. The fax makes possible an actual picture of a document. This may be preferable to retyping it or sending it by paper mail because it can go immediately. Sometimes people who are exchanging contracts will use the fax to cut down on the time it takes to get them signed and sent back and forth. The scanner will do the same thing but will produce a document that can be e-mailed.

Skill 11.8 Recognize strategies for analyzing and communicating with diverse audiences.

Guidelines for Assessing your Audience

- **Values**- What is important to this group of people? What is their background and how will that affect their perception of your speech?
- **Needs**- Find out in advance what the audience's needs are. Why are they listening to you? Find a way to satisfy their needs.
- **Constraints**- What might hold the audience back from being fully engaged in what you are saying, or agreeing with your point of view, or processing what you are trying to say? These could be political reasons, which make them wary of your presentation's ideology from the start, or knowledge reasons, in which the audience lacks the appropriate background information to grasp your ideas. Avoid this last constraint by staying away from technical terminology, slang, or abbreviations that may be unclear to your audience.
- **Demographic Information**- Take the audience's size into account, as well as the location of the presentation.

Skill 11.9 Recognize that communication choices should be made with sensitivity to listeners' backgrounds.

Political correctness is a concept frequently bandied about in the twenty-first century. It has always existed, of course. The successful speaker of the nineteenth century understood and was sensitive to audiences. However, that person was typically a man, of course, and the only audience that was important was a male audience, and more often than not, the only important audience was a white one.

Many things have changed in discourse since the nineteenth century just as the society the speaker lives in and addresses has changed, and the speaker who disregards the existing conventions for political correctness usually finds himself in trouble. Rap music makes a point of ignoring those conventions, particularly with regard to gender, and is often the target of hostile attacks. On the other hand, rap performers often intend to be revolutionary and have developed their own audiences and have become outrageously wealthy by exploiting those newly developed audiences based primarily on thumbing their noses at establishment conventions.

Even so, the successful speaker must understand and be sensitive to what is current in political correctness. The "n word" is a case in point. There was a time when politicians and other public speakers used that word, but they no longer can do so. Nothing could spell the end of a politician's career more certainly than using that term in his campaign or public addresses.

References to gender have become particularly sensitive in the twentieth century as a result of the women's rights movement, and the speaker who disregards these sensitivities does so at his peril. The generic "he" is no longer acceptable, and this requires a strategy to deal with pronominal references without repetitive he/she, his/her, etc. There are several ways to approach this issue: switch to a passive construction that does not require a subject; switch back and forth, using the male pronoun in one reference and the female pronoun in another one, being sure to sprinkle them reasonably evenly; or switch to the plural. The last alternative is the one most often chosen. This requires some care and the speaker should spend time developing these skills before stepping in front of an audience.

Skill 11.10 Recognize the difference between supportive and non-supportive audiences and appropriate strategies for addressing those audiences.

There are several ways to persuade audiences to accept speakers' points of view. They may ingratiate themselves with by identifying with the audience in some way. For example, for an audience of farmers, a childhood spent on a grandparent's farm during the summers may bridge the gap between the speaker's experience and that of the audience. Building credibility is another way and may be accomplished with such things as degrees in the area being addressed or years of experience.

Emotional appeal is best exerted by presenting examples of suffering people or animals or by painting a picture of devastation, etc. The descriptive language used to evoke an emotional response must somehow be available through one of the five senses: the audience must be able to see with its own eyes, hear with its own ears, smell with its own nose, touch with its own fingers, taste with its own tongue, so to speak, if the emotions are to be aroused.

An argument must be reasonable. Reasoning does not necessarily change minds or bring about action, but people like to believe that they do not make decisions on the basis of emotion or being impressed with a person. The reasoning also must be sound because even people who are not high-level thinkers are likely to be insulted by flaws in reasoning. It's always risky to use flawed reasoning to persuade. While many speakers, particularly religious or political ones, rely on emotional appeal to gain a following, it's a calculated risk. The followers may not be the ones desired, and the ones who are recruited may not last long. Relying on emotional appeal alone is more likely to be suspect as far as ethics are concerned.

If an audience is already well disposed toward the speaker, emotional appeal may be used only to reestablish the connection between him/her and the audience. Also, it may not be necessary to establish credibility in these cases. Even so, it should never be ignored, even with an audience that is disposed to accept the message being delivered.

If the audience is hostile, then more time will need to be spent on emotional appeal and establishing credibility. Also, in the reasoning part of the argument, opposing points of view will need to be refuted, which is generally not necessary when the audience is favorable.

Skill 11.11 Demonstrate knowledge of strategies for recognizing when a message is not understood and for making adjustments to presentations to clarify and promote understanding.

Effective speakers connect with their audiences and make it a point to be aware of how they are responding. The most effective speeches include audience response of one kind or another. Audiovisuals can help the audience follow the points the speaker is making. PowerPoint, for example, has many devices that make it possible for text, pictures, and illustrations, to move on the screen. Some presentation software makes animation possible. The serious speaker learns and uses these devices.

The speaker who is paying attention to how an audience is responding should look for the following signs that attention has waned:
- People are shifting in their seats.
- Heads are down instead of looking forward.
- Eyes seem to be glazed over.
- A few people get up to leave. If only one or two do so, there may be an explanation, but if more leave, it is an indication that the speaker has lost the audience.
- People are talking to each other. A little of this may not be a bad sign—people may be commenting on what is being said—but if very much is going on, it's a sign that minds are either puzzled or elsewhere.

What can be done?
- If the speaker has dwelled too long on one point, moving on to something else is a good idea.
- Call attention to what is on the screen.
- An interactive activity that has been planned ahead of time and will test understanding can be introduced at this point.
- Break into small groups who will discuss the points being dealt with and have them report what they have concluded. Make sure the groups have an assignment and understand what they are to do during the discussion. Appointing a leader of each group is a good idea.
- When the groups come back, discuss in the larger group what the small groups have reported.
- If there are misunderstandings, they should come out in the small groups and the speaker can clarify.

Skill 11.12   Understand the differences among the purposes for speaking and appropriate strategies for each purpose.

Listening to students sitting on the steps that lead into the building that houses their classrooms, teachers will hear dialogue that may not even be understandable to them. The student who is writing to his peers will need to know and understand the peculiarities of that discourse in order to be very effective with them. This is a good example for students of what it means to tailor language for a particular audience and for a particular person.

This is a good time to teach the concept of jargon. Writing to be read by a lawyer is a different thing from writing to be read by a medical doctor. Writing to be read by parents is different from writing to be read by the administrator of the school. Not only are the vocabularies different, but also the formality/informality of the discourse will need to be adjusted.

The things to be aware of in determining what the language should be for a particular audience, then, hinge on two things: vocabulary and formality/informality. The most formal language does not use contractions or slang. The most informal language will certainly use contractions and the slang that is appropriate for the particular audience. Formal language will use longer sentences and will not sound like a conversation. The most informal language will use shorter sentences—not necessarily simple sentences—but shorter constructions and will sound like a conversation.

Novels use formal language only when it is in the mouth of a character who would speak that way, such as a lawyer or a school superintendent. It's jarring to read a novel that has a construction worker using formal language. Using examples of various characters and their dialogues from fiction is useful in helping students understand this crucial aspect of writing.

COMPETENCY 12.0 DEMONSTRATE KNOWLEDGE OF THE COMMUNICATION PROCESS COMPONENTS FOR EVALUATING ORAL MESSAGES

Skill 12.1 Recognize the responsibilities of listeners and the role of feedback in communication.

A successful speech requires three stages of preparation and/or adaptation: pre-speech, during the speech, and post-speech.

Pre-speech Preparation

- Know the audience. In order to generate positive feedback, one must know to whom it is that he or she will be speaking. Factors such as the audience's size, background/s, relationship to the speaker, and the audience's knowledge of the speech's topic must be considered when preparing the presentation.
- If the speaker has the opportunity to discuss the topic with an audience member or members prior to the speech, do so in order to learn about their backgrounds, experiences, expectations, and knowledge of the subject.
- If the audience addressed is primarily homogenous, try to incorporate material and references relevant to that group into the speech. Doing so can help to persuade people and establish rapport with them. But take care to not say anything that might exclude or demean any member of the audience.
- If the speaker is unfamiliar with the audience that he or she will be addressing, ask the relevant person—the boss, one's contact person, the event organizer, etc.—for information about the audience.
- When preparing the speech topic, keep in mind just what the speech's goal is and how it might best be achieved.
- Anticipate disagreement. If one is promoting a particular product, course of action, or viewpoint, think beforehand about any possible objections that might be raised in response to the speech. Then prepare clear and appropriate answers.

During the Speech

When delivering a speech before a live audience one must be aware of non-verbal feedback that may be given by the listeners: eye contact or no eye contact, nodding or shaking of the head, facial expressions indicating engagement or boredom, and raised hands indicating the desire to make comments or ask questions. In order to reciprocate and respond to these types of feedback, the speaker should:
- Make clear at the beginning of the speech if questions will be fielded during or after the speech, or both.

- Make sustained eye contact with all audience members or, if speaking to a large group, with all parts of the room, hall, etc.
- Decide whether or not the speech will be given from a fixed point—from behind a podium, for instance—or if one is going to work the audience by moving about the room, up and down aisles, etc. Doing the latter can enhance the audience's sense of closeness to the speaker.
- If using Powerpoint or a blackboard during the speech, be careful not to spend too much time facing away from the audience.
- Make sure that the speech doesn't conclude abruptly. Otherwise the audience may be surprised or left with the impression that the speaker was overly eager to conclude.
- When concluding a speech make clear to the audience that questions or comments are welcome.

Post-speech

- Answer any audience member's questions or comments forthrightly. If a speaker doesn't know the answer to a question, he or she should tell the questioner that an answer would be quickly provided. Get the questioner's contact information, then respond accordingly.
- If relevant, speakers should provide audience members with contact information in case further questions or comments arise.
- As the question-and-answer session comes to a close, be sure to thank the audience for their time and attention.

An excellent guide to all facets of speech preparation and performance is *The St. Martin's Guide to Public Speaking* by Joseph S. Tuman and Douglas M. Fraleigh.

Skill 12.2   Demonstrate knowledge of various types and purposes of listening and the skills unique to each type of purpose.

Different situations call for different types of listening:

Informative Listening: With informative listening, the listener's main goal is to simply understand the speaker's message. A successful informative listener takes away the closest possible message to what the speaker intended for. This kind of listening is used predominantly in learning and classroom situations, but is also essential in the workplace. Having an informed vocabulary in the subject area of the message is crucial. Unfamiliar words should be clarified to ensure understanding. Concentration is also essential. The listener should avoid distracting interferences. Memory is the final component, as it allows you to recall the information you received.

Relationship Listening: During relationship listening, the listener is attempting to either help someone or improve interpersonal relationships. This kind of listening is used in counseling, medicinal clinics, and most frequently, between friends. The three major aspects of relationship listening are attending (paying attention and focusing on speech, demonstrated with eye contact and attentive body language), supporting (knowing when to talk and when to listen, not interrupting, and providing thoughtful advice when needed), and empathizing (feeling and thinking with the other person or putting yourself in his or her shoes).

Appreciative Listening: This type of listening is employed simply for enjoyment. It is focused more on the response of the listener, rather than the source of the message. The quality of appreciative listening depends on presentation (the setting, style and personality of the speaker), and perception (expectations and prior experiences' influence).

Critical Listening: Critical listening is used in many situations, from job sites to church to political rallies to family dinner tables. Aristotle outlined the three main features that affect critical listening; ethos, or the credibility of the speaker, logos, or the logic of the argument, and pathos, the emotional appeal of the argument. Listeners should watch out for manipulative strategies and lack of evidence to back up claims.

Skill 12.3 Recognize the roles and responsibilities of the listener and know appropriate and effective listening responses across a variety of communication situations.

The foundation of listening responsibilities lies in the ability to be a discriminating listener. This refers to the ability to respond to the speaker's rate, volume, force, pitch, and emphasis, thereby detecting meaningful changes and hints at the speaker's true intentions. Discriminative listening also includes sensitivity to pauses as well as body language. While informative listening focuses on what is said, discriminative listening focuses on *how* it is said.

Also, see Skill 12.1.

Skill 12.4 Demonstrate knowledge of strategies for analyzing spoken messages to understand and evaluate stated and implied meanings.

Questions: Ask students what strategies the spoken message uses, how well those strategies respond to the requirements of the situation, and how well the speaker responded to spontaneous occurrences, questions, or problems.

Perception Checking: This is a feedback technique. It refers to the effort to understand the feelings behind the words.

Ask students to describe their impressions of the speaker's feelings. They should not relay any feelings of approval or disapproval.

Paraphrasing: When students paraphrase, it is significant to stress that the resulting summary reflects what the spoken message meant to the student, not what it actually meant or was intended to mean. Have students practice different types of paraphrasing, such as restating the original statement in more specific terms, using an example, or restating it in more general terms.

Skill 12.5 **Recognize criteria for evaluating the content, organization, and support of communication strategies and for evaluating oral messages on the basis of their purpose, quality, and appropriateness.**

See Skills 11.3, 11.5, and 11.6.

Skill 12.6 **Recognize the effects of physical and physiological conditions on listening.**

Any audience, no matter the age, will have a mixture of hearing capabilities. Because so many young people are listening to loud music and hearing other eardrum-damaging sounds, it's no longer reasonable to assume that everyone in any audience can hear clearly. For that reason, even smaller rooms should be equipped with good sound systems. There have been many technological advances in these systems in recent years, making them very affordable. If the speech is to be delivered outdoors, a sound system is a requirement. High ceilings make hearing difficult, and adjustments should be made to compensate.

If the presentation is to senior citizens or if older people are likely to be in the audience, it's important to remember that most people suffer hearing loss as they age. It's also good to know that the loss is in the upper ranges most often, so a female speaker will need more augmentation than a male with a low voice. If the sound system is sufficiently sophisticated, it can be adjusted so bass tones are lower and soprano tones are higher.

Providing the sound system is effective, a speaker should always make it her business to check out the environment where a presentation is to be delivered. Is the temperature moderate—not too warm, not too cold? When people are shivering, they can think of little else. If they are sweating in a too-warm room, their discomfort will interfere with their ability to listen.

Are there ambient sounds that will compete with the voice of the speaker? For example, if the room is in a busy building with conversations and other noises going on in the hallways, the doors must be closed if the presentation is to be a success. Even so, there may still be a lot of interference, so the speaker will need to compensate. If the crowd does not fill the room, they might be moved away from the door or doors.

Sometimes, in conference centers the walls are very thin or are only divided with temporary dividers, and the meeting in the next room will interfere. Some of these factors can be determined ahead of time and if necessary the meeting can be moved elsewhere.

Skill 12.7 **Demonstrate knowledge of listening barriers such as bias, close-mindedness, preconceived attitudes, indifference, and emotional involvement in communication situations.**

The more information a speaker has about an audience, the more likely she is to communicate effectively with them. Several factors figure into the speaker/audience equation: age, ethnic background, educational level, knowledge of the subject, and interest in the subject.

Speaking about computers to senior citizens who have rudimentary knowledge at best about the way computers work must take that situation into account. Perhaps handing out a glossary would be useful for this audience. Speaking to first-graders about computers presents its challenges. On the other hand, the average high-school student has more experience with computers than most adults and that should be taken into account. Speaking to a room full of computer systems engineers requires a rather thorough understanding of the jargon related to the field.

In considering the age of the audience, it's best not to make assumptions. The gathering of senior citizens might include retired systems engineers or people who have made their livings using computers, so research about the audience is important. It might not be wise to assume that high-school students have a certain level of understanding, either.

With an audience that is primarily Hispanic with varying levels of competence in English, the speaker is obligated to adjust the presentation to fit that audience. The same would be true when the audience is composed of people who may have been in the country for a long time but whose families speak their first language at home. Black English presents its own peculiarities, and if the audience is composed primarily of African-Americans whose contacts in the larger community are not great, some efforts need to be made to acquaint oneself with the specific peculiarities of the community those listeners come from.

It's unwise to condescend to an audience; they will almost certainly be insulted. On the other hand, speaking to an audience of college graduates will require different skills than speaking to an audience of people who have never attended college.

Finally, has the audience come because of an interest in the topic or because they have been influenced or forced to come to the presentation?

If the audience comes with an interest in the subject already, efforts to motivate or draw them into the discussion might not be necessary. On the other hand, if the speaker knows the audience does not have a high level of interest in the topic, it would be wise to use devices to draw them into it, to motivate them to listen.

Skill 12.8 Demonstrate knowledge of the effects of listener appreciation.

An appreciative audience is the joy of any speaker; the opposite is the bane. How to know if what is being said is appreciated? The following are the major factors:

- Applause
- Nodding of heads
- Carefully listening with a pleasant look on their faces
- Upright, alert posture
- No one is leaving

In other words, body language is the best clue and the successful speaker will be attuned to it.

Skill 12.9 Demonstrate knowledge of questioning skills for interviewing and gathering firsthand information.

There are many very good models for becoming a top-notch interviewer. Much can be learned from watching a lawyer interview a witness, for example. Also, television reporters are excellent interviewers and one who wants to become a good interviewer would be well advised to pay attention to them.

There are several principles and approaches that can be used to conduct a successful interview.

- Make the interviewee comfortable. Establishing good faith is the first order of business. If the person being interviewed doesn't trust the interviewer, little is likely to come from it. Remember, though, once that trust is established, to be careful to follow through. A betrayed interviewee can do a lot of damage.
- Research. Know as much about the interviewee as possible ahead of time.
- Plan. Determine what you want to find out long before the interview begins. Just as a good lawyer always knows what he wants to hear before a question is asked, so should the interviewer. An outline of the presentation to which the interview will contribute should already be in the interviewer's head as well as in writing. When a reporter interviews a person, the story is already taking place in his mind. How will the information from this interview fit into the story?
- Write the questions ahead of time. Based on what your story will say, what do you want from the interviewee?

- Be flexible. Although preparing ahead of time is extremely important, it's also important to be loose enough to allow the story to lead elsewhere; but don't let don't let digressions take over.
- Huge amounts of tape can be expended on material that the interviewer will have to go through and eliminate if the interview is not controlled. Interviewers are more likely to make this mistake than to fail to get everything they need.

COMPETENCY 13.0 UNDERSTAND THAT COMMUNICATION MAY INFLUENCE AND BE INFLUENCED BY PEOPLE AND THEIR RELATIONSHIPS WITH ONE ANOTHER AND BY COMMUNICATION ANXIETY AND UNDERSTAND THE IMPORTANCE AND ETHICAL RESPONSIBILITIES OF ADAPTING COMMUNICATION TO AUDIENCE NEEDS, THE SITUATION, AND THE SETTING

Skill 13.1   Recognize the influence of context on communication.

See Skills 11.3, 11.5, and 11.12.

Skill 13.2   Recognize and understand the individual and social factors that may lead to communication anxiety.

Anxiety about standing up in front of a group and making a speech is common to most people until they have quite a bit of experience. This anxiety has many sources:

- Memory of times the person has failed or has felt foolish in the past.
- Fear of saying something that will reveal a lack of knowledge.
- Fear of criticism by peers and others.
- Fear that those of higher social standing may ridicule efforts.

Careful preparation and the confidence that comes with a broad understanding of the subject can go a long way to calm public speaking anxiety. Also, deep-breathing strategies are helpful for some people. Recognizing that there are other points of view, but that this one is valid is also helpful. Everyone is entitled to a point of view, even if there are opposing ones. Sometimes opening a speech with humor helps to calm the speaker, providing the audience laughs at the humor, of course. It's worth trying.

Anxiety in conversing with others comes from many of the same sources. A very good antidote to this kind of anxiety is a genuine interest in the other person. Questions that will lead the other to talk about his or her own point of view, own background and interests, or job or family often goes a long way to ameliorate this kind of anxiety. When people feel that another is genuinely interested in what they have to say, they are less likely to be critical. Talking about the weather has become a butt of jokes; even so, it is sometimes a good way to get a conversation started since it's something everyone has in common.

Skill 13.3 Recognize strategies to help minimize and/or manage communication anxiety.

Negative emotions, including anxiety, are usually acquired through punishment, and the negative reinforcement used to shape the social skills of children sometimes has drawbacks. Parents and teachers feel responsible for socializing the children under their care—that is, helping them develop the skills necessary to live in a civilized community. Punishment for speaking out of turn is one of those socializing efforts that tend to result in associations between speaking and fear. Punishment for not waiting one's turn is another. It has also been found that certain people are particularly susceptible to the development of this kind of anxiety as the result of such conditioning.

At the same time, an atmosphere of encouragement and reward for communicating in the home or elementary classroom is inversely related to the level of apprehension about speaking in public that subjects report as adults.

There are several things that teachers can do to help students overcome their fear of speaking in public. One very important thing is to teach students to do thorough research on their topics and to construct speeches they feel confident about. The second thing teachers can do is assure that students have as many opportunities as possible to practice giving speeches. Participating in group discussions has been shown to help students overcome this anxiety about public speaking. It may help students to know that the time of greatest anxiety is during the minute prior to speaking and the first minute of speaking. In other words, if they have prepared, and if they have been practicing, when they stand up to speak, they can have some assurance that if they persevere, the anxiety will subside. Most speakers become progressively more comfortable while presenting a public speech, a process called habituation.

Skill 13.4 Recognize strategies for appropriate and effective small group communication, including components and group variables (e.g., roles, norms, leadership).

Research shows that students who work together in groups or teams develop their skills in organizing, leadership, research, communication, and problem solving. Working in teams can help students to overcome anxiety in distance learning courses and contribute a sense of community and belonging for the students.

What is Cooperative/Collaborative Learning?

When students work together in small groups, research shows that students tend to learn more material being taught and retain the information longer than when the same information is taught using different methods.

The process in both cooperative and collaborative learning is that students work in groups or teams to reach a goal. Cooperative and collaborative discussions actively involve the student to interact with faculty, other students, and the material in meaningful ways. Providing opportunities for students to communicate with each other what they are learning in an online environment is one highly effective way to engage students in the active learning process.

Some collaborative or cooperative learning strategies include:

- **Panel discussion** - A panel/group of students is given a set of questions from which they prepare a group response.
- **Case study** - A group of students is given a narrative description of a problematic situation and then asked to identify and/or solve the problem.
- **Action maze** - A group of students is given a description of an incident that requires analysis and action. They provide a brief response and then forward it to another group. The group that received that response must determine the consequences of the first group's response and either agree or come up with a better response. This process can go on through as many levels as the instructor feels is meaningful.
- **Role-playing** - A team of students is asked to take on the parts of characters in a dramatic representation of a real situation or organizational unit. Role-playing can take place in a chat room or via bulletin board response to questions. Students respond as their character would respond throughout the planned dialog.
- **Students as teachers** - A group of students develops the presentation of a course topic for the rest of the class, perhaps posing one or more interesting questions for class discussion.
- **Formal debate** - Students are divided into teams to present opposing viewpoints; some students may act as respondents or judges.
- **Writing groups** - Students present drafts of written assignments to one another for critique and then revise their drafts based on other student comments.

Group Interactions

Assign a student in each group a specific role they will take on for the source of the activity:

- Leader—the leader directs the action for the day once the teacher has given the instructions.
- Recorder—this group member does the writing for the entire group; he or she uses one sheet, which saves paper.
- Encourager—the encourager gives compliments related to how the group is working, such as "That was a great answer!"
- Checker—this member checks and hands in the work for the group.

Collaboration

- Students decide on goals and the means to accomplish those goals.
- Students decide which roles to play to reach goals.
- Students practice negotiation and social skills and evaluate both their own contributions and those of the other group members.
- Students learn to collaborate and reinforce one another's strengths and observe that people with different strengths may accomplish goals differently or more efficiently.

A good activity to enforce the importance of collaboration breaks the students into groups of four. They use a problem-solving plan and work together during class time as well as outside of class. A recent problem: Would it be cheaper to get to New York City from Long Island by car, bus, or plane? The students show their plans and all their work for each mode of transportation so there are no questions about their answers. The groups may have a little trouble getting started and getting all parties involved, but the final outcome will ensure improved cooperation skills as well as real world training.

Skill 13.5 **Demonstrate knowledge of problem-solving strategies that can be used in group situations.**

See Skills 13.10 and 13.11.

Skill 13.6 **Demonstrate knowledge of the relationship between nonverbal and verbal communication and how vocal qualities and verbal and nonverbal cues can help clarify the meaning, organization, and goals of speaking.**

Posture: Maintain a straight, but not stiff posture. Instead of shifting weight from hip to hip, point your feet directly at the audience and distribute your weight evenly. Keep shoulders aligned towards the audience. If you have to turn your body to use a visual aid, turn 45 degrees and continue speaking towards the audience.

Movement: Instead of staying glued to one spot or pacing back and forth, stay within four to eight feet of the front row of your audience, and take a step or half-step to the side every once in a while. If you are using a lectern, feel free to move to the front or side of it to engage your audience more. Avoid distancing yourself from the audience; you want them to feel involved and connected.

Gestures: Using gestures are a great way to appear natural when speaking publicly. Use them just as you would when speaking to a friend. They shouldn't be exaggerated, but they should be utilized for added emphasis. Avoid keeping your hands in your pockets or locked behind your back, wringing your hands and fidgeting nervously, or keeping your arms crossed.

Eye Contact: Many people are intimidated by using eye contact when speaking to large groups. Interestingly, eye contact usually *helps* the speaker overcome speech anxiety by connecting with their attentive audience and easing feelings of isolation. Instead of looking at a spot on the back wall or at your notes, scan the room and make eye contact for one to three seconds per person.

Voice: Many people fall into one of two traps when speaking: using a monotone or talking too fast, both of which are caused by anxiety. A monotone restricts your natural inflection, but can be remedied by releasing tension in upper and lower body muscles. Subtle movement will keep you loose and natural. Talking too fast, on the other hand, is not necessarily a bad thing if the speaker is exceptionally articulate. If not, though, or if the speaker is talking about very technical things, it becomes far too easy for the audience to become lost. When you talk too fast and begin tripping over your words, consciously pause after every sentence you say. Don't be afraid of brief silences. The audience needs time to absorb what you are saying.

Volume: Problems with volume, whether too soft or too loud, can usually be combated with practice. If you tend to speak too softly, have someone stand in the back of the room and give you a signal when your voice is loud enough. If possible, have someone in the front of the room as well to make sure you're not overcompensating with excessive volume. Conversely, if you have a problem with speaking too loudly, have the person in the front of the room signal you when your voice is soft enough and check with the person in the back to make sure it is still loud enough to be heard. In both cases, note your volume level for future reference. Don't be shy about asking your audience, "Can you hear me in the back?" Suitable volume is beneficial for both you and the audience.

Pitch: Pitch refers to the length, tension and thickness of a person's vocal cords. As your voice gets higher, the pitch gets higher. In oral performance, pitch reflects upon the emotional arousal level. More variation in pitch typically corresponds to more emotional arousal, but can also be used to convey sarcasm or highlight specific words.

Skill 13.7   **Recognizes the importance of freedom of speech and ethical communication in a democratic society.**

In Rome, the censor had two duties: to count the citizens and to supervise their morals. Today's teacher sometimes fits that definition. However, "supervising morals" becomes increasingly complicated as heated discussions over the role of religion in the classroom, freedom of speech, and maintaining discipline mount.

Issues concerning censorship of the curriculum are usually decided by the administrators and sometimes by the board members of a particular school. Issues involved in making those decisions are religion, race, sex, and politics. It is not permissible to use federal funds to promote a particular religion. Even so, any definition of "promote" is debatable. Does a reference to the history of a particular religion fall under the definition? How about an objective comparison of religions? Does the very mention of the names of particular religious figures constitute promotion?

Is it permissible for a student to refer to his own religion in a discussion of literature? Is it permissible for a student to refer to a religion not his own in such a discussion? If students are asked to select a work of literature for a report, is it permissible for that work to reflect a particular religion?

Young people are often very sensitive to issues regarding race and may perceive that there is discrimination where none exists. Nevertheless, a work of literature that seems to present a character of a particular race in a demeaning or critical way should be avoided. Students should be advised of these matters when they are allowed to select what they will read and report on.

Knowing what is too mature sexually for students of a particular age is problematic. Most popular literature includes sexually explicit treatment of characters, plot, conflicts, etc. The safest course is to avoid these resources as much as possible, which amounts to downright censorship. What is lost if this is the course taken? Overprotecting students may not be the best preparation for the world they live in or will be moving into as adults. Discussions of some of these matters may be useful in helping them grow and understand what is going on in their lives. Children are becoming sexually active at much earlier ages than ever in the history of public education and that fact must be taken into account. If material that is sexually explicit is used in the classroom, some parents will surely object. Carefully following the guidelines of a particular school or school district is the safest route to take.

Skill 13.8 Recognize the ethical responsibility to challenge harmful stereotypical or prejudicial communication and to use inclusive language when addressing others.

See Skill 11.9.

Skill 13.9 Demonstrate knowledge of the differences among oral, written, and electronic communication processes.

Although widely different in many aspects, written and spoken English share a common basic structure or syntax (subject, verb, object) and the common purpose of fulfilling the need to communicate—but the similarities end there.

Spoken English does follow the basic word order mentioned above (subject, verb object) as does written English. We would write as we would speak, "I sang a song." It is usually only in poetry or music that that word order or syntax is altered: "Sang I a song." However, beyond that, spoken English is freed from the constraints and expectations imposed upon the written word.

Because of these restraints, in the form of rules of grammar and punctuation, learning to read and write occupy years of formal schooling, whereas learning to speak is a natural developmental stage, much like walking, that is accomplished before the tedious process of learning to write what we speak is endured.

These rules are imposed upon the written language in part because of necessity. Written English is an isolated event. The writer must use an expected, ordered structure, complete with proper spacing and punctuation in order to be understood by an audience that he or she may never see.

In contrast, the speaker of English can rely on hand gestures, facial expressions, and tone of voice to convey information and emotions beyond that which is conveyed in his or her words alone. In addition, speaking is not usually an isolated event. A speaker has a listener who can interrupt, ask questions, or provide additional information, ensuring that the communication is understood.

Thus, spoken English is a much more fluid form of communication and is more directly suited to meeting the needs of the particular audience. This gives rise to regional dialects and forms of expressions that with time and usage may find their way into formal written English.

However, with technology, there are new avenues for communication that are resulting in a synthesis of these two forms of communication: text messaging and chat room dialogues. In these forms, written English is not bound by the formal rules of spelling, grammar, and punctuation—rather, it is free to more closely mimic its spoken counterpart.

Want to shout your answer? USE ALL CAPS! Saying something with a smile? Then show it! ☺ The limited space on cell phones and the immediacy of Internet chat rooms has also led to adaptations in spelling, where, for example, "text message" becomes "txt msg." Other abbreviated spellings and expressions have gained such popular usage that in 2005 the world's first dxNRE & glosRE (dictionary and glossary), "transl8it!" (Translate!) was published to help in the translation of standard English into text speak. Although these unorthodox forms of communication may frighten formal grammarians, this brave new world of communicating, as employed online and via cell phones, is far from being the death knell for "proper" English. Rather, it is just one more indication of the versatility of our language and the ingenuity and creativity of the individuals who employ it.

Skill 13.10 Recognize the roles of interpersonal skills in maintaining relationships.

In dealing with high-school students, it's important to remember that they are in launch mode. Their major developmental task at this stage is to separate themselves from their parents. The struggle between the teenager and the parents complicates the job of the teacher during this period, but it is not nearly so great a factor as the constant struggle to develop relationships with peers. First, there is self-definition. Teenagers are seeking to be part of a group that will fit their own developing self-definition. They make statements about who they are by the friends they choose. It's no accident that this is the age when gangs begin to develop.

In any high school, there are embryonic gangs although most of them never develop into the actual gang phenomenon that is seen on the streets. On the other hand, in some cities, there is an actual connection between the grouping in high school and the actual well-formed and often ominous gangs. Teachers need to be aware of the behaviors and appearances that suggest gang behavior.

However, for most of the students in a classroom, interpersonal relationships are just as powerful but not quite so threatening. The most difficult thing for a teacher is getting the attention of the students so they can be taught what they need to know, always keeping in mind the role of the high school experience in preparing them to go on to college and to succeed there.

Add in the reality that many of these students are already sexually active, long before they are in a position to take responsibility for the consequences of their behavior. Pregnancy, of course, is always a threat—one that has the potential for closing the doors of developmental opportunity, at least for girls. It also has developmental implications for the young men. The second threat is STDs, some of which, like herpes, will complicate lives forever, and like AIDS, which will threaten very lives.

So what can teachers do to achieve in the classroom what must be achieved, and also assist students to get through this developmental stage so they can be ready for the next one?

The study of literature is a good way for students to experience life, emotions, relationships, etc., without actually living them. Using stories, plots, characters, etc., as a way to involve students emotionally and mentally in the realities related to living in the world can be very helpful to these young people. It's possible to discover solutions to relationship problems that might never occur to them any other way without the serious consequences that often go with learning through direct experience.

It has been demonstrated in some of the studies of programs to prevent risky sexual behavior that the only programs that are truly effective in impacting the statistics are those that include either a job component, where students work at something, or a community-service component, where students perform community service, such as working with the elderly or with children.

Research projects that explore social problems might suggest opportunities for students to serve others, such as the elderly poor or children in institutional care because their parents either cannot or will not provide for them This has been demonstrated to have very positive effects on young people who are trying to make their way through this stage when they are preparing to launch themselves into a life of independence from their parents. Teenagers want to make their own decisions and make their own way, but separating from parents who have long guided them is the most difficult step many will ever take. It's also an opportunity for the English teacher to play a significant role in helping them find meaning and purpose.

Skill 13.11   Demonstrate knowledge of strategies for appropriately and effectively negotiating and solving problems in various situations and settings.

Negotiation is in order if two parties share the same objective but have significant differences in how to achieve it. The purpose, of course, is to find a compromise that both parties can live with. What comes out of it may be a compromise satisfactory to sides (the best possible outcome), a standoff (the worst outcome), or a standoff with an agreement to try again at a later time. Negotiation is not influencing. Group decision-making is also a different thing.

An advocate can represent one party or the other in negotiating with the purpose of gaining the most favorable outcomes for that party. The process goes like this: the negotiator tries to determine the minimum outcome or outcomes the other party is willing to accept and then adjusts demands accordingly. If the advocate manages to get most if not all of the outcomes the represented party desires without pushing the other party to break off negotiations, he has succeeded.

In the best of all possible worlds of negotiation, both parties win, sometimes called a win/win situation. This is usually achieved by looking behind the positions of the parties to the interests of each. This is usually achieved by looking at options.

Negotiation is a process. The **first stage** is the definition of objectives and conflicts of both parties.

The **second stage** is determining what each side is willing to trade, what they will offer. It's important to remember that the name of the game in negotiating is give and take.

Bargaining chips are those things that are of low value to the one who offers but of high value to the receiver. Non-negotiables are those that are valuable to the offerer but cheap to the other side.

The **third stage** is determining the best alternative to a negotiated agreement. The following question must be asked: What are the consequences of a failure to come to a compromise? The answer will measure how eager a party is to settle.

The **fourth** stage has to do with how much to ask at the outset. Those who ask for more and support their demands with reasonable arguments usually get more. However, there is also the risk of deadlock. It's important at this stage to administer a heavy dose of patience.

The **fifth** stage involves considering options before the negotiating conference. A party can refuse to come to the conference table unless a condition has been met. For example, a party might require first place in the presentation of demands. This may signal that the other side is not interested in negotiating and that it would be a waste of time to meet. Also, who will be doing the negotiating, the party or a representative?

The **sixth stage** is preparing for the conference. It's important not to let pressure impact how you go about preparing. For example, it's better to avoid deadlines for completion of negotiations; they should move forward at their own pace. Also, keep in mind that there is some empowerment simply in the willingness of the other party to meet because it's a signal that they want something. Bullying, irrationality, and citing principles and regulations are devices often used to achieve the success of the opposing party and should not be yielded to. The negotiator must refuse to be intimidated. It's important to remember that more asked for will yield more received.

The **seventh stage** is the conference itself. Giving the opposing party the opportunity to speak first may be the best possible outcome because the offer may be more than anticipated. In any case, it's not a good idea to open with an offer. Going into the background and stating the problem is a better way to go before discussing terms. Offering the least is the best place to start. Using threats or revealing weaknesses is not helpful. If things do not progress to the satisfaction of one side or the other, a party may step out of the room. Also, one party may set a deadline for reaching an agreement.

After the conference, regardless of the outcome, it's important to analyze what happened and think about what has been learned. It's a good idea to keep notes so the process can be reviewed for the purpose of improving negotiating skills.

Most negotiating is informal. Even so, it's important to think of it in the terms stated above, even breaking it down into steps. Dealing with conflicts and problems almost always calls for negotiation and compromise. Learning and applying formal negotiating skills is useful for dealing with day-to-day situations that require such solutions.

TEACHER CERTIFICATION STUDY GUIDE

| DOMAIN IV. | LITERATURE |

COMPETENCY 14.0 RECOGNIZE AND ANALYZE THE DISTINCTIVE FEATURES AND HISTORICAL DEVELOPMENT OF VARIOUS GENRES AND RECOGNIZE RECURRENT THEMES IN ALL GENRES

Skill 14.1   Identify and analyze the defining characteristics of a variety of literary forms and genres.

Allegory: A story in verse or prose with characters representing virtues and vices. There are two meanings, symbolic and literal. John Bunyan's *The Pilgrim's Progress* is the most renowned of this genre.

Ballad: In *medias res* story told or sung, usually in verse and accompanied by music. Literary devices found in ballads include the refrain, or repeated section, and incremental repetition, or anaphora, for effect. Earliest forms were anonymous folk ballads. Later forms include Coleridge's Romantic masterpiece, "The Rime of the Ancient Mariner."

Drama: Plays – comedy, modern, or tragedy - typically in five acts. Traditionalists and neoclassicists adhere to Aristotle's unities of time, place and action. Plot development is advanced via dialogue. Literary devices include asides, soliloquies and the chorus representing public opinion. Greatest of all dramatists/playwrights is William Shakespeare. Other dramaturges include Ibsen, Williams, Miller, Shaw, Stoppard, Racine, Moliére, Sophocles, Aeschylus, Euripides, and Aristophanes.

Epic: Long, often book length poem reflecting values inherent in the generative society. Epic devices include an invocation to a Muse for inspiration, purpose for writing, universal setting, protagonist and antagonist who possess supernatural strength and acumen, and interventions of a God or the gods. Understandably, there are very few epics: Homer's *Iliad* and *Odyssey*, Virgil's *Aeneid*, Milton's *Paradise Lost*, Spenser's *The Fairie Queene*, Barrett Browning's *Aurora Leigh*, and Pope's mock-epic, *The Rape of the Lock*.

Epistle: A letter that is not always originally intended for public distribution, but due to the fame of the sender and/or recipient, becomes public domain. Paul wrote epistles that were later placed in the Bible.

Essay: Typically a limited length prose work focusing on a topic and propounding a definite point of view and authoritative tone. Great essayists include Carlyle, Lamb, DeQuincy, Emerson and Montaigne, who is credited with defining this genre.

Fable: Terse tale offering up a moral or exemplum. Chaucer's "The Nun's Priest's Tale" is a fine example of a *bete fabliau* or beast fable in which animals speak and act in characteristically human ways, illustrating human foibles.

Legend: A traditional narrative or collection of related narratives, popularly regarded as historically factual but actually a mixture of fact and fiction.

Myth: Stories that are more or less universally shared within a culture to explain its history and traditions.

Novel: The longest form of fictional prose containing a variety of characterizations, settings, local color and regionalism. Most have complex plots, expanded description, and attention to detail. Some of the great novelists include Austin, the Brontes, Twain, Tolstoy, Hugo, Hardy, Dickens, Hawthorne, Forster, and Flaubert.

Poem: The only requirement is rhythm. Sub-genres include fixed types of literature such as the sonnet, elegy, ode, pastoral, and villanelle. Unfixed types of literature include blank verse and dramatic monologue.

Romance: A highly imaginative tale set in a fantastical realm dealing with the conflicts between heroes, villains and/or monsters. "The Knight's Tale" from Chaucer's *Canterbury Tales*, *Sir Gawain and the Green Knight* and Keats' "The Eve of St. Agnes" are prime representatives.

Short Story: Typically a terse narrative, with less developmental background about characters. May include description, author's point of view, and tone. Poe emphasized that a successful short story should create one focused impact. The following are considered to be great short story writers: Hemingway, Faulkner, Twain, Joyce, Shirley Jackson, Flannery O'Connor, de Maupasssant, Saki, Edgar Allen Poe, and Pushkin.

Skill 14.2   Identify, compare, and contrast recurring themes across diverse literary works from a variety of societies, eras, cultures, traditions, and genres.

An archetype is an idealized model of a person, object, or concept from which similar instances are derived, copied, patterned, or emulated. In psychology, an archetype is a model of a person, personality or behavior. Archetypes often appear in literature. William Shakespeare, for example, is known for popularizing many archetypal characters. Although he based many of his characters on existing archetypes from fables and myths, Shakespeare's characters stand out as original by their contrast against a complex, social literary landscape. An image, character, or pattern of circumstances that reoccurs frequently in literature can be considered an archetype.

For example, *Oedipus Rex* has a structure that appears to be repeated in the lives of all men in the sense that all sons are replacements for their fathers. In "Barn Burning" Faulkner provides an original example that calls forth this archetype.

There are many archetypes and skillful and creative writers often rely on them to create successful fiction. Some examples of **action archetypes**:

- The search for the killer
- The search for salvation (or the holy grail)
- The search for the hero
- The descent into hell

Some examples of **character archetypes**:
- The double
- The scapegoat
- The prodigal son
- The Madonna and the Magdalene

The family has often been used as a recurring archetypal theme in literature including the Greek play *Oedipus Rex* and other Greek literature such as the *Medea.* Many of Shakespeare's plays also used this archetype: *Hamlet, Romeo and Juliet,* and *King Lear*, for example. Modern writers also use the family archetype, such as *Desire Under the Elms* by Eugene O'Neill and *A Streetcar Named Desire* by Tennessee Williams. In her popular novel *Beloved,* Toni Morrison uses the archetype of family by chronicling the difficulties the protagonist Sethe and her family face before the Civil War as well as during the conflict and afterward. The result is a compelling picture of a family's response to the devastation brought on by slavery.

Skill 14.3   Analyze the development of form, style, and point of view and their purpose in American, British, and world literature.

See Skills 14.4 and 15.3.

Skill 14.4   Analyze the form, content, purpose, and major themes of American, British, and world literature in their historical perspectives.

American Literature is defined by a number of clearly identifiable periods.

Native American works from various tribes

These were originally part of a vast oral tradition that spanned most of continental America from as far back as before the fifteenth century.

- Characteristics of native Indian literature include
  - reverence for and awe of nature.
  - interconnectedness of elements in the life cycle.

- Themes of Indian literature often reflect
  - the hardiness of the native body and soul.
  - remorse for the destruction of a way of life.
  - the genocide of many tribes by the encroaching settlement and Manifest Destiny policies of the U. S. government.

The Colonial Period in New England and the South

Stylistically, early colonists' writings were neo-classical, emphasizing order, balance, clarity, and reason. Schooled in England, their writing and speaking was still decidedly British even as their thinking became entirely American.

Early American literature reveals the lives and experiences of the New England expatriates who left England to find religious freedom.

William Bradford's excerpts from *The Mayflower Compact* relate vividly the hardships of crossing the Atlantic in such a tiny vessel, the misery and suffering of the first winter, the approaches of the American Indians, the decimation of their ranks, and the establishment of the Bay Colony of Massachusetts.

Anne Bradstreet's poetry relates much concerning colonial New England life. From her journals, modern readers learn of the everyday life of the early settlers, the hardships of travel, and the responsibilities of different groups and individuals in the community,

Early American literature also reveals the commercial and political adventures of the Cavaliers who came to the New World with King George's blessing.

William Byrd's journal, *A History of the Dividing Line,* concerning his trek into the Dismal Swamp separating the Carolinian territories from Virginia and Maryland makes quite lively reading. A privileged insider to the English Royal Court, Byrd, like other Southern Cavaliers, was given grants to pursue business ventures.

The Revolutionary Period contains non-fiction genres: essay, pamphlet, speech, famous document, and epistle.

Major writers and works of the Revolutionary Period:

Thomas Paine's pamphlet, *Common Sense*, which, though written by a recently transplanted Englishman, spoke to the American patriots' common sense in dealing with the issues in the cause of freedom.

Other contributions are Benjamin Franklin's essays from *Poor Richard's Almanac* and satires such as "How to Reduce a Great Empire to a Small One" and "A Letter to Madame Gout."

There were great orations such as Patrick Henry's *Speech to the Virginia House of Burgesses* - the "Give me liberty or give me death" speech - and George Washington's *Farewell to the Army of the Potomac.* Less memorable and thought rambling by modern readers are Washington's inaugural addresses.

The *Declaration of Independence*, the brainchild predominantly of Thomas Jefferson, with some prudent editing by Ben Franklin, is a prime example of neoclassical writing -- balanced, well crafted, and focused.

Epistles include the exquisitely written, moving correspondence between John Adams and Abigail Adams. The poignancy of their separation - she in Boston, he in Philadelphia - is palpable and real.

The Romantic Period

Early American folktales and the emergence of a distinctly American writing, not just a stepchild to English forms, constitute the next period.

Washington Irving's characters, Ichabod Crane and Rip Van Winkle, create a uniquely American folklore devoid of English influences. Their environment and the superstitions of the New Englander indelibly mark the characters. The early American writings of James Fenimore Cooper and his Leatherstocking Tales with their stirring accounts of drums along the Mohawk and the French and Indian Wars, the futile British defense of Fort William Henry and the brutalities of this time frame allow readers a window into their uniquely American world. Natty Bumppo, Chingachgook, Uncas, and Magua are unforgettable characters that reflect the American spirit in thought and action.

The poetry of Fireside Poets James Russell Lowell, Oliver Wendell Holmes, Henry Wadsworth Longfellow, and John Greenleaf Whittier was recited by American families and read in the long New England winters. In "The Courtin'," Lowell used Yankee dialect to tell a narrative. Spellbinding epics by Longfellow such as *Hiawatha*, *The Courtship of Miles Standish*, and *Evangeline* told of adversity, sorrow, and ultimate happiness in a uniquely American warp. "Snowbound" by Whittier relates the story of a captive family isolated by a blizzard, stressing family closeness. Holmes' "The Chambered Nautilus" and his famous line, "Fired the shot heard round the world," put American poetry on a firm footing with other world literature.

Nathaniel Hawthorne and Herman Melville are the preeminent early American novelists, writing on subjects definitely regional, specific and American, yet sharing insights about human foibles, fears, loves, doubts, and triumphs. Hawthorne's writings range from children's stories, like the Cricket on the Hearth series, to adult fare of dark, brooding short stories such as "Dr. Heidegger's Experiment," "The Devil and Tom Walker," and "Rapuccini's Daughter." His masterpiece, *The Scarlet Letter*, takes on the society of hypocritical Puritan New Englanders who ostensibly left England to establish religious freedom but who have become entrenched in judgmental finger wagging. They ostracize Hester and condemn her child, Pearl, as a child of Satan. Great love, sacrifice, loyalty, suffering, and related epiphanies add universality to this tale. *The House of the Seven Gables* also deals with kept secrets, loneliness, societal pariahs, and love ultimately triumphing over horrible wrong. Herman Melville's great opus, *Moby Dick*, follows a crazed Captain Ahab on his Homeric odyssey to conquer the great white whale that has outwitted him and his whaling crews time and again. The whale has even taken Ahab's leg and according to Ahab, wants all of him. Melville recreates in painstaking detail and with insider knowledge the harsh life of a whaler out of New Bedford, by way of Nantucket. For those who don't want to learn about every guy rope or all parts of the whaler's rigging, Melville offers up the succinct tale of Billy Budd and his Christ-like sacrifice to the black and white maritime laws on the high seas. An accident results in the death of one of the ship's officers, a slug of a fellow, who had taken a dislike to the young, affable, shy Billy. Captain Vere must hang Billy for the death of Claggert, but knows that this is not right. However, an example must be given to the rest of the crew so that discipline can be maintained.

Edgar Allan Poe creates a distinctly American version of romanticism with his 16-syllable line in "The Raven," the classical "To Helen," and his Gothic "Annabelle Lee." The horror short story can be said to originate from Poe's pen. "The Tell-Tale Heart," "The Cask of Amontillado," "The Fall of the House of Usher," and "The Masque of the Red Death" are exemplary short stories. The new genre of detective story also emerges with Poe's "Murders in the Rue Morgue."

American Romanticism has its own offshoot in the Transcendentalism of Ralph Waldo Emerson and Henry David Thoreau. One wrote about transcending the complexities of life; the other, who wanted to get to the marrow of life, pitted himself against nature at Walden Pond and wrote an inspiring autobiographical account of his sojourn, aptly titled *On Walden Pond*. He also wrote passionately on his objections to the interference of government on the individual in "On the Duty of Civil Disobedience."

Emerson's elegantly crafted essays and war poetry still validate several important universal truths. Probably most remembered for his address to Thoreau's Harvard graduating class, "The American Scholar," he defined the qualities of hard work and intellectual spirit required of Americans in their growing nation.

The Transition between Romanticism and Realism

The Civil War period ushers in the poignant poetry of Walt Whitman and his homages to all who suffer from the ripple effects of war and presidential assassination. His "Come up from the Fields, Father" about a Civil War soldier's death and his family's reaction and "When Lilacs Last in the Courtyard Bloom'd" about the effects of Abraham Lincoln's death on the poet and the nation should be required readings in any American literature course. Further, his *Leaves of Grass* gave America its first poetry truly unique in form, structure, and subject matter.

Emily Dickinson, like Walt Whitman, leaves her literary fingerprint on a vast array of poems, all but three of which were unpublished in her lifetime. Her themes of introspection and attention to nature's details and wonders are, by any measurement, world-class works. Her posthumous recognition reveals the timeliness of her work. American writing had most certainly arrived!

During this period such legendary figures as Paul Bunyan and Pecos Bill rose from the oral tradition. Anonymous storytellers around campfires told tales of a huge lumberman and his giant blue ox, Babe, whose adventures were explanations of natural phenomena like those of footprints filled with rainwater becoming the Great Lakes. Or the whirling-dervish speed of Pecos Bill explaining the tornadoes of the Southwest. Just as ancient peoples found reasons for the events in their lives, these American pioneer storytellers created a mythology appropriate to the vast reaches of the unsettled frontier.

Mark Twain also left a giant footprint with his unique blend of tall tale and fable. "The Celebrated Jumping Frog of Calaveras County" and "The Man who Stole Hadleyburg" are epitomes of short story writing. Move to the novel and Twain again rises head and shoulders above others with his bold, still disputed, oft-banned *The Adventures of Huckleberry Finn*, which examines such taboo subjects as a white person's love of a slave, the issue of leaving children with abusive parents, and the outcomes of family feuds. Written partly in dialect and southern vernacular, *The Adventures of Huckleberry Finn* is touted by some as the greatest American novel.

The Realistic Period

The late nineteenth century saw a reaction against the tendency of Romantic writers to look at the world through rose-colored glasses. Writers like Frank Norris (*The Pit*) and Upton Sinclair (*The Jungle*) used their novels to decry conditions for workers in slaughterhouses and wheat mills. In *The Red Badge of Courage*, Stephen Crane wrote of the daily sufferings of the common soldier in the Civil War. Realistic writers wrote of common, ordinary people and events using detail that would reveal the harsh realities of life. They broached taboos by creating protagonists whose environments often destroyed them. Romantic writers would have only protagonists whose indomitable wills helped them rise above adversity.

Crane's *Maggie: A Girl of the Streets* deals with a young woman forced into prostitution to survive. In "The Occurrence at Owl Creek Bridge," Ambrose Bierce relates the unfortunate hanging of a Confederate soldier.

Short stories, like Bret Harte's "The Outcasts of Poker Flat" and Jack London's "To Build a Fire," deal with unfortunate people whose luck in life has run out. Many writers, sub-classified as naturalists, believed that man was subject to a fate over which he had no control.

The Modern Era
Twentieth century American writing can be classified into the following three genres.

America Drama
The greatest and most prolific of American playwrights include
Eugene O'Neill -- *Long Day's Journey into Night, Mourning Becomes Electra,* and *Desire Under the Elms*
Arthur Miller -- *The Crucible, All My Sons,* and *Death of a Salesman*
Tennessee Williams -- *Cat on a Hot Tin Roof, The Glass Menagerie,* and *A Street Car Named Desire*
Edward Albee -- *Who's Afraid of Virginia Woolf?, Three Tall Women,* and *A Delicate Balance*

American Fiction
The renowned American novelists of this century include
John Updike -- *Rabbit Run* and *Rabbit Redux*
Sinclair Lewis -- *Babbit* and *Elmer Gantry*
F. Scott Fitzgerald -- *The Great Gatsby* and *Tender is the Night*
Ernest Hemingway -- *A Farewell to Arms* and *For Whom the Bell Tolls*
William Faulkner -- *The Sound and the Fury* and *Absalom, Absalom*
Bernard Malamud -- *The Fixer* and *The Natural*

American Poetry
The poetry of the twentieth century is multifaceted, as represented by Edna St. Vincent Millay, Marianne Moore, Richard Wilbur, Langston Hughes, Maya Angelou, and Rita Dove. Head and shoulders above all others are the many-layered poems of Robert Frost. His New England motifs of snowy evenings, birches, apple picking, stonewall-mending, hired hands, and detailed nature studies relate universal truths in exquisite diction, polysyllabic words, and rare allusions to either mythology or the *Bible*.

Anglo-Saxon
The Anglo-Saxon period spans six centuries but produced only a smattering of literature. The first British epic is *Beowulf,* anonymously written by Christian monks many years after the events in the narrative supposedly occurred.

This Teutonic saga relates the triumph three times over of monsters by the hero, Beowulf. "The Seafarer," a shorter poem, some history, and some riddles are the rest of the Anglo-Saxon canon.

Medieval

The Medieval period introduces Geoffrey Chaucer, the father of English literature, who's *Canterbury Tales* are written not in Latin but in the vernacular, or street language, of England. Thus, the tales are said to be the first work of British literature. Next, Thomas Malory's *Le Morte d'Arthur* culls the extant tales from Europe as well as England concerning the legendary King Arthur, Merlin, Guenevere, and the Knights of the Round Table. This is the generative work that gave rise to the many Arthurian legends that stir the chivalric imagination.

Renaissance and Elizabethan

The Renaissance, the most important period since it is synonymous with William Shakespeare, begins with importing the Petrarchan or Italian sonnet into England. Sir Thomas Wyatt and Sir Philip Sydney wrote English versions. Next, Sir Edmund Spenser invented a variation on this Italian sonnet form, aptly called the Spenserian sonnet. His masterpiece is the epic, *The Fairie Queene*, honoring Queen Elizabeth I's reign. He also wrote books on the Red Cross Knight, St. George and the Dragon, and a series of Arthurian adventures. Spenser was dubbed the Poet's Poet. He created a nine-line stanza, eight lines of iambic pentameter and an extra-footed ninth line, an alexandrine. Thus, he invented the Spenserian stanza as well.

William Shakespeare, the Bard of Avon, wrote 154 sonnets, 39 plays, and two long narrative poems. The sonnets are justifiably called the greatest sonnet sequence in all literature. Shakespeare dispensed with the octave/sestet format of the Italian sonnet and invented his three quatrains, one heroic couplet format. His plays are divided into comedies, history plays, and tragedies. Great lines from these plays are more often quoted than those of any other author. The Big Four tragedies, *Hamlet*, *Macbeth*, *Othello*, and *King Lear* are acknowledged to be the most brilliant examples of this genre.

Seventeenth century

John Milton's devout Puritanism was the wellspring of his creative genius that closes the remarkable productivity of the English Renaissance. His social commentary in such works as *Aereopagitica*, *Samson Agonistes*, and his elegant sonnets would be enough to solidify his stature as a great writer. It is his masterpiece based in part on the Book of Genesis that places Milton very near the top of the rung of a handful of the most renowned of all writers. *Paradise Lost*, written in balanced, elegant Neoclassic form, truly does justify the ways of God to man. The greatest allegory about man's journey to the Celestial City (Heaven) was written at the end of the English Renaissance, as was John Bunyan's *The Pilgrim's Progress*, which describes virtues and vices personified.

This work is, or was for a long time, second only to the *Bible* in numbers of copies printed and sold.

The Jacobean Age gave us the marvelously witty and cleverly constructed conceits of John Donne's metaphysical sonnets, as well as his insightful meditations, and his version of sermons or homilies. "Ask not for whom the bell tolls", and "No man is an island unto himself" are famous epigrams from Donne's *Meditations*. His most famous conceit is that which compares lovers to a footed compass, traveling seemingly separate, but always leaning towards one another and conjoined in "A Valediction Forbidding Mourning."

Eighteenth century
Ben Jonson, author of the wickedly droll play, *Volpone,* and the Cavalier *carpe diem* poets Robert Herrick, Sir John Suckling, and Richard Lovelace also wrote during King James I's reign.

The Restoration and Enlightenment reflect the political turmoil of the regicide of Charles I, the Interregnum Puritan government of Oliver Cromwell, and the restoring of the monarchy to England by the coronation of Charles II, who had been given refuge by the French King Louis. Neoclassicism became the preferred writing style, especially for Alexander Pope. New genres, such as *The Diary of Samuel Pepys*, the novels of Daniel Defoe, the periodical essays and editorials of Joseph Addison and Richard Steele, and Pope's mock epic, *The Rape of the Lock*, demonstrate the diversity of expression during this time.

Writers who followed were contemporaries of Dr. Samuel Johnson, the lexicographer of *The Dictionary of the English Language*. Fittingly, this Age of Johnson, which encompasses James Boswell's biography of Dr. Johnson, Robert Burns' Scottish dialect and regionalism in his evocative poetry and the mystical pre-Romantic poetry of William Blake usher in the Romantic Age and its revolution against Neoclassicism.

Romantic period
The Romantic Age encompasses what is known as the First Generation Romantics, William Wordsworth and Samuel Taylor Coleridge, who collaborated on *Lyrical Ballads,* which defines and exemplifies the tenets of this style of writing. The Second Generation includes George Gordon, Lord Byron, Percy Bysshe Shelley, and John Keats. These poets wrote sonnets, odes, epics, and narrative poems, most dealing with homage to nature. Wordsworth's most famous other works are "Intimations on Immortality" and "The Prelude." Byron's satirical epic, *Don Juan*, and his autobiographical *Childe Harold's Pilgrimage* are irreverent, witty, self-deprecating and, in part, cuttingly critical of other writers and critics. Shelley's odes and sonnets are remarkable for sensory imagery.

Keats' sonnets, odes, and longer narrative poem, *The Eve of St. Agnes*, are remarkable for their introspection and the tender age of the poet, who died when he was only twenty-five. In fact, all of the Second Generation died before their times. Wordsworth, who lived to be eighty, outlived them all, as well as his friend and collaborator, Coleridge. Others who wrote during the Romantic Age are the essayist, Charles Lamb, and the novelist, Jane Austin. The Bronte sisters, Charlotte and Emily, penned two of the finest novels ever written, *Jane Eyre* and *Wuthering Heights*. Marianne Evans, also known as George Eliot, wrote several important novels: her masterpiece, *Middlemarch*, plus *Silas Marner*, *Adam Bede*, and *Mill on the Floss*.

Nineteenth century
The Victorian Period is remarkable for the diversity and proliferation of work in three major areas. Poets who are typified as Victorians include Alfred, Lord Tennyson, who wrote *Idylls of the King*, twelve narrative poems about the Arthurian legend, and Robert Browning, who wrote chilling dramatic monologues, such as "My Last Duchess," as well as long poetic narratives such as *The Pied Piper of Hamlin*. His wife Elizabeth wrote two major works, the epic feminist poem, *Aurora Leigh*, and her deeply moving and provocative *Sonnets from the Portuguese,* in which she details her deep love for Robert and her amazement that he reciprocated that love. Gerard Manley Hopkins, a Catholic priest, wrote poetry with sprung rhythm. (See Glossary of Literary Terms in 4.2). A. E. Housman, Matthew Arnold, and the Pre-Raphaelites, especially the brother and sister duo, Dante Gabriel Rosetti and Christina Rosetti, contributed much to round out the Victorian Era poetic scene. The Pre-Raphaelites, a group of nineteenth-century English painters, poets, and critics, reacted against Victorian materialism and the neoclassical conventions of academic art by producing earnest, quasi-religious works. Medieval and early Renaissance painters up to the time of the Italian painter Raphael inspired the group. Robert Louis Stevenson, the great Scottish novelist, wrote his adventure/history lessons for young adults. Victorian prose ranges from the incomparable, keenly woven plot structures of Charles Dickens to the deeply moving Dorset/Wessex novels of Thomas Hardy, in which women are repressed and life is more struggle than euphoria. Rudyard Kipling wrote about colonialism in India in works like *Kim* and *The Jungle Book,* that create exotic locales and a distinct main point concerning the Raj, the British colonial government during Queen Victoria's reign. Victorian drama is a product mainly of Oscar Wilde, whose satirical masterpiece, *The Importance of Being Earnest*, farcically details and lampoons Victorian social mores.

Twentieth century

The early twentieth century is represented mainly by the towering achievement of George Bernard Shaw's dramas: *St. Joan*, *Man and Superman*, *Major Barbara*, and *Arms and the Man*, to name a few. Novelists are too numerous to list, but Joseph Conrad, E. M. Forster, Virginia Woolf, James Joyce, Nadine Gordimer, Graham Greene, George Orwell, and D. H. Lawrence comprise some of the century's very best.

Twentieth century poets of renown and merit include W. H. Auden, Robert Graves, T. S. Eliot, Edith Sitwell, Stephen Spender, Dylan Thomas, Philip Larkin, Ted Hughes, Sylvia Plath, and Hugh MacDarmid. This list is by no means complete.

North American Literature

North American literature is divided between the United States, Canada, and Mexico. The American writers have been amply discussed in 1.0. Canadian writers of note include feminist Margaret Atwood, (*The Hand Maid's Tale*); Alice Munro, a remarkable short story writer; and W. P. Kinsella, another short story writer whose two major subjects are North American Indians and baseball. Mexican writers include 1990 Nobel Prize winning poet, Octavio Paz, (*The Labyrinth of Solitude*) and feminist Rosarian Castillanos (*The Nine Guardians*).

Central American/Caribbean Literature

The Caribbean and Central America encompass a vast area and cultures that reflect oppression and colonialism by England, Spain, Portugal, France, and The Netherlands. The Caribbean writers include Samuel Selvon from Trinidad and Armado Valladres of Cuba. Central American authors include dramatist Carlos Solorzano, from Guatemala, whose plays include *Dona Beatriz, The Hapless, The Magician,* and *The Hands of God.*

South American Literature

Chilean Gabriela Mistral was the first Latin American writer to win the Nobel Prize for literature. She is best known for her collections of poetry, *Desolation and Feeling*. Chile was also home to Pablo Neruda, who, in 1971, also won the Nobel Prize for literature for his poetry. His 29 volumes of poetry have been translated into more than 60 languages, attesting to his universal appeal. *Twenty Love Poems* and *Song of Despair* are justly famous. Isabel Allende is carrying on the Chilean literary standards with her acclaimed novel, *House of Spirits*. Argentine Jorge Luis Borges is considered by many literary critics to be the most important writer of his century from South America. His collections of short stories, *Ficciones*, brought him universal recognition. Also from Argentina, Silvina Ocampo, a collaborator with Borges on a collection of poetry, is famed for her poetry and short story collections, which include *The Fury* and *The Days of the Night*.

Noncontinental European Literature

Horacio Quiroga represents Uruguay, and Brazil has Joao Guimaraes Rosa, whose novel, *The Devil to Pay*, is considered first-rank world literature.

Germany

German poet and playwright Friedrich von Schiller is best known for his history plays, *William Tell* and *The Maid of Orleans*. He is a leading literary figure in Germany's Golden Age of Literature.

Also from Germany, Rainer Maria Rilke, the great lyric poet, is one of the poets of the unconscious, or stream of consciousness. Germany also has given the world Herman Hesse, (*Siddartha*), Gunter Grass (*The Tin Drum*), and arguably the greatest of all German writers, Goethe.

Scandinavia

Scandinavia has encouraged the work of Hans Christian Andersen in Denmark, who advanced the fairy tale genre with such wistful tales as "The Little Mermaid" and "Thumbelina." The social commentary of Henrik Ibsen in Norway startled the world of drama with such issues as feminism (*The Doll's House* and *Hedda Gabler*) and the effects of sexually transmitted diseases (*The Wild Duck* and *Ghosts*). Sweden's Selma Lagerlof is the first woman to ever win the Nobel Prize for literature. Her novels include *Gosta Berling's Saga* and the world-renowned *The Wonderful Adventures of Nils*, a children's work.

Russia

Russian literature is vast and monumental. Who has not heard of Fyodor Dostoyevsky's *Crime and Punishment*, or *The Brothers Karamazov*, or Count Leo Tolstoy's *War and Peace*? These are examples of psychological realism. Dostoyevsky's influence on modern writers cannot be overly stressed. Tolstoy's *War and Peace* is the sweeping account of the invasion of Russia and Napoleon's taking of Moscow, abandoned by the Russians. This novel is called the national novel of Russia. Further advancing Tolstoy's greatness is his ability to create believable, unforgettable female characters, especially Natasha in *War and Peace* and the heroine of *Anna Karenina*. Pushkin is famous for great short stories; Anton Chekhov for drama, (*Uncle Vanya*, *The Three Sisters*, *The Cherry Orchard*); Yevtushenko for poetry (*Babi Yar*). Boris Pasternak won the Nobel Prize (*Dr. Zhivago*). Aleksandr Solzhenitsyn (*The Gulag Archipelago*) is only recently back in Russia after years of expatriation in Vermont. Ilya Varshavsky, who creates fictional societies that are dystopias, or the opposite of utopias, represents the genre of science fiction.

France

France has a multifaceted canon of great literature that is universal in scope, almost always championing some social cause: the poignant short stories of Guy de Maupassant; the fantastic poetry of Charles Baudelaire (*Fleurs du Mal);* the groundbreaking lyrical poetry of Rimbaud and Verlaine; and the existentialism of Jean-Paul Sartre (*No Exit, The Flies, Nausea*), Andre Malraux, (*The Fall*), and Albert Camus (*The Stranger, The Plague*), the recipient of the 1957 Nobel Prize for literature. Drama in France is best represented by Rostand's *Cyrano de Bergerac*, and the neo-classical dramas of Racine and Corneille (*El Cid*). Feminist writings include those of Sidonie-Gabrielle Colette, known for her short stories and novels, as well as Simone de Beauvoir.

The great French novelists include Andre Gide, Honore de Balzac (*Cousin Bette*), Stendhal (*The Red and the Black*), the father/son duo of Alexandre Dumas (*The Three Musketeers* and *The Man in the Iron Mask*. Victor Hugo is the Charles Dickens of French literature, having penned the masterpieces, *The Hunchback of Notre Dame* and the French national novel, *Les Miserables*. The stream of consciousness of Proust's *Remembrance of Things Past*, and the Absurdist theatre of Samuel Beckett and Eugene Ionesco (*Rhinoceros*) attest to the groundbreaking genius of the French writers.

Slavic nations

Austrian writer Franz Kafka (*The Metamorphosis, The Trial,* and *The Castle*) is considered by many to be the literary voice of the first half of the twentieth century. Representing the Czech Republic is the poet Vaclav Havel. Slovakia has dramatist Karel Capek (*R.U.R.*) Romania is represented by Elie Weisel (*Night*), a Nobel Prize winner.

Spain

Spain's great writers include Miguel de Cervantes (*Don Quixote*) and Juan Ramon Jimenez. The anonymous national epic, *El Cid*, has been translated into many languages.

Italy

Italy's greatest writers include Virgil, who wrote the great epic, *The Aeneid*; Giovanni Boccaccio (*The Decameron*); Dante Alighieri (*The Divine Comedy*); and Alberto Moravia.

Ancient Greece

Greece will always be foremost in literary assessments due to Homer's epics, *The Iliad* and *The Odyssey*. No one except Shakespeare is more often cited. Add to these the works of Plato and Aristotle for philosophy; the dramatists Aeschylus, Euripides, and Sophocles for tragedy, and Aristophanes for comedy. Greece is the cradle not only of democracy, but of literature as well.

Africa

African literary greats include South Africans Nadine Gordimer (Nobel Prize for literature) and Peter Abrahams (*Tell Freedom: Memories of Africa*), an autobiography of life in Johannesburg. Chinua Achebe (*Things Fall Apart*) and the poet, Wole Soyinka, hail from Nigeria. Mark Mathabane's autobiography, *Kaffir Boy,* is about growing up in South Africa. Egyptian writer, Naguib Mahfouz, and Doris Lessing from Zimbabwe (the former Rhodesia), write about race relations in their respective countries. Because of her radical politics, Lessing was banned from her homeland and The Union of South Africa, as was Alan Paton, whose seemingly simple story, *Cry, the Beloved Country*, brought the plight of blacks and the whites' fear of blacks under apartheid to the rest of the world.

Far East

Asia has many modern writers who are being translated for the Western reading public. India's Krishan Chandar has authored more than 300 stories. Rabindranath Tagore won the Nobel Prize for literature in 1913 (*Song Offerings*). Narayan, India's most famous writer (*The Guide*), is highly interested in mythology and legends of India. Santha Rama Rau's work, *Gifts of Passage*, is her true story of life in a British school where she tries to preserve her Indian culture and traditional home.

Revered as Japan's most famous female author, Fumiko Hayashi (*Drifting Clouds*) had written more than 270 literary works at the time of her death. The classical Age of Japanese literary achievement includes the father Kiyotsugu Kan ami and the son Motokkiyo Zeami, who developed the theatrical experience known as Noh drama to its highest aesthetic degree. The son is said to have authored over 200 plays, of which 100 still are extant.

In 1968 the Nobel Prize for literature was awarded to Yasunari Kawabata. *The Sound of the Mountain* and *The Snow Country* are considered to be his masterpieces. His Palm-of-the-Hand Stories take the essentials of Haiku poetry and transform them into the short story genre.

Katai Tayama (*The Quilt*) is touted as the father of the genre known as the Japanese confessional novel. He also wrote in the "ism" of naturalism. His works are definitely not for the squeamish.

The slice of life psychological writings of Ryunosuke Akutagawa gained him acclaim in the Western world. His short stories, especially "Rashamon" and "In a Grove," are greatly praised for style as well as content.

China, too, has given to the literary world. Li Po, the T'ang dynasty poet from the Chinese Golden Age, revealed his interest in folklore by preserving the folk songs and mythology of China. Po further allows his reader to enter into the Chinese philosophy of Taoism and to know this feeling against expansionism during the T'ang dynastic rule. As far back as the T'ang dynasty, which was one of great diversity in the arts, the Chinese version of a short story was created with the help of Jiang Fang. His themes often express love between a man and a woman. Modern feminist and political concerns are written eloquently by Ting Ling, who used the pseudonym Chiang Ping-Chih. Her stories reflect her concerns about social injustice and her commitment to the women's movement.

COMPETENCY 15.0 RECOGNIZE AND ANALYZE LITERARY ELEMENTS AND TECHNIQUES AND HOW THEY CONVEY MEANING IN CLASSIC AND CONTEMPORARY LITERATURE FROM A VARIETY OF ERAS, CULTURES, TRADITION, GENRES, AND MEDIA

Skill 15.1 Identify and analyze literary elements and understand their influence on the effectiveness of a literary piece.

It's no accident that **plot** is sometimes called action. If the plot does not *move*, the story quickly dies. Therefore, the successful writer of stories uses a wide variety of active verbs in creative and unusual ways. If a reader is kept on her toes by the movement of the story, the experience of reading it will be pleasurable. That reader will probably want to read more of this author's work. Careful, unique, and unusual choices of active verbs will bring about that effect. William Faulkner is a good example of a successful writer whose stories are lively and memorable because of his use of unusual active verbs. In analyzing the development of plot, it's wise to look at the verbs. However, the development of believable conflicts is also vital. If there is no conflict, there is no story. What devices does a writer use to develop the conflicts and are they real and believable?

Character is portrayed in many ways: description of physical characteristics, dialogue, interior monologue, the thoughts of the character, the attitudes of other characters toward this one, etc. Descriptive language depends on the ability to recreate a sensory experience for the reader. If the description of the character's appearance is a visual one, then the reader must be able to *see* the character. What's the shape of the nose? What color are the eyes? How tall or how short is this character? Thin or chubby? How does the character move? How does the character walk? Terms must be chosen that will create a picture for the reader. It's not enough to say the eyes are blue, for example. What blue? Often the color of eyes is compared to something else to enhance the readers' ability to visualize the character. A good test of characterization is the level of emotional involvement of the reader in the character. If the reader is to become involved, the description must provide an actual experience—seeing, smelling, hearing, tasting, or feeling.

Dialogue will reflect characteristics. Is it clipped? Is it highly dialectal? Does a character use a lot of colloquialisms? The ability to portray the speech of a character can make or break a story. The kind of person the character is in the mind of the reader is dependent on impressions created by description and dialogue. How do other characters feel about this one as revealed by their treatment of him, their discussions of him with each other, or their overt descriptions of the character? For example, "John, of course, can't be trusted with another person's possessions." In analyzing a story, it's useful to discuss the devices used to produce character.

Setting may be visual, temporal, psychological, or social. Descriptive words are often used here also. In Edgar Allan Poe's description of the house in "The Fall of the House of Usher" as the protagonist/narrator approaches it, the air of dread and gloom that pervades the story is caught in the setting and sets the stage for the story. A setting may also be symbolic, as it is in Poe's story, where the house is a symbol of the family that lives in it. As the house disintegrates, so does the family.

The language used in all of these aspects of a story—plot, character, and setting—work together to create the **mood** of a story. Poe's first sentence establishes the mood of the story: "During the whole of a dull, dark, and soundless day in the autumn of the year, when the clouds hung oppressively low in the heavens, I had been passing alone, on horseback, through a singularly dreary tract of country; and at length found myself, as the shades of the evening drew on, within view of the melancholy House of Usher."

Skill 15.2   **Identify a variety of literary techniques and devices in classic and contemporary literature representing a variety of genres and media.**

Essential terminology and literary devices germane to literary analysis include alliteration, allusion, antithesis, aphorism, apostrophe, assonance, blank verse, caesura, conceit, connotation, consonance, couplet, denotation, diction, epiphany, exposition, figurative language, free verse, hyperbole, iambic pentameter, inversion, irony, kenning, metaphor, metaphysical poetry, metonymy, motif, onomatopoeia, octava rima, oxymoron, paradox, parallelism, personification, quatrain, scansion, simile, soliloquy, Spenserian stanza, synecdoche, terza rima, tone, and wit.

The more basic terms and devices, such as alliteration, allusion, analogy, aside, assonance, atmosphere, climax, consonance, denouement, elegy, foil, foreshadowing, metaphor, simile, setting, symbol, and theme are defined and exemplified in the English 5-9 Study Guide.

Antithesis: Balanced writing about conflicting ideas, usually expressed in sentence form. Some examples are expanding from the center, shedding old habits, and searching, never finding.

Aphorism: A focused, succinct expression about life from a sagacious viewpoint. Writings by Ben Franklin, Sir Francis Bacon, and Alexander Pope contain many aphorisms. "Whatever is begun in anger ends in shame" is an aphorism.

Apostrophe: Literary device of addressing an absent or dead person, an abstract idea, or an inanimate object. Sonneteers, such as Sir Thomas Wyatt, John Keats, and William Wordsworth, address the moon, stars, and the dead Milton.

For example, in William Shakespeare's *Julius Caesar*, Mark Antony addresses the corpse of Caesar in the speech that begins: "O, pardon me, thou bleeding piece of earth, that I am meek and gentle with these butchers! Thou art the ruins of the noblest man that ever lived in the tide of times. Woe to the hand that shed this costly blood!"

Blank Verse: Poetry written in iambic pentameter but unrhymed. Works by Shakespeare and Milton are epitomes of blank verse. Milton's *Paradise Lost* states, "Illumine, what is low raise and support,/ That to the height of this great argument I may assert Eternal Providence/ And justify the ways of God to men."

Caesura: A pause, usually signaled by punctuation, in a line of poetry. The earliest usage occurs in *Beowulf*, the first English epic dating from the Anglo-Saxon era. "To err is human,/ to forgive, divine" (Pope).

Conceit: A comparison, usually in verse, between seemingly disparate objects or concepts. John Donne's metaphysical poetry contains many clever conceits. For instance, Donne's "The Flea" (1633) compares a flea bite to the act of love; and in "A Valediction: Forbidding Mourning" (1633) separated lovers are likened to the legs of a compass, the leg drawing the circle eventually returning home to "the fixed foot."

Connotation: The ripple effect surrounding the implications and associations of a given word, distinct from the denotative, or literal, meaning. For example, "Good night, sweet prince, and flights of angels sing thee to thy *rest*" in which "rest" refers to a burial.

Consonance: The repeated usage of similar consonant sounds, most often used in poetry. "Sally sat sifting seashells by the seashore" is a familiar example.

Couplet: Two rhyming lines of poetry. Shakespeare's sonnets end in heroic couplets written in iambic pentameter. Pope is also a master of the couplet. His *Rape of the Lock* is written entirely in heroic couplets.

Denotation: What a word literally means, as opposed to its connotative meaning. For example, "Good night, sweet prince, and flights of angels sing thee to thy *rest*" in which "rest" refers to sleep.

Diction: The right word in the right spot for the right purpose. The hallmark of a great writer is precise, unusual, and memorable diction.

Epiphany: The moment when the proverbial lightbulb goes off in one's head and comprehension sets in.

Exposition: Fill-in or background information about characters meant to clarify and add to the narrative; the initial plot element, which precedes the buildup of conflict.

Figurative Language: Not meant in a literal sense, but to be interpreted through symbolism. Figurative language is made up of such literary devices as hyperbole, metonymy, synecdoche, and oxymoron. A synecdoche is a figure of speech in which the word for part of something is used to mean the whole; for example, "sail" for "boat," or vice versa.

Free Verse: Poetry that does not have any predictable meter or patterning. Margaret Atwood, e. e. cummings, and Ted Hughes write in this form.

Hyperbole: Exaggeration for a specific effect. For example, "I'm so hungry that I could eat a million of these."

Iambic Pentameter: The two elements in a set five-foot line of poetry. An iamb is two syllables, unaccented and accented, per foot or measure. Pentameter means five feet of these iambs per line or ten syllables.

Inversion: A typical sentence order to create a given effect or interest. Bacon and Milton's work use inversion successfully. Emily Dickinson was fond of arranging words outside of their familiar order. For example in "Chartless" she writes "Yet know I how the heather looks" and "Yet certain am I of the spot." Instead of saying "Yet I know" and "Yet I am certain" she reverses the usual order and shifts the emphasis to the more important words.

Irony: An unexpected disparity between what is written or stated and what is really meant or implied by the author. Verbal, situational, and dramatic are the three literary ironies. Verbal irony is when an author says one thing and means something else. Dramatic irony is when an audience perceives something that a character in the literature does not know. Irony of situation is a discrepancy between the expected result and actual results. Shakespeare's plays contain numerous and highly effective use of irony. O. Henry's short stories have ironic endings.

Kenning: Another way to describe a person, place, or thing so as to avoid prosaic repetition. The earliest examples can be found in Anglo-Saxon literature such as *Beowulf* and "The Seafarer." Instead of writing King Hrothgar, the anonymous monk wrote, great Ring-Giver, or Father of his people. A lake becomes the swans' way, and the ocean or sea becomes the great whale's way. In ancient Greek literature, this device was called an "epithet."

Metaphysical Poetry: Verse characterization by ingenious wit, unparalleled imagery, and clever conceits. The greatest metaphysical poet is John Donne. Henry Vaughn and other seventeenth century British poets contributed to this movement as in *Words*, "I saw eternity the other night, like a great being of pure and endless light."

Metonymy: Use of an object or idea closely identified with another object or idea to represent the second. "Hit the books" means "go study." Washington, D.C. means the U.S. government and the White House means the U.S. President.

Motif: A key, oft-repeated phrase, name, or idea in a literary work. Dorset/Wessex in Hardy's novels and the moors and the harsh weather in the Bronte sisters' novels are effective use of motifs. Shakespeare's *Romeo and Juliet* represents the ill-fated young lovers' motif.

Onomatopoeia: Word used to evoke the sound in its meaning. The early Batman series used *pow, zap, whop, zonk* and *eek* in an onomatopoetic way.

Octava rima: A specific eight-line stanza of poetry whose rhyme scheme is abababcc. Lord Byron's mock epic, *Don Juan*, is written in this poetic way.

Oxymoron: A contradictory form of speech, such as jumbo shrimp, unkindly kind, or John Mellencamp's song lyric, "It hurts so good."

Paradox: Seemingly untrue statement, which when examined more closely proves to be true. John Donne's sonnet "Death Be Not Proud" postulates that death shall die and humans will triumph over death, at first thought not true, but ultimately explained and proven in this sonnet.

Parallelism: A type of close repetition of clauses or phrases that emphasize key topics or ideas in writing. The psalms in the King James Version of the *Bible* contain many examples.

Personification: Giving human characteristics to inanimate objects or concepts. Great writers, with few exceptions, are masters of this literary device.

Quatrain: A poetic stanza composed of four lines. A Shakespearean or Elizabethan sonnet is made up of three quatrains and ends with a heroic couplet.

Scansion: The two-part analysis of a poetic line. Count the number of syllables per line and determine where the accents fall. Divide the line into metric feet. Name the meter by the type and number of feet. Much is written about scanning poetry. Try not to inundate your students with this jargon; rather allow them to feel the power of the poets' words, ideas, and images instead.

Soliloquy: A highlighted speech, in drama, usually delivered by a major character expounding on the author's philosophy or expressing, at times, universal truths. This is done with the character alone on the stage.

Spenserian Stanza: Invented by Sir Edmund Spenser for usage in *The Fairie Queene*, his epic poem honoring Queen Elizabeth I.

Each stanza consists of nine lines, eight in iambic parameter. The ninth line, called an alexandrine, has two extra syllables or one additional foot.

Sprung Rhythm: Invented and used extensively by the poet Gerard Manley Hopkins. It consists of variable meter, which combines stressed and unstressed syllables fashioned by the author. See "Pied Beauty" or "God's Grandeur."

Stream of Consciousness: A style of writing which reflects the mental processes of the characters expressing at times jumbled memories, feelings, and dreams. Major writers who use this type of expression are James Joyce, Virginia Woolf, and William Faulkner.

Terza Rima: A series of poetic stanzas utilizing the recurrent rhyme scheme of aba, bcb, cdc, ded, and so forth. The second-generation Romantic poets - Keats, Byron, Shelley, and, to a lesser degree, Yeats - used this Italian verse form, especially in their odes. Dante used this stanza in *The Divine Comedy*.

Tone: The discernible attitude inherent in an author's work regarding the subject, readership, or characters. Swift or Pope's tone is satirical. Boswell's tone toward Johnson is admiring.

Wit: Writing of genius, keenness, and sagacity expressed through clever use of language. Alexander Pope and the Augustans wrote about and were said to possess wit.

In addition to these terms, there are four major time periods of writings. They are neoclassicism, romanticism, realism, and naturalism. Certain authors, among these Chaucer, Shakespeare, Whitman, Dickinson, and Donne, though writing during a particular literary period, are considered to have a style all their own.

Neoclassicism: Patterned after the greatest writings of classical Greece and Rome, this type of writing is characterized by balanced, graceful, well-crafted, refined, elevated style. Major proponents of this style are poet laureates John Dryden and Alexander Pope. The eras in which they wrote are called the Ages of Dryden and Pope. The self is not exalted and focus is on the group, not the individual, in neoclassic writing.

Romanticism: Writings emphasizing the individual. Emotions and feelings are validated. Nature acts as an inspiration for creativity; it is a balm of the spirit. Romantics harken back to medieval, chivalric themes and ambiance. They also emphasize supernatural, Gothic themes and settings, which are characterized by gloom and darkness. Imagination is stressed. New types of writings include detective and horror stories (Poe) and autobiographical introspection (Wordsworth and Thoreau). There are two generations in British Literature: First Generation includes William Wordsworth and Samuel Taylor Coleridge, whose collaboration, *Lyrical Ballads*, defines romanticism and its exponents.

Wordsworth maintained that the scenes and events of everyday life and the speech of ordinary people were the raw material of which poetry could and should be made. Romanticism spread to the United States, where Ralph Waldo Emerson and Henry David Thoreau adopted it in their transcendental romanticism, emphasizing reasoning. Further extensions of this style are found in Edgar Allen Poe's Gothic writings. Second Generation romantics include the ill-fated Englishmen Lord Byron, John Keats, and Percy Bysshe Shelley. Byron and Shelley, who for some most typify the romantic poet (in their personal lives as well as in their work), wrote resoundingly in protest against social and political wrongs and in defense of the struggles for liberty in Italy and Greece. The Second Generation romantics stressed personal introspection and the love of beauty and nature as requisites of inspiration.

Realism: Unlike classical and neoclassical writing, which often deal with aristocracies and nobility or the gods, realistic writers deal with the common man and his socioeconomic problems in a non-sentimental way. Muckraking, social injustice, domestic abuse, and inner city conflicts are examples of writings by writers of realism. Realistic writers include Stephen Crane, Ernest Hemingway, Thomas Hardy, George Bernard Shaw, and Henrik Ibsen.

Naturalism: This is realism pushed to the maximum, writing which exposes the underbelly of society, usually the lower class struggles. This is the world of penury, injustice, abuse, ghetto survival, hungry children, single parenting, and substance abuse. Émile Zola was inspired by his readings in history and medicine and attempted to apply methods of scientific observation to the depiction of pathological human character, notably in his series of novels devoted to several generations of one French family.

Skill 15.3 **Identify and analyze the ways in which an author uses language structure, literary form, point of view, word choice, style, and format to convey a viewpoint and to elicit an emotional response from the reader.**

There are at least thirteen possible choices for point of view (voice) in literature as demonstrated and explained by Wallace Hildick in his *13 Types of Narrative* (London: MacMillan and Co., 1968). However, for purposes of helping students write essays about literature, three, or possibly four, are adequate. The importance of teaching students to use this aspect of a piece of literature to write about it is not just as an analytic exercise but also should help them research how a writer's choices impact the overall effect of the work.

Point of view or voice is essentially through whose eyes the reader sees the action. The most common is the third-person objective. If the story is seen from this point of view, the reader watches the action, hears the dialogue, reads descriptions and from all of those must deduce characterization—what sort of person a character is.

In this point of view, an unseen narrator tells the reader what is happening, using the third person—he, she, it, they. The effect of this point of view is usually a feeling of distance from the plot. More responsibility is on the reader to make judgments than in other points of view. However, the author may intrude and evaluate or comment on the characters or the action.

The voice of the first-person narrator is often used as well. The reader sees the action through the eyes of an actor who is also telling the story. In writing about a story that uses this voice, the narrator must be analyzed as a character. What sort of person is this? What is this character's position in the story—observer, commentator, and actor? Can the narrator be believed or is he or she biased? The value of this voice is that while the reader is able to follow the narrator around and see the action from his point of view, the reader is also able to feel what the narrator feels. For this reason, the writer can involve the reader more intensely in the story itself and move the reader by invoking feelings—pity, sorrow, anger, hate, confusion, disgust, etc. Many of the most memorable novels are written from this point of view.

Another voice often used may best be titled "omniscient" because the reader is able to get into the mind of more than one character or sometimes all the characters. This point of view can also bring greater involvement of the reader in the story. By knowing what a character is thinking and feeling, the reader is able to empathize when a character feels great pain and sorrow, which tends to make a work memorable. On the other hand, knowing what a character is thinking makes it possible to get into the mind of a pathological murderer and may elicit horror or disgust.

"Omniscient" can be broken down into third-person omniscient or first-person omniscient. In third-person omniscient, the narrator is not seen or known or acting in the story but is able to watch and record not only what is happening or being said, but also what characters are thinking. In first-person omniscient, on the other hand, the narrator plays a role in the story but can also record what other characters are thinking. It is possible, of course, that the narrator is the pathological murderer, which creates an effect quite different than a story in which the thoughts of the murderer are known but the narrator is standing back and reporting his behavior, thoughts, and intents.

Point of view or voice is a powerful tool in the hands of a skillful writer. The questions to be answered in writing an essay about a literary work are: What point of view has this author used? What effect does it have on the story? If it had been written in a different voice, how would the story be different?

COMPETENCY 16.0 UNDERSTAND GENERAL SKILLS, STRATEGIES, AND PURPOSES FOR READING LITERATURE AND KNOW HOW TO SELECT AND USE LITERARY MATERIALS APPROPRIATE TO THE AGE AND DEVELOPMENT LEVEL OF LEARNERS

Skill 16.1 Recognize the importance of using a wide variety of print and electronic materials throughout the curriculum, including high quality children's and young adults' literature and diverse expository materials appropriate to the age, developmental level, and interests of the learner.

See Skills 2.1, 2.2, 2.3, and 2.4.

Skill 16.2 Recognize the value of reading aloud to learners using a variety of genres and the importance of providing time for reading entire texts for authentic purposes.

Reading, whether aloud or silently, evokes responses that can be verbalized. For young or below grade level readers, some sight-reading may be necessary. This should be done in small groups of two or three without teacher intervention. Students should feel free to discuss the text as they read. Most high school students should be able to participate in small group discussions of literature that has been read outside of class. During silent or at-home reading, the students should take notes of key elements as they read to enable them to contribute to subsequent discussions. Teacher guided discussion should transpire only after students have had a chance to think through the elements of the literature which are under study. Teacher led discussions should evolve from student responses to the reading not from preconceived interpretations by the teacher or recognized critics. Perceptive assessment of student comments will lead to questioning that probes the student's personal reactions and can ultimately be as analytical as any discussion the teacher might have planned.

Rather than involving the whole class, which favors the loquacious and inhibits the shy, let the students form into four or five discussion groups. After the initial discussion, have two groups join to share their reactions.

Skill 16.3 Recognize how making inferences; drawing conclusions making comparisons from personal, creative, and critical points of view; and sharing responses with peers encourages learners to respond personally to literature.

A common fallacy in reasoning is the *post hoc ergo propter hoc* ("after this, therefore because of this") or the false-cause fallacy. These occur in cause/effect reasoning, which may either go from cause to effect or effect to cause. They happen when an inadequate cause is offered for a particular effect; when the possibility of more than one cause is ignored; and when a connection between a particular cause and a particular effect is not made.

An example of a *post hoc*: Our sales shot up thirty-five percent after we ran that television campaign; therefore, the campaign caused the increase in sales. It might have been a cause, of course, but more evidence is needed to prove it.

An example of an inadequate cause for a particular effect: An Iraqi truck driver reported that Saddam Hussein had nuclear weapons; therefore, Saddam Hussein is a threat to world security. More causes are needed to prove the conclusion.

An example of ignoring the possibility of more than one possible cause: John Brown was caught out in a thunderstorm and his clothes were wet before he was rescued; therefore, he developed influenza the next day because he got wet. Being chilled may have played a role in the illness, but Brown would have had to contract the influenza virus before he would come down with it whether or not he had gotten wet.

An example of failing to make a connection between a particular cause and an effect assigned to it. Anna fell into a putrid pond on Saturday; on Monday she came down with polio; therefore, the polio was caused by the pond. This, of course, is not acceptable unless the poliovirus is found in a sample of water from the pond. A connection must be proven.

Skill 16.4 Recognize that learners have a variety of responses to literature.

Reading literature involves a reciprocal interaction between the reader and the text.

Types of responses

Emotional: The reader can identify with the characters and situations so as to project himself into the story. The reader feels a sense of satisfaction by associating aspects of his own life with the people, places, and events in the literature. Emotional responses are observed in a reader's verbal and non-verbal reactions - laughter, comments on its effects, and retelling or dramatizing the action.

Interpretive: Interpretive responses result in inferences about character development, setting, or plot; analysis of style elements - metaphor, simile, allusion, rhythm, tone; outcomes derivable from information provided in the narrative; and assessment of the author's intent. Interpretive responses are made verbally or in writing.

Critical: Critical responses involve making value judgments about the quality of a piece of literature. Reactions to the effectiveness of the writer's style and language use are observed through discussion and written reactions.

Evaluative: Some reading response theory researchers also add a response that considers the readers considerations of such factors as how well the piece of literature represents its genre, how well it reflects the social/ethical mores of society, and how well the author has approached the subject for freshness and slant.

Middle school readers will exhibit both emotional and interpretive responses. Naturally, making interpretive responses depends on the degree of knowledge the student has of literary elements. A child's being able to say why a particular book was boring or why a particular poem made him sad evidences critical reactions on a fundamental level. Adolescents in ninth and tenth grades should begin to make critical responses by addressing the specific language and genre characteristics of literature. Evaluative responses are harder to detect and are rarely made by any but a few advanced high school students. However, if the teacher knows what to listen for, she can recognize evaluative responses and incorporate them into discussions.

For example, if a student says, "I don't understand why that character is doing that," he is making an interpretive response to character motivation. However, if he goes on to say, "What good is that action?" he is giving an evaluative response that should be explored in terms of "What good should it do and why isn't that positive action happening?"

At the emotional level, the student says, "I almost broke into a sweat when he was describing the heat in the burning house." An interpretive response says, "The author used descriptive adjectives to bring his setting to life." Critically, the student adds, "The author's use of descriptive language contributes to the success of the narrative and maintains reader interest through the whole story." If he goes on to wonder why the author allowed the grandmother in the story to die in the fire, he is making an evaluative response.

Levels of response
The levels of reader response will depend largely on the reader's degree of social, psychological, and intellectual development. Most middle school students have progressed beyond merely involving themselves in the story enough to be able to retell the events in some logical sequence or describe the feeling that the story evoked. They are aware to some degree that the feeling evoked was the result of a careful manipulation of good elements of fiction writing. They may not explain that awareness as successfully as a high school student, but they are beginning to grasp the concepts and not just the personal reactions. They are beginning to differentiate between responding to the story itself and responding to a literary creation.

Fostering self-esteem and empathy for others and the world in which one lives

All-important is the use of literature as "bibliotherapy" that allows the reader to identify with others and become aware of alternatives, yet not feeling directly betrayed or threatened. For the high school student the ability to empathize is an evaluative response, a much desired outcome of literature studies. Use of these books either individually or as a thematic unit of study allows for discussion or writing. The titles are grouped by theme, not by reading level.

ABUSE:
    Blair, Maury and Brendel, Doug. *Maury, Wednesday's Child*
    Dizenzo, Patricia. *Why Me?*
    Parrot, Andrea. *Coping with Date Rape and Acquaintance Rape*

NATURAL WORLD CONCERNS:
    Caduto, M. and Bruchac, J. *Keepers of Earth*
    Gay, Kathlyn. *Greenhouse Effect*
    Johnson, Daenis. *Fiskadaro*
    Madison, Arnold. *It Can't Happen to Me*

EATING DISORDERS:
    Arnold, Caroline. *Too Fat, Too Thin, Do I Have a Choice?*
    DeClements, Barthe. *Nothing's Fair in Fifth Grade*
    Snyder, Anne. *Goodbye, Paper Doll*

FAMILY:
    Chopin, Kate. *The Runner*
    Cormier, Robert. *Tunes for Bears to Dance to*
    Danzinger, Paula. *The Divorce Express*
    Neufield, John. *Sunday Father*
    Okimoto, Jean Davies. *Molly by any Other Name*
    Peck, Richard. *Don't Look and It Won't Hurt*
    Zindel, Paul. *I Never Loved Your Mind*

STEREOTYPING:
    Baklanov, Grigory. (Trans. by Antonina W. Bouis) *Forever Nineteen*
    Kerr, M.E. *Gentle Lands*
    Greene, Betty. *Summer of My German Soldier*
    Reiss, Johanna. *The Upstairs Room*
    Taylor, Mildred D. *Roll of Thunder, Hear Me Cry*
    Wakatsuki-Houston, Jeanne and Houston, James D. *Farewell to Manzanar*

SUICIDE AND DEATH:
    Blume, Judy. *Tiger Eyes*
    Bunting, Eve. *If I Asked You, Would You Stay?*
    Gunther, John. *Death Be Not Proud*
    Mazer, Harry. *When the Phone Rings*
    Peck, Richard. *Remembering the Good Times*
    Richter, Elizabeth. *Losing Someone You Love*
    Strasser, Todd. *Friends Till the End*

Cautions: *There is always a caution when reading materials of a sensitive or controversial nature. The teacher must be cognizant of events in her school and surrounding community to spare students undue suffering. A child who has known a recent death in his family or circle of friends may need to distance himself from classroom discussion. Whenever open discussion of a topic brings pain or embarrassment, the child should not be further subjected. Older children and young adults will be able to discuss issues with greater objectivity and without making blurted, insensitive comments. The teacher must be able to gauge the level of emotional development of her students when selecting subject matter and the strategies for studying it. The student or his parents may consider some material objectionable. Should a student choose not to read assigned material, it is the teacher's responsibility to allow the student to select an alternate title. It is always advisable to notify parents if a particularly sensitive piece is to be studied.*

Skill 16.5   Recognize that literature can be a means of transmitting moral and cultural values within a community.

Literature is powerful in influencing the thinking of individual readers and all of society. Waves of philosophical ideas have swept over the reading world almost from the time of the invention of the printing press. It's possible to trace the emergence of a particular set of values over centuries. Feminism is a case in point. While the matter of women's rights didn't reach a boiling point until the 1960s, it can be traced through history for many years.

For example, Empress Theodora of Byzantium was a proponent of legislation that would afford greater protections and freedoms to her female subjects, and Christine de Pizan, the first professional female writer, advanced many feminist ideas as early as the 1300s in the face of attempts to restrict female inheritance and guild membership. In 1869, John Stuart Mill published *The Subjection of Women* to demonstrate that "the legal subordination of one sex to the other is wrong…and…one of the chief hindrances to human improvement." Norwegian playwright Henrik Ibsen wrote the highly controversial play, *A Doll's House,* in 1879, a scathing criticism of the traditional roles of men and women in Victorian marriages. These and many other works with feminist themes led to changes in the way society viewed women throughout the civilized world. The impact of the literature and the changes in thinking on this issue led to many countries' granting of the vote to women in the late 1800s and the early years of the twentieth century.

Regional literature has played an important role in the themes of popular literature, particularly in American literature. The best-known of the regional American writers is Samuel Langhorne Clemens, better known as Mark Twain, with his stories about the Mississippi River and the state of Missouri.

Although his home state was a slave state and considered by many to be part of the South, it declined to join the Confederacy and remained loyal to the Union. He wrote sympathetic slave characters in many of his stories.

Some regional American writers:
Harriet Beecher Stowe
Sarah Orne Jewett
George Washington Cable
Joel Chandler Harris
Edward Eggleston
James Whitcomb Riley
Bret Harte

Ethnic themes are also very popular in American literature. Toni Morrison, who writes African-American stories, is considered to be the most important American writer of the last 25 years and won the Nobel Prize for Literature in 1993 for her collected works. Saul Bellow wrote of his own Jewish background and also won the Nobel Prize in 1976.

James Michener wrote history as fiction in his many novels: *Tales of the South Pacific* (for which he won the Pulitzer Prize for Fiction in 1948), *Hawaii*, *The Drifters*, *Centennial*, *The Source*, *The Fires of Spring*, *Chesapeake*, *Caribbean*, *Caravans*, *Alaska*, *Texas*, and *Poland*.

Literature about a particular period has also been very popular with American writers. The Civil War era has been a very successful subject for novelists, most notably Margaret Mitchell, who wrote *Gone With the Wind*.

Some novels about the American Civil War:
- *The Red Badge of Courage* by Stephen Crane
- *Cold Mountain* by Charles Frazier
- *Love and War* by John Jakes
- *Gods and Generals*; *The Last Full Measure* by Jeffrey Shaara
- *By Valour and Arms* by James Street
- *Fort Pillow* by Harry Turtledove
- *Lincoln* by Gore Vidal

Skill 16.6 Recognize how literary works can be related to people, perspectives, and personal experiences.

It's no coincidence that when studying ancient civilizations to learn about their way of life, we rely on their art just as heavily as their more concrete, technological achievements. A society's creative output is a direct glimpse into the heart and soul of its people. We can glean so much more about the Middle Ages, for example, by looking at the literature of the time, than by studying a goblet owned by a king.

Why is this? Literature is the result of people expressing themselves, or their *experience* of life, in written word. Therefore, it can be argued that literature is a more accurate gauge of human life than historical documents, which can be fabricated or biased.

Pass this philosophy along to students by using historical literature as a way to glimpse each author's human experience. Ask students questions such as, "What does the tone of this piece say about the way of life for the author?" or "How is the way of life depicted in this story different from your own life experience?" Getting students to think about literature as a way to document a certain period's human experience may inspire them to document their own!

Skill 16.7 Recognize how knowledge gained from literature can be used to understand contemporary historical economic, social, and political issues and events.

The literature teacher teaches an appreciation for and knowledge of the literature of the past and present. He or she also teaches skills for understanding authors' intentions as well as those matters that creep into works that reflect the convictions, intentions, and philosophies of an author that are not necessarily intentional. In other words, through the study of literature, students have an opportunity to know people of the sort they will probably never meet and to understand their innermost feelings and purposes. They also have an opportunity to participate in events that will forever be beyond their actual physical sphere.

An understanding of literature can change lives. Growth and development that will not come any other way are possible through these studies. Students who have never thought deeply about what is happening to them and what goes on in the world around them begin to see and understand important concepts and possibilities. Teachers often see in some students a sort of blossoming, an "aha" about the world that is the best possible reward for this kind of teaching.

It only comes about if students learn the skills for looking below the surface and learn to trust their own abilities to participate in this process. Nowhere is this more apparent than in the study of poetry. Teachers are sometimes puzzled but more often than not delighted by the responses of students to a certain poem. They have the capacity to see things in the poem that the professional critics have missed, and what they see often delights. Seeing war through the eyes of a poet who has experienced its awfulness is an eye- and soul-opener for many students. They will forever see war through the screen of this experience, and it will color how they look at their worlds.

It is these capabilities and proclivities that teachers evoke in students that turn them into thinking adults—citizens who will look beyond the surface and search for motivation and meanings.

All high-school teachers need to see their roles as teaching certain subject matter in a certain curriculum but also as preparing students to be successful college students and/or successful citizens of the world.

It is particularly in the analysis of motivation that the study of literature leads readers/students to be willing to think beyond surface events. So many Americans accept that what is happening is not their responsibility. They trust elected officials to make all the decisions. For the most part, they do not see any role for themselves in what goes on in the world beyond their front doors. A high percentage never vote because they can't see that elections of leaders have anything to do with them. By helping students explore human motivations as depicted in literature—in protagonists and antagonists, for example—their understanding of what drives people becomes a part of how they view others and deal with them. They become more thoughtful about the world they live in and more likely to think about decisions made by government leaders more analytically. They will also be more likely to become involved in the process.

Approached in this way, a story that deals with the aftermath of war in terms of a soldier who experienced it provides a way of looking at other wars, even contemporary ones, in a more realistic way. Reading *The Grapes of Wrath* with an interest in what motivated the many players in the Great Depression reveals much of what the contemporary political, social, and economic situation truly looks like. What was the role of the church in John Steinbeck's novel? Are there parallels in the church of today? What about business owners? Etc.

Students who become serious about reading and understanding literature are destined to become more involved in their college curricula, in making choices for their own lives, and ultimately for becoming involved in those processes in their own communities, states, and country.

RESOURCES

1. Abrams, M. H. ed. *The Norton Anthology of English Literature*. 6th ed. 2 vols. New York: Norton, 1979.

    A comprehensive reference for English literature, containing selected works from *Beowulf* through the twentieth century and information about literary criticism.

2. Beach, Richard. "Strategic Teaching in Literature." *Strategic Teaching and Learning: Cognitive Instruction in the Content Areas*. Edited by Beau Fly Jones and others. ASCD Publications, 1987: 135-159.

    A chapter dealing with a definition of and strategic teaching strategies for literature studies.

3. Brown, A. C. and others. *Grammar and Composition 3rd Course*. Boston: Houghton Mifflin, 1984.

    A standard ninth-grade grammar text covering spelling, vocabulary, and reading, listening, and writing skills.

4. Burmeister, L. E. *Reading Strategies for Middle and Secondary School Teachers*. Reading, MA: Addison-Wesley, 1978.

    A resource for developing classrooms strategies for reading and content area classes, using library references, and adapting reading materials to all levels of students.

5. Carrier, W. and B. Neumann, eds. *Literature from the World*. New York: Scribner, 1981.

    A comprehensive world literature text for high school students, with a section on mythology and folklore.

6. Cline, R. K. J. and W. G. McBride. *A Guide to Literature for Young Adults: Background, Selection, and Use*. Glenview, IL: Scott Foresman, 1983.

    A literature reference containing sample readings and an overview of adolescent literature and the developmental changes that affect reading.

7. Coater, Jr. R. B., ed. *Reading Research and Instruction.* Journal of the College Research Association. Pittsburgh, PA : 1995.

   A reference tool for reading and language arts teachers, covering the latest research and instructional techniques.

8. Corcoran, B. and E. Evans, eds. *Readers, Texts, Teachers.* Upper Montclair, NJ: Boynton/Cook, 1987.

   A collection of essays concerning reader response theory, including activities that help students interpret literature and help the teacher integrate literature into the course study.

9. Cutting, Brian. *Moving on in Whole Language: the Complete Guide for Every Teacher.* Bothell, WA: Wright Group, 1992.

   A resource of practical knowledge in whole language instruction.

10. Damrosch, L. and others. *Adventures in English Literature.* Orlando, FL: Harcourt, Brace, Jovanovich, 1985.

    One of many standard high school English literature textbooks with a solid section on the development of the English language.

11. Davidson, A. *Literacy 2000 Teacher's Resource. Emergent Stages 1&2.* 1990.

12. Devine, T. G. *Teaching Study Skills: A Guide for Teachers.* Boston: Allyn and Bacon, 1981.

13. Duffy, G. G. and others. *Comprehension Instruction: Perspectives and Suggestions.* New York: Longman, 1984.

    Written by researchers at the Institute of Research on Teaching and the Center for the Study of Reading, this reference includes a variety of instructional techniques for different levels.

14. Fleming, M. ed. *Teaching the Epic.* Urbana, IL: NCTE, 1974.

    Methods, materials, and projects for the teaching of epics with examples of Greek, religious, national, and American epics.

15. Flood, J. ed. *Understanding Reading Comprehension: Cognition, Language, and the Structure of Prose.* Newark, DE: IRA, 1984.

    Essays by preeminent scholars dealing with comprehension for learners of all levels and abilities.

16. Fry, E. B. and others. *The Reading Teacher's Book of Lists.* Edgewood Cliffs, NJ: Prentice-Hall, 1984.

    A comprehensive list of book lists for students of various reading levels.

17. Garnica, Olga K. and Martha L. King. *Language, Children, and Society.* New York: Pergamon Press, 1981.

18. Gere, A. R. and E. Smith. *Attitude, Language and Change.* Urbana, IL: NCTE, 1979.

    A discussion of the relationship between standard English and grammar and the vernacular usage, including various approaches to language instruction.

19. Hayakawa, S. I. *Language in Thought and Action.* 4th ed. Orlando, Fl: Harcourt, Brace, Jovanovich, 1979.

20. Hook, J. N. and others. *What Every English Teacher Should Know.* Champaign, IL: NCTE, 1970.

    Research based text that summarizes methodologies and specific application for us with students.

21. Johnson, D. D. and P. D. Pearson. *Teaching Reading Vocabulary.* 2nd ed. New York: Holt, Rinehart, and Winston, 1984.

    A student text that stresses using vocabulary study in improving reading comprehension, with chapters on instruction components in the reading and content areas.

22. Kaywell, I. F. ed. *Adolescent Literature as a Complement to the Classics.* Norwood, MA: Christopher-Gordon Pub., 1993.

    A correlation of modern adolescent literature to classics of similar themes.

23. Mack, M. ed. *World Masterpieces*. 3rd ed. 2 vols. New York: Norton, 1973.

    A standard world literature survey, with good introductory material on a critical approach to literature study.

24. McLuhan, M. *Understanding Media: The Extensions of Man*. New York: Signet, 1964.

    The most classic work on the effect media has on the public and the power of the media to influence thinking.

25. McMichael, G. ed. *Concise Anthology of American Literature*. New York: Macmillan, 1974.

    A standard survey of American literature text.

26. Moffett, J. *Teaching the Universe of Discourse*. Boston: Houghton Mifflin, 1983.

    A significant reference text that proposes the outline for a total language arts program, emphasizing the reinforcement of each element of the language arts curriculum to the other elements.

27. Moffett, James and Betty Jane Wagner. *Student - Centered Language Arts K-12*. 4th ed. Boston: Houghton Mifflin, 1992.

28. Nelms, B. F. ed. *Literature in the Classroom: Readers, Texts, and Contexts*. Urbana, IL: NCTE, 1988.

    Essays on adolescent and multicultural literature, social aspects of literature, and approaches to literature interpretation.

29. Nilsen, A. P. and K. L. Donelson. *Literature for Today's Young Adults*. 2nd ed. Glenview, IL: Scott, Foresman, and Co., 1985.

    An excellent overview of young adult literature - its history, terminologies, bibliographies, and book reviews.

30. Perrine, L. *Literature: Structure, Sound, and Sense*. 5th ed. Orlando, FL: Harcourt, Brace, Jovanovich, 1988.

    A much revised text for teaching literature elements, genres, and interpretation.

31. Piercey, Dorothy. *Reading Activities in Content Areas: An Ideabook for Middle and Secondary Schools.* 2nd ed. Boston: Allyn and Bacon, 1982.

32. Pooley, R. C. *The Teaching of English Usage.* Urbana, IL: NCTE, 1974.

    A revision of the important 1946 text that discusses the attitudes toward English usage through history and recommends specific techniques for usage instruction.

33. Probst, R. E. *Response and Analysis: Teaching Literature in Junior and Senior High School.* Upper Montclair, NJ: Boynton/Cook, 1988.

    A resource that explores reader response theory and discusses student-centered methods for interpreting literature. Contains a section on the progress of adolescent literature.

34. Pyles, T. and J. Alges. *The Origin and Development of the English Language.* 3rd ed. Orlando, FL: Harcourt, Brace, Jovanovich, 1982.

    A history of the English language; sections on social, personal, historical, and geographical influences on language usage.

35. Readence, J. E. and others. *Content Area Reading: an integrated approach.* 2nd ed. Dubuque, IA: Kendall/Hunt, 1985.

    A practical instruction guide for teaching reading in the content areas.

36. Robinson, H. Alan. *Teaching Reading and Study Strategies: The Content Areas.* Boston: Allyn and Bacon, 1978.

37. Roe, B. D. and others. *Secondary School Reading Instruction: The Content Areas.* 3rd ed. Boston: Houghton Mifflin, 1987.

    A resource of strategies for the teaching of reading for language arts teachers with little reading instruction background.

38. Rosenberg, D. *World Mythology: An Anthology of the Great Myths and Epics.* Lincolnwood, IL: National Textbook, 1986.

    Presents selections of main myths from which literary allusions are drawn. Thorough literary analysis of each selection.

39. Rosenblatt, L. M. *The Reader, the Text, the Poem. The Transactional Theory of the Literary Work.* Southern Illinois University Press, 1978.

    A discussion of reader response theory and reader-centered methods for analyzing literature.

40. Santeusanio, Richard P. *A Practical Approach to Content Area Reading.* Reading, MA.: Addison-Wesley Publishing Co., 1983.

41. Shepherd, David L. *Comprehensive High School Reading Methods.* 2nd ed. Columbus, OH: Charles F. Merrill Publishing, 1978.

42. Strickland, D. S. and others. *Using Computers in the Teaching of Reading.* New York: Teachers College Press, 1987.

    Resource for strategies for teaching and learning language and reading with computers and recommendations for software for all grades.

43. Sutherland, Zena and others. *Children and Books.* 6th ed. Glenview, IL: Scott, Foresman, and Co., 1981.

    Thorough study of children's literature, with sections on language development theory and chapters on specific genres with synopses of specific classic works for child/adolescent readers.

44. Tchudi, S. and D. Mitchell. *Explorations in the Teaching of English.* 3rd ed. New York: Harper Row, 1989.

    A thorough source of strategies for creating a more student-centered involvement in learning.

45. Tompkins, Gail E. *Teaching Writing: Balancing Process and Product.* 2nd ed. New York: Macmillan, 1994.

    A tool to aid teachers in integrating recent research and theory about the writing process, writing reading connections, collaborative learning, and across the curriculum writing with practices in the fourth through eighth grade classrooms.

46. Warriners, J. E. *English Composition and Grammar.* Benchmark ed. Orlando, FL: Harcourt, Brace, Jovanovich, 1988.

    Standard grammar and composition textbook, with a six book series for seventh through twelfth grades; includes vocabulary study, language history, and diverse approaches to writing process.

SAMPLE TEST

Section I: Essay Test

Given are several prompts, reflecting the need to exhibit a variety of writing skills. In most testing situations, 30 minutes would be allowed to respond to each of the prompts. Some tests may allow 60 minutes for the essay to incorporate more than one question or allow for greater preparation and editing time. Read the directions carefully and organize your time wisely.

Section II: Multiple Choice Test

This section contains 125 questions. In most testing situations, you would be expected to answer from 35-40 questions within 30 minutes. If you time yourself on the entire battery, take no more than 90 minutes.

Section III: Answer Key

Section I: Essay Prompts

Prompt A

Write an expository essay discussing effective teaching strategies for developing literature appreciation with a heterogeneous class of ninth graders. Select any appropriate piece(s) of world literature to use as examples in the discussion.

Prompt B

After reading the following passage from Aldous Huxley's *Brave New World,* discuss the types of reader responses possible with a group of eighth graders.

> "He hated them all - all the men who came to visit Linda. One afternoon, when he had been playing with the other children - it was cold, he remembered, and there was snow on the mountains - he came back to the house and heard angry voices in the bedroom. They were women's voices, and they were words he didn't understand; but he knew they were dreadful words. Then suddenly, crash! something was upset; he heard people moving about quickly, and there was another crash and then a noise like hitting a mule, only not so bony; then Linda screamed. 'Oh, don't, don't, don't!' she said. He ran in. There were three women in dark blankets. Linda was on the bed. One of the women was holding her wrists. Another was lying across her legs, so she couldn't kick. The third was hitting her with a whip. Once, twice, three times; and each time Linda screamed."

Prompt C

Write a persuasive letter to the editor on any contemporary topic of special interest. Employ whatever forms of discourse, style devices, and audience appeal techniques that seem appropriate to the topic.

Section II: Sample Questions

Part A

Each underlined portion of sentences 1-10 contains one or more errors in grammar, usage, mechanics, or sentence structure. Circle the choice which best corrects the error without changing the meaning of the original sentence

1. Joe didn't hardly know his cousin Fred who'd had a rhinoplasty. (Skill 7.4, Easy)

   A. hardly did know his cousin Fred
   B. didn't know his cousin Fred hardly
   C. hardly knew his cousin Fred
   D. didn't know his cousin Fred
   E. didn't hardly know his cousin Fred

2. There were fewer pieces of evidence presented during the second trial (Skill 7.4, Easy)

   A. fewer peaces
   B. less peaces
   C. less pieces
   D. fewer pieces

3. Mixing the batter for cookies, the cat licked the Crisco from the cookie sheet. (Skill 7.4, Average Rigor)

   A. While mixing the batter for cookies
   B. While the batter for cookies was mixing
   C. While I mixed the batter for cookies
   D. While I mixed the cookies
   E. Mixing the batter for cookies

4. Mr. Smith respectfully submitted his resignation and had a new job. (Skill 7.4, Average Rigor)

   A. respectfully submitted his resignation and has
   B. respectfully submitted his resignation before accepting
   C. respectfully submitted his resignation because of
   D. respectfully submitted his resignation and had

5. The teacher **implied** from our angry words that there was conflict **between you and me**. (Skill 7.4, Average Rigor)

   A. Implied... between you and I

   B. Inferred... between you and I

   C. Inferred... between you and me

   D. Implied... between you and me

6. Wally **groaned, "Why** do I have to do an oral interpretation **of "The Raven."** (Skill 7.4, Average Rigor)

   A. groaned "Why... of 'The Raven'?"

   B. groaned "Why... of "The Raven"?

   C. groaned ", Why... of "The Raven?"

   D. groaned, "Why... of "The Raven."

7. **The coach offered her assistance but the athletes** wanted to practice on their own. (Skill 7.4, Rigorous)

   A. The coach offered her assistance, however, the athletes wanted to practice on their own.

   B. The coach offered her assistance: furthermore, the athletes wanted to practice on their own.

   C. Having offered her assistance, the athletes wanted to practice on their own.

   D. The coach offered her assistance; however, the athletes wanted to practice on their own.

   E. The coach offered her assistance, and the athletes wanted to practice on their own.

8. **Walt Whitman was famous for his composition, Leaves of Grass, serving as a nurse during the Civil War, and a devoted son (Skill 7.4, Rigorous)**

   A. *Leaves of Grass*, his service as a nurse during the Civil War, and a devoted son

   B. composing *Leaves of Grass*, serving as a nurse during the Civil War, and being a devoted son

   C. his composition, *Leaves of Grass*, his nursing during the Civil War, and his devotion as a son

   D. his composition *Leaves of Grass,* serving as a nurse during the Civil War and a devoted son

   E. his composition *Leaves of Grass*, serving as a nurse during the Civil War. and a devoted son

9. **A teacher must know not only her subject matter but also the strategies of content teaching. (Skill 7.4, Rigorous)**

   A. must not only know her subject matter but also the strategies of content teaching

   B. not only must know her subject matter but also the strategies of content teaching

   C. must not know only her subject matter but also the strategies of content teaching

   D. must know not only her subject matter but also the strategies of content teaching

10. The Taj Mahal has been designated one of the Seven Wonders of the World, and people know it for its unique architecture. (Skill 7.4, Rigorous)

   A. The Taj Mahal has been designated one of the Seven Wonders of the World, and it is known for its unique architecture.

   B. People know the Taj Mahal for its unique architecture, and it has been designated one of the Seven Wonders of the World.

   C. People have known the Taj Mahal for its unique architecture, and it has been designated of the Seven Wonders of the World.

   D. The Taj Mahal has designated itself one of the Seven Wonders of the World.

Part B

Directions: Select the best answer in each group of multiple choices.

11. The literary device of personification is used in which example below? (Skill 1.2, Easy)

    A. "Beg me no beggary by soul or parents, whining dog!"

    B. "Happiness sped through the halls cajoling as it went."

    C. "O wind thy horn, thou proud fellow."

    D. "And that one talent which is death to hide."

12. The Elizabethans wrote in (Skill 1.3 Easy)

    A. Celtic

    B. Old English

    C. Middle English

    D. Modern English

13. The synonyms *gyro, hero,* and *submarine* reflect which influence on language usage? (Skill 1.3, Average Rigor)

    A. Social

    B. Geographical

    C. Historical

    D. Personal

14. Middle and high school students are more receptive to studying grammar and syntax (Skill 1.3, Average Rigor)

    A. through worksheets and end of lessons practices in textbooks.

    B. through independent, homework assignment.

    C. through analytical examination of the writings of famous authors.

    D. through application to their own writing.

15. **Which event triggered the beginning of Modern English? (Skill 1.3, Average Rigor)**

    A. Conquest of England by the Normans in 1066

    B. Introduction of the printing press to the British Isles

    C. Publication of Samuel Johnson's lexicon.

    D. American Revolution

16. **Which of the following is not true about the English language? (Skill 1.3, Average Rigor)**

    A. English is the easiest language to learn.

    B. English is the least inflected language.

    C. English has the most extensive vocabulary of any language.

    D. English originated as a Germanic tongue.

17. **What was responsible for the standardizing of dialects across America in the 20th century? (Skill 1.3, Rigorous)**

    A. With the immigrant influx, American became a melting pot of languages and cultures.

    B. Trains enabled people to meet other people of different languages and cultures.

    C. Radio, and later, television, used actors and announcers who spoke without pronounced dialects.

    D. Newspapers and libraries developed programs to teach people to speak English with an agreed-upon common dialect.

18. **Latin words that entered the English language during the Elizabethan age include (Skill 1.3, Rigorous)**

    A. allusion, education, and esteem

    B. vogue and mustache

    C. canoe and cannibal

    D. alligator, cocoa, and armadillo

19. The most significant drawback to applying learning theory research to classroom practice is that (Skill 1.3, Rigorous)

   A. today's students do not acquire reading skills with the same alacrity as when greater emphasis was placed on reading classical literature.

   B. development rates are complicated by geographical and cultural In analyzing literature and in looking for ways to bring a work to life for an audience, the use of comparable themes and ideas from other pieces of literature and from one's own life experiences, including from reading the daily newspaper, is very important and useful.

   C. homogeneous grouping has contributed to faster development of some age groups.

   D. social and environmental conditions have contributed to an escalated maturity level than research done twenty of more years ago would seem to indicate.

20. Which aspect of language is innate? (Skill 1.3, Rigorous)

   A. Biological capability to articulate sounds understood by other humans

   B. Cognitive ability to create syntactical structures

   C. Capacity for using semantics to convey meaning in a social environment

   D. Ability to vary inflections and accents

21. The English department is developing strategies to encourage all students to become a community of readers. From the list of suggestions below, which would be the least effective way for teachers to foster independent reading? (Skill 1.4, Average Rigor)

    A. Each teacher will set aside a weekly 30-minute in-class reading session during which the teacher and students read a magazine or book for enjoyment.

    B. Teacher and students develop a list of favorite books to share with each other.

    C. The teacher assigns at least one book report each grading period to ensure that students are reading from the established class list.

    D. The students gather books for a classroom library so that books may be shared with each other.

22. Modeling is a practice that requires students to (Skill 1.7, Average Rigor)

    A. create a style unique to their own language capabilities.

    B. emulate the writing of professionals.

    C. paraphrase passages from good literature.

    D. peer evaluate the writings of other students.

23. Which of the following reading strategies calls for higher order cognitive skills? (Skill 1.8, Average Rigor)

    A. Making predictions

    B. Summarizing

    C. Monitoring

    D. Making inferences

24. Before reading a passage, a teacher gives her students an anticipation guide with a list of statements related to the topic they are about to cover in the reading material. She asks the students to indicate their agreement or disagreement with each statement on the guide. This activity is intended to (Skill 1.8, Rigorous)

   A. elicit students' prior knowledge of the topic and set a purpose for reading.

   B. help students to identify the main ideas and supporting details in the text.

   C. help students to synthesize information from the text.

   D. help students to visualize the concepts and terms in the text.

25. Among junior-high school students of low-to-average readability levels, which work would most likely stir reading interest? (Skill 2.1, Easy)

   A. *Elmer Gantry*, Sinclair Lewis

   B. *Smiley's People*, John Le Carre

   C. *The Outsiders*, S.E. Hinton

   D. *And Then There Were None*, Agatha Christie.

26. Which of the following would be the most significant factor in teaching Homer's *Iliad* and *Odyssey* to any particular group of students? (Skill 2.3, Average Rigor)

   A. Identifying a translation on the appropriate reading level

   B. Determining the students' interest level

   C. Selecting an appropriate evaluative technique

   D. Determining the scope and delivery methods of background study

27. Which of the following is a formal reading-level assessment? (Skill 2.5, Average Rigor)

   A. A standardized reading test

   B. A teacher-made reading test

   C. An interview

   D. A reading diary

28. Read the following passage and identify the main idea. (Skill 2.5, Rigorous)

Sometimes too much of a good thing can become a very bad thing indeed. In an earnest attempt to consume a healthy diet, dietary supplement enthusiasts have been known to overdose. Vitamin C, for example, long thought to help people ward off cold viruses, is currently being studied for its possible role in warding off cancer and other disease that cases tissue degeneration. Unfortunately, an overdose of vitamin C—more than 10,000 mg—on a daily basis can cause nausea and diarrhea. Calcium supplements, commonly taken by women, are helpful in warding off osteoporosis. More than just a few grams a day, however, can lead to stomach upset and even kidney and bladder stones. Niacin, proven useful in reducing cholesterol levels, can be dangerous in large doses to those who suffer from heart problems, asthma or ulcers.

A. Supplements taken in excess can be a bad thing indeed.

B. Dietary supplement enthusiasts have been known to overdose.

C. Vitamins can cause nausea, diarrhea, and kidney or bladder stones.

D. People who take supplements are preoccupied with their health.

29. Which teaching method would best engage underachievers in the required senior English class? (Skill 2.8, Average Rigor)

A. Assign use of glossary work and extensively footnoted excerpts of great works.

B. Have students take turns reading aloud the anthology selection

C. Let students choose which readings they'll study and write about.

D. Use a chronologically arranged, traditional text, but assigning group work, panel presentations, and portfolio management

30. To understand the origins of a word, one must study the (Skill 3.1, Easy)

A. synonyms

B. inflections

C. phonetics

D. etymology

31. Which word in the following sentence is a bound morpheme: "The quick brown fox jumped over the lazy dog"? (Skill 3.1, Rigorous)

   A. The

   B. fox

   C. lazy

   D. jumped

32. If a student has a poor vocabulary, the teacher should recommend first that (Skill 3.4 Average Rigor)

   A. the student read newspapers, magazines and books on a regular basis.

   B. the student enroll in a Latin class.

   C. the student write the words repetitively after looking them up in the dictionary.

   D. the student use a thesaurus to locate synonyms and incorporate them into his/her vocabulary

33. In a class of non-native speakers of English, which type of activity will help students the most? (Skill 4.1, Rigorous)

   A. Have students make oral presentations so that they can develop a phonological awareness of sounds.

   B. Provide students more writing opportunities to develop their written communication skills.

   C. Encourage students to listen to the new language on television and radio.

   D. Provide a variety of methods to develop speaking, writing, and reading skills.

34. Regularly requiring students to practice reading short, instructional-level texts at least three times to a peer and to give and receive peer feedback about these readings mainly addresses which reading skill? (Skill 4.4, Rigorous)

   A. Comprehension

   B. Fluency

   C. Evaluation

   D. Word-solving

35. To determine the credibility of information, researchers should do all of the following except (Skill 4.6, Rigorous)

   A. establish the authority of the document.

   B. disregard documents with bias.

   C. evaluate the currency and reputation of the source.

   D. use a variety of research sources and methods.

36. Which of the following is the least preferable strategy for teaching literature? (Skill 5.1, Average Rigor)

   A. teacher-guided total class discussion

   B. small group discussion

   C. teacher lecture

   D. dramatization of literature selections

37. Sometimes readers can be asked to demonstrate their understanding of a text. This might include all of the following except (Skill 5.1, Average Rigor)

   A. role playing.

   B. paraphrasing.

   C. storyboarding a part of the story with dialogue bubbles.

   D. reading the story aloud

38. The students in Mrs. Cline's seventh grade language arts class were invited to attend a performance of Romeo and Juliet presented by the drama class at the high school. To best prepare, they should (Skill 5.4, Average Rigor)

   A. read the play as a homework exercise.

   B. read a synopsis of the plot and a biographical sketch of the author.

   C. examine a few main selections from the play to become familiar with the language and style of the author.

   D. read a condensed version of the story and practice attentive listening skills.

39. In writing a report, Hector has to explain where acid rain comes from and what it has done to the environment. What is the most likely form of organizational structure? (Skill 5.6, Easy)

    A. Cause and effect

    B. Problem and solution

    C. Exposition

    D. Definition

40. Students returning from a field trip to the local newspaper want to thank their hosts for the guided tour. As their teacher, what form of communication should you encourage them to use? (Skill 6.1, Average Rigor)

    A. Each student will send an email expressing his or her appreciation.

    B. As a class, students will create a blog, and each student will write about what they learned.

    C. Each student will write a thank you letter that the teacher will fax to the newspaper.

    D. Each student will write a thank you note that the teacher will mail to the newspaper.

41. Which of the following is the least effective procedure for promoting consciousness of audience? (Skill 6.1, Average Rigor)

    A. Pairing students during the writing process

    B. Reading all rough drafts before the students write the final copies

    C. Having students compose stories or articles for publication in school literary magazines or newspapers

    D. Writing letters to friends or relatives

42. In "inverted triangle" introductory paragraphs, the thesis sentence occurs (Skill 6.2, Easy)

    A. at the beginning of the paragraph.

    B. in the middle of the paragraph.

    C. at the end of the paragraph.

    D. in the second paragraph.

43. What is the main form of discourse in this passage? (Skill 6.2, Average Rigor)

   It would have been hard to find a passer-by more wretched in appearance. He was a man of middle height, stout and hardy, in the strength of maturity; he might have been forty-six or seven. A slouched leather cap hid half his face, bronzed by the sun and wind, and dripping with sweat.

   A. Description

   B. Narration

   C. Exposition

   D. Persuasion

44. Regarding the study of poetry, select the answer which is least applicable to all types of poetry. (Skill 6.2, Average Rigor)

   A. Setting and audience

   B. Theme and tone

   C. Pattern and diction

   D. Diction and rhyme scheme

45. Which sentence below best minimizes the impact of bad news? (Skill 6.2, Rigorous)

   A. We have denied you permission to attend the event.

   B. Although permission to attend the event cannot be given, you are encouraged to buy the video.

   C. Although you cannot attend the event, we encourage you to buy the video.

   D. Although attending the event is not possible, watching the video is an option.

46. The new teaching intern is developing a unit on creative writing and is trying to encourage her students to write poetry. Which of the following would not be an effective technique? (Skill 6.2, Average Rigor)

    A. In groups, students will draw pictures to illustrate "The Love Song of J. Alfred Prufrock" by T.S. Eliot.

    B. Either individually or in groups, students will compose a song, writing lyrics that try to use poetic devices.

    C. Students will bring to class the lyrics of a popular song and discuss the imagery and figurative language.

    D. Students will read aloud their favorite poems and share their opinions of and responses to the poems.

47. Writing ideas quickly without interruption of the flow of thoughts or attention to conventions is called (Skill 6.3, Easy)

    A. brainstorming.

    B. mapping.

    C. listing.

    D. free writing.

48. Which of the following is most true of expository writing? (Skill 6.5, Easy)

    A. It is mutually exclusive of other forms of discourse.

    B. It can incorporate other forms of discourse in the process of providing supporting details.

    C. It should never employ informal expression.

    D. It should only be scored with a summative evaluation.

49. Explanatory or informative discourse is (Skill 6.5, Easy)

    A. exposition.

    B. narration.

    C. persuasion.

    D. description.

50. Which of the following is not a technique of prewriting? (Skill 7.1, Easy)

    A. Clustering

    B. Listing

    C. Brainstorming

    D. Proofreading

51. In the following excerpt from "Civil Disobedience," what type of reasoning does Henry David Thoreau use? (Skill 7.1, Rigorous)

> Unjust laws exist; shall we be content to obey them, or shall we endeavor to amend them, and obey them until we have succeeded, or shall we transgress them at once? Men generally, under such a government as this, think that they ought to wait until they have persuaded the majority to alter them. They think that, if they should resist, the remedy would be worse than the evil. But it is the fault of the government itself that the remedy *is* worse than the evil. ... Why does it always crucify Christ, and excommunicate Copernicus and Luther, and pronounce Washington and Franklin rebels?
> --"Civil Disobedience" by Henry David Thoreau

A. Ethical reasoning

B. Inductive reasoning

C. Deductive reasoning

D. Intellectual reasoning

52. Which of the following sentences is properly punctuated? (Skill 7.4, Easy)

A. The more you eat; the more you want.

B. The authors—John Steinbeck, Ernest Hemingway, and William Faulkner—are staples of modern writing in American literature textbooks.

C. Handling a wild horse, takes a great deal of skill and patience.

D. The man, who replaced our teacher, is a comedian.

53. Which of the following sentences contains a subject-verb agreement error? (Skill 7.4, Average Rigor)

A. Both mother and her two sisters were married in a triple ceremony.

B. Neither the hen nor the rooster is likely to be served for dinner.

C. My boss, as well as the company's two personnel directors, have been to Spain.

D. Amanda and the twins are late again.

54. In general, the most serious drawback of using a computer in writing is that (Skill 7.7, Rigorous)

   A. the copy looks so good that students tend to overlook major mistakes.

   B. the spell check and grammar programs discourage students from learning proper spelling and mechanics.

   C. the speed with which corrections can be made detracts from the exploration and contemplation of composing.

   D. the writer loses focus by concentrating on the final product rather than the details.

55. Which transition word would show contrast between these two ideas? (Skill 8.1, Average Rigor)

   We are confident in our skills to teach English. We welcome new ideas on this subject.

   A. We are confident in our skills to teach English, and we welcome new ideas on this subject.

   B. Because we are confident in our skills to teach English, we welcome new ideas on the subject.

   C. When we are confident in our skills to teach English, we welcome new ideas on the subject.

   D. We are confident in our skills to teach English; however, we welcome new ideas on the subject.

56. Which of the following should students use to improve coherence of ideas within an argument? (Skill 8.2, Rigorous)

   A. Transitional words or phrases to show relationship of ideas.

   B. Conjunctions like "and" to join ideas together.

   C. Direct quotes to improve credibility.

   D. Adjectives and adverbs to provide stronger detail.

57. n preparing your high school freshmen to write a research paper about a social problem, what recommendation can you make so they can determine the credibility of their information? (Skill 9.2, Average Rigor)

   A. Assure them that information on the Internet has been peer-reviewed and verified for accuracy.

   B. Find one solid source and use that exclusively.

   C. Use only primary sources.

   D. Cross check your information with another credible source.

58. Which of the following are secondary research materials? (Skill 9.2, Average Rigor)

   A. The conclusions and inferences of other historians.

   B. Literature and nonverbal materials, novels, stories, poetry and essays from the period, as well as coins, archaeological artifacts, and art produced during the period.

   C. Interviews and surveys conducted by the researcher.

   D. Statistics gathered as the result of the research's experiments.

59. Which of the following is not correct? (Skill 9.4, Easy)

   A. Because most students have wide access to media, teachers should refrain from using it in their classrooms to diminish the overload.

   B. Students can use CD-ROMs to explore information using a virtual reality experience.

   C. Teacher can make their instruction more powerful by using educational media.

   D. The Internet enables students to connect with people across cultures and to share interests.

60. Which of the following statements indicates an instructional goal for using multimedia in the classroom? (Skill 9.4 Average Rigor)

    A. Audio messages invite the listener to form mental images consistent with the topic of the audio.

    B. Print messages appeal almost exclusively to the mind and push students to read with more thought.

    C. Listening to an audio message is more passive than reading a print message.

    D. Teachers who develop activities to foster a critical perspective on audiovisual presentation will decrease passivity.

61. Which of the following should not be included in the opening paragraph of an informative essay? (Skill 10.2, Easy)

    A. Thesis sentence

    B. Details and examples supporting the main idea

    C. Broad general introduction to the topic

    D. A style and tone that grabs the reader's attention

62. For their research paper on the effects of the Civil War on American literature, students have brainstormed a list of potential online sources and are seeking your authorization. Which of these represent the strongest source? (Skill 10.1, Rigorous)

    A. http://www.wikipedia.org/

    B. http://www.google.com

    C. http://www.nytimes.com

    D. http://docsouth.unc.edu/southlit/civilwar.html

63. In the paragraph below, which sentence does not contribute to the overall task of supporting the main idea? (Skill 10.2 Easy)

   1) The Springfield City Council met Friday to discuss new zoning restrictions for the land to be developed south of the city. 2) Residents who opposed the new restrictions were granted 15 minutes to present their case. 3) Their argument focused on the dangers that increased traffic would bring to the area. 4) It seemed to me that the Mayor Simpson listened intently. 5) The council agreed to table the new zoning until studies would be performed.

   A. Sentence 2

   B. Sentence 3

   C. Sentence 4

   D. Sentence 5

64. In this paragraph from a student essay, identify the sentence that provides a detail. (Skill 10.2 Rigorous)

   (1) The poem concerns two different personality types and the human relation between them. (2) Their approach to life is totally different. (3) The neighbor is a very conservative person who follows routines. (4) He follows the traditional wisdom of his father and his father's father. (5) The purpose in fixing the wall and keeping their relationship separate is only because it is all he knows.

   A. Sentence 1

   B. Sentence 3

   C. Sentence 4

   D. Sentence 5

65. Which part of a classical argument is illustrated in this excerpt from the essay "What Should Be Done About Rock Lyrics?" (Skill 10.3, Rigorous)

> But violence against women is greeted by silence. It shouldn't be.
>
> This does not mean censorship, or book (or record) burning. In a society that protects free expression, we understand a lot of stuff will float up out of the sewer. Usually, we recognize the ugly stuff that advocates violence against any group as the garbage it is, and we consider its purveyors as moral lepers. We hold our nose and tolerate it, but we speak out against the values it proffers.
> --"What Should Be Done About Rock Lyrics?" Caryl Rivers

A. Narration

B. Confirmation

C. Refutation and concession

D. Summation

66. Which of the following situations is not an ethical violation of intellectual property? (Skill 10.5, Rigorous)

A. A student visits ten different websites and writes a report to compare the costs of downloading music. He uses the names of the websites without their permission.

B. A student copies and pastes a chart verbatim from the Internet but does not document it because it is available on a public site.

C. From an online article found in a subscription database, a student paraphrases a section on the problems of music piracy. She includes the source in her Works Cited but does not provide an in-text citation.

D. A student uses a comment from M. Night Shyamalan without attribution claiming the information is common knowledge.

67. Which of the following would not be a major concern in an oral presentation? (Skill 11.1, Easy)

   A. Establishing the purpose of the presentation

   B. Evaluating the audience's demographics and psychographics.

   C. Creating a PowerPoint slide for each point.

   D. Developing the content to fit the occasion.

68. If students use slang and expletives, what is the best course of action to take in order to improve their formal communication skills? (Skill 11.5, Average Rigor)

   A. Ask the students to paraphrase their writing, that is, translate it into language appropriate for the school principal to read.

   B. Refuse to read the students' papers until they conform to a more literate style.

   C. Ask the students to read their work aloud to the class for peer evaluation.

   D. Rewrite the flagrant passages to show the students the right form of expression.

69. Oral debate is most closely associated with which form of discourse? (Skill 11.6, Easy)

   A. Description

   B. Exposition

   C. Narration

   D. Persuasion

70. In presenting a report to peers about the effects of Hurricane Katrina on New Orleans, the students wanted to use various media in their argument to persuade their peers that more needed to be done. Which of these would be the most effective? (Skill 11.7, Rigorous)

   A. A PowerPoint presentation showing the blueprints of the levees before the flood and redesigned now for current construction..

   B. A collection of music clips made by the street performers in the French Quarter before and after the flood.

   C. A recent video showing the areas devastated by the floods and the current state of rebuilding.

   D. A collection of recordings of interviews made by the various government officials and local citizens affected by the flooding.

71. In preparing a speech for a contest, your student has encountered problems with gender specific language. Not wishing to offend either women or men, she seeks your guidance. Which of the following is not an effective strategy? (Skill 11.9, Rigorous)

   A. Use the generic "he" and explain that people will understand and accept the male pronoun as all-inclusive.

   B. Switch to plural nouns and use "they" as the gender-neutral pronoun.

   C. Use passive voice so that the subject is not required.

   D. Use male pronouns for one part of the speech and then use female pronouns for the other part of the speech.

72. Mr. Ledbetter has instructed his students to prepare a slide presentation that illustrates an event in history. Students are to include pictures, graphics, media clips and links to resources. What competencies will students exhibit at the completion of this project? (Skill 11.11, Rigorous)

   A. Analyze the impact of society on media.

   B. Recognize the media's strategies to inform and persuade.

   C. Demonstrate strategies and creative techniques to prepare presentations using a variety of media.

   D. Identify the aesthetic effects of a media presentation.

73. Students have been asked to evaluate the message in several television commercials for credit cards. Which type of listening skill would be most appropriate? (Skill 12.2, Average Rigor)

   A. Informative listening

   B. Critical listening

   C. Appreciative listening

   D. Relationship listening

74. In literature, evoking feelings of pity or compassion is to create (Skill 12.2, Average Rigor)

   A. colloquy.

   B. irony.

   C. pathos.

   D. paradox

75. Identify the type of appeal used by Molly Ivins's in this excerpt from her essay "Get a Knife, Get a Dog, But Get Rid of Guns." (Skill 12.3, Rigorous)

   As a civil libertarian, I, of course, support the Second Amendment. And I believe it means exactly what it says: *A well regulated militia being necessary to the security of a free state, the right of the people to keep and bear arms shall not be infringed.*

   A. Ethical

   B. Emotional

   C. Rational

   D. Literary

76. What is not one of the advantages of collaborative or cooperative learning? (Skill 13.4, Easy)

   A. Students that work together in groups or teams develop their skills in organizing, leadership, research, communication, and problem solving.

   B. Working in teams can help students overcome anxiety in distance learning courses and contribute a sense of community and belonging for the students.

   C. Students tend to learn more material being taught and retain the information longer than when the same information is taught using different methods.

   D. Teachers reduce their workload and the time spent on individuals the assignments, and grading.

77. Overcrowded classes prevent the individual attention needed to facilitate language development. This drawback can be best overcome by (Skill 13.4, Average Rigor)

    A. dividing the class into independent study groups.

    B. assigning more study time at home.

    C. using more drill practice in class.

    D. Team teaching.

78. In preparing students for their oral presentations, the instructor provided all of these guidelines, except one. Which is not an effective guideline? (Skill 13.6, Average Rigor)

    A. Even if you are using a lectern, feel free to move about. This will connect you to the audience.

    B. Your posture should be natural, not stiff. Keep your shoulders toward the audience.

    C. Gestures can help communicate as long as you don't overuse them or make them distracting.

    D. You can avoid eye contact if you focus on your notes. This will make you appear more knowledgeable.

79. Which of the following is not an advantage of oral communication over written communication? (Skill 13.9, Average Rigor)

    A. Oral communication provides immediate feedback.

    B. Oral communication relies on non-verbal clues to express meaning.

    C. Oral communication is carefully prepared and presented.

    D. Oral communication is more social than written communication.

80. The arrangement and relationship of words in sentences or sentence structures best describes (Skill 13.9, Rigorous)

    A. style.

    B. discourse.

    C. thesis.

    D. syntax.

81. A traditional, anonymous story, ostensibly having a historical basis, usually explaining some phenomenon of nature or aspect of creation, defines a/an (Skill 14.1, Easy)

   A. proverb.

   B. idyll.

   C. myth.

   D. epic.

82. Which of the following is not a characteristic of a fable? (Skill 14.1, Easy)

   A. Animals that feel and talk like humans.

   B. Happy solutions to human dilemmas.

   C. Teaches a moral or standard for behavior.

   D. Illustrates specific people or groups without directly naming them.

83. The following lines from Robert Browning's poem "My Last Duchess" come from an example of what form of dramatic literature? (Skill 14.1, Rigorous)

   That's my last Duchess painted on the wall,
   Looking as if she were alive. I call
   That piece a wonder
   now: Frà Pandolf's hands
   Worked busily a day
   and there she stands.
   Will 't please you sit and look at her?

   A. Tragedy

   B. Comic opera

   C. Dramatis personae

   D. Dramatic monologue

84. Hoping to take advantage of the popularity of the Harry Potter series, a teacher develops a unit on mythology comparing the story and characters of Greek and Roman myths with the story and characters of the Harry Potter books. Which of these is a commonality that would link classical literature to popular fiction? (Skill 14.2, Rigorous)

   A. The characters are gods in human form with human-like characteristics.

   B. The settings are realistic places in the world where the characters interact as humans would.

   C. The themes center on the universal truths of love and hate and fear.

   D. The heroes in the stories are young males and only they can overcome the opposing forces.

85. Charles Dickens, Robert Browning, and Robert Louis Stevenson were (Skill 14.4, Easy)

   A. Victorians.

   B. Medievalists.

   C. Elizabethans.

   D. Absurdists.

86. What is considered the first work of English literature because it was written in the vernacular of the day? (Skill 14.4, Easy)

   A. *Beowulf*

   B. *Le Morte d'Arthur*

   C. *The Faerie Queene*

   D. *Canterbury Tales*

87. Considered one of the first feminist plays, this Ibsen drama ends with a door slamming symbolizing the lead character's emancipation from traditional societal norms. (Skill 14.4, Average Rigor)

   A. *The Wild Duck*

   B. *Hedda Gabler*

   C. *Ghosts*

   D. *The Doll's House*

88. American colonial writers were primarily (Skill 14.4, Average Rigor)

   A. Romanticists.

   B. Naturalists.

   C. Realists.

   D. Neo-classicists.

89. Arthur Miller wrote *The Crucible* as a parallel to what twentieth century event? (Skill 14.4, Average Rigor)

   A. Sen. McCarthy's House un-American Activities Committee Hearing

   B. The Cold War

   C. The fall of the Berlin wall

   D. The Persian Gulf War

90. Which of the writers below is a renowned Black poet? (Skill 14.4, Average Rigor)

   A. Maya Angelou

   B. Sandra Cisneros

   C. Richard Wilbur

   D. Richard Wright

91. Which of the following is not a theme of Native American writing? (Skill 14.4, Average Rigor)

   A. Emphasis on the hardiness of the human body and soul

   B. The strength of multi-cultural assimilation

   C. Contrition for the genocide of native peoples

   D. Remorse for the love of the Indian way of life

92. The writing of Russian naturalists is (Skill 14.4, Average Rigor)

   A. optimistic.

   B. pessimistic.

   C. satirical.

   D. whimsical.

93. In the following poem, what literary movement is reflected? (Skill 14.4, Rigorous)

   "My Heart Leaps Up" by William Wordsworth

   My heart leaps up when I behold
     A rainbow in the sky:
   So was it when my life began;
   So is it now I am a man;
   So be it when I shall grow old,
     Or let me die!
   The Child is father of the Man;
   And I could wish my days to be
   Bound each to each by natural piety

   A. Neo-classicism

   B. Victorian literature

   C. Romanticism

   D. Naturalism

94. "Every one must pass through Vanity Fair to get to the celestial city" is an allusion from a (Skill 14.4, Rigorous)

    A. Chinese folk tale.

    B. British allegory.

    C. Norse sage.

    D. German fairy tale.

95. Which author did not write satire? (Skill 14.4, Rigorous)

    A. Joseph Addison

    B. Richard Steele

    C. Alexander Pope

    D. John Bunyan

96. What were two major characteristics of the first American literature? (Skill 14.4, Rigorous)

    A. Vengefulness and arrogance

    B. Bellicosity and derision

    C. Oral delivery and reverence for the land

    D. Maudlin and self-pitying egocentricism

97. Which of the following is the best definition of existentialism? (Skill 14.4, Rigorous)

    A. The philosophical doctrine that matter is the only reality and that everything in the world, including thought, will and feeling, can be explained only in terms of matter.

    B. Philosophy that views things as they should be or as one would wish them to be.

    C. A philosophical and literary movement, variously religious and atheistic, stemming from Kierkegaard and represented by Sartre.

    D. The belief that all events are determined by fate and are hence inevitable.

98. Which sonnet form describes the following? (Skill 14.4, Rigorous)

> My galley charg'd with forgetfulness,
> Through sharp seas, in winter night doth pass
> 'Tween rock and rock; and eke mine enemy, alas,
> That is my lord steereth with, cruelness.
> And every oar a thought with readiness,
> As though that death were light in such a case.
> An endless wind doth tear the sail apace
> Or forc'ed sighs and trusty fearfulness.
> A rain of tears, a cloud of dark disdain,
> Hath done the wearied cords great hinderance,
> Wreathed with error and eke with ignorance.
> The stars be hid that led me to this pain
> Drowned is reason that should me consort,
> And I remain despairing of the poet

A. Petrarchan or Italian sonnet

B. Shakespearian or Elizabethan sonnet

C. Romantic sonnet

D. Spenserian sonnet

99. Which is the least true statement concerning an author's literary tone? (Skill 15.2, Average Rigor)

A.. Tone is partly revealed through the selection of details.

B. Tone is the expression of the author's attitude towards his/her subject.

C. Tone in literature is usually satiric or angry.

D. Tone in literature corresponds to the tone of voice a speaker uses.

100. In the following quotation, addressing the dead body of Caesar as though he were still a living being is to employ an (Skill 15.2, Average Rigor)

> O, pardon me, though
> Bleeding piece of earth
> That I am meek and gentle with
> These butchers.
>   -Marc Antony from *Julius Caesar*

A. apostrophe

B. allusion

C. antithesis

D. anachronism

101. An extended metaphor comparing two very dissimilar things (one lofty one lowly) is a definition of a/an (Skill 15.2, Average Rigor)

    A. antithesis.

    B. aphorism.

    C. apostrophe.

    D. conceit.

102. Which of the following is a characteristic of blank verse? (Skill 15.2, Average Rigor)

    A. Meter in iambic pentameter

    B. Clearly specified rhyme scheme

    C. Lack of figurative language

    D. Unspecified rhythm

103. Which is the best definition of free verse, or *vers libre*? (Skill 15.2, Average Rigor)

    A. Poetry, which consists of an unaccented syllable followed by an unaccented sound.

    B. Short lyrical poetry written to entertain but with an instructive purpose.

    C. Poetry, which does not have a uniform pattern of rhythm.

    D. A poem which tells the story and has a plot

104. Which level of meaning is the hardest aspect of a language to master? (Skill 15.2, Rigorous)

    A. Denotation

    B. Jargon

    C. Connotation

    D. Slang

105. Which of the following would not help students understand the concept of connotation and its impact of conveying tone? (Skill 13.2, Rigorous)

    A. A world atlas

    B. The poems of Robert Frost

    C. A dictionary of synonyms and antonyms

    D. Real estate advertisements

106. Which choice below best defines naturalism? (Skill 15.2, Rigorous)

   A. A belief that the writer or artist should apply scientific objectivity in his/her observation and treatment of life without imposing value judgments.

   B. The doctrine that teaches that the existing world is the best to be hoped for.

   C. The doctrine that teaches that God is not a personality, but that all laws, forces and manifestations of the universe are God-related.

   D. A philosophical doctrine that professes that the truth of all knowledge must always be in question.

107. Which term best describes the form of the following poetic excerpt? (Skill 15.2, Rigorous)

   And more to lulle him in his slumber soft,
   A trickling streake from high rock
   tumbling downe,
   And ever-drizzling raine upon the loft.
   Mixt with a murmuring winde, much like a swowne
   No other noyse, nor peoples troubles cryes.
   As still we wont t'annoy the walle'd towne,
   Might there be heard: but careless Quiet lyes,
   Wrapt in eternall silence farre from enemyes.

   A. Ballad

   B. Elegy

   C. Spenserian stanza

   D. *Octava rima*

108. In the phrase "The Cabinet conferred with the President," Cabinet is an example of a/an (Skill 15.2, Rigorous)

   A. metonym

   B. synecdoche

   C. metaphor

   D. allusion

109. What syntactic device is most evident from Abraham Lincoln's "Gettysburg Address"? (Skill 15.2, Rigorous)

It is rather for us to be here dedicated to the great task remaining before us -- that from these honored dead we take increased devotion to that cause for which they gave the last full measure of devotion— that we here highly resolve that these dead shall not have died in vain -- that this nation, under God, shall have a new birth of freedom—and that government of the people, by the people, for the people, shall not perish from the earth.

A. Affective connotation

B. Informative denotations

C. Allusion

D. Parallelism

110. What is the salient literary feature of this excerpt from an epic? (Skill 15.2, Rigorous)

Hither the heroes and the nymphs resorts,
To taste awhile the pleasures of a court;
In various talk th'instructive hours they passed,
Who gave the ball, or paid the visit last;
One speaks the glory of the English Queen,
And another describes a charming Indian screen;
A third interprets motion, looks, and eyes;
At every word a reputation dies.

A. Sprung rhythm

B. Onomatopoeia

C. Heroic couplets

D. Motif

111. **The following passage is written from which point of view? (Skill 15.3, Easy)**

> As she mused the pitiful vision of her mother's life laid its spell on the very quick of her being—that life of commonplace sacrifices closing in final craziness. She trembled as she heard again her mother's voice saying constantly with foolish insistence: *Dearevaun Seraun! Dearevaun Seraun!**

"The end of pleasure is pain!" (Gaelic)

A. First person, narrator

B. Second person, direct address

C. Third person, omniscient

D. First person, omniscient

112. **Which of the following is not a fallacy in logic? (Skill 16.3, Rigorous)**

A. All students in Ms. Suarez's fourth period class are bilingual.
   Beth is in Ms. Suarez's fourth period.
   Beth is bilingual.

B. All bilingual students are in Ms. Suarez's class.
   Beth is in Ms. Suarez's fourth period.
   Beth is bilingual.

C. Beth is bilingual.
   Beth is in Ms. Suarez's fourth period.
   All students in Ms. Suarez's fourth period are bilingual.

D. If Beth is bilingual, then she speaks Spanish.
   Beth speaks French.
   Beth is not bilingual.

113. Which of the following is an example of the post hoc fallacy? (Skill 16.3, Rigorous)

A. When the new principal was hired, student-reading scores improved; therefore, the principal caused the increase in scores.

B. Why are we spending money on the space program when our students don't have current textbooks?

C. You can't give your class a 10-minute break. Once you do that, we'll all have to give our students a 10-minute break.

D. You can never believe anything he says because he's not from the same country as we are.

114. Based on the excerpt below from Kate Chopin's short story "The Story of an Hour," what can students infer about the main character? (Skill 16.3, Rigorous)

She did not stop to ask if it were or were not a monstrous joy that held her. A clear and exalted perception enabled her to dismiss the suggestion as trivial. She knew that she would weep again when she saw the kind, tender hands folded in death; the face that had never looked save with love upon her, fixed and gray and dead. But she saw beyond that bitter moment a long procession of years to come that would belong to her absolutely. And she opened and spread her arms out to them in welcome.

A. She dreaded her life as a widow.

B. Although she loved her husband, she was glad that he was dead for he had never loved her.

C. She worried that she was too indifferent to her husband's death.

D. Although they had both loved each other, she was beginning to appreciate that opportunities had opened because of his death.

115. Written on the sixth grade reading level, most of S. E. Hinton's novels (for instance, *The Outsiders*) have the greatest reader appeal with (Skill 16.4, Average Rigor)

    A. sixth graders.

    B. ninth graders.

    C. twelfth graders.

    D. adults.

116. What is the best course of action when a child refuses to complete a reading/ literature assignment on the grounds that it is morally objectionable? (Skill 16.4, Average Rigor)

    A. Speak with the parents and explain the necessity of studying this work

    B. Encourage the child to sample some of the text before making a judgment

    C. Place the child in another teacher's class where they are studying an acceptable work

    D. Provide the student with alternative selections that cover the same performance standards that the rest of the class is learning.

117. Which of the following responses to literature typically give middle school students the most problems? (Skill 16.4, Average Rigor)

    A. Interpretive

    B. Evaluative

    C. Critical

    D. Emotional

118. **How will literature help students in a science class able understand the following passage? (Skill 16.4, Rigorous)**

    Just as was the case more than three decades ago, we are still sailing between the Scylla of deferring surgery for too long and risking irreversible left ventricular damage and sudden death, and the Charibdas of operating too early and subjecting the patient to the early risks of operation and the later risks resulting from prosthetic valves.
    --E. Braunwald, *European Heart Journal,* July 2000

    A. They will recognize the allusion to Scylla and Charibdas from Greek mythology and understand that the medical community has to select one of two unfavorable choices.

    B. They will recognize the allusion to sailing and understand its analogy to doctors as sailors navigating unknown waters.

    C. They will recognize that the allusion to Scylla and Charibdas refers to the two islands in Norse mythology where sailors would find themselves shipwrecked and understand how the doctors feel isolated by their choices.

    D. They will recognize the metaphor of the heart and relate it to Eros, the character in Greek mythology who represents love. Eros was the love child of Scylla and Charibdas.

119. **In preparing a report about William Shakespeare, students are asked to develop a set of interpretive questions to guide their research. Which of the following would not be classified as an interpretive question? (Skill 3.1, Rigorous)**

    A. What would be different today if Shakespeare had not written his plays?

    B. How will the plays of Shakespeare affect future generations?

    C. How does the Shakespeare view nature in *A Midsummer's Night Dream* and *Much Ado About Nothing*?

    D. During the Elizabethan age, what roles did young boys take in dramatizing Shakespeare's plays?

120. Which is not a Biblical allusion? (Skill 16.4, Rigorous)

   A. The patience of Job

   B. Thirty pieces of silver

   C. "Man proposes; God disposes"

   D. "Suffer not yourself to be betrayed by a kiss"

121. Recognizing empathy in literature is mostly a/an (Skill 16.4, Rigorous)

   A. emotional response.

   B. interpretive response.

   C. critical response.

   D. evaluative response.

122. The tendency to emphasize and value the qualities and peculiarities of life in a particular geographic area exemplifies (Skill 16.5, Easy)

   A. pragmatism.

   B. regionalism.

   C. pantheism.

   D. abstractionism.

123. In preparing a unit on 20th century immigration you prepare a list of books for students to read. Which book would not be appropriate for this topic? (Skill 16.7, Average Rigor)

   A. *The Things They Carried* by Tim O'Brien

   B. *Exodus* by Leon Uris

   C. *The Joy Luck Club* by Amy Tan

   D. *Tortilla Flats* by John Steinbeck

124. To explore the relationship of literature to modern life, which of these activities would not enable students to explore comparable themes? (Skill 16.7, Average Rigor)

   A. After studying various world events, such as the Palestinian-Israeli conflict, students write an updated version of *Romeo and Juliet* using modern characters and settings.

   B. Before studying *Romeo and Juliet*, students watch *West Side Story*.

   C. Students research the major themes of *Romeo and Juliet* by studying news stories and finding modern counterparts for the story.

   D. Students would explore compare the romantic themes of *Romeo and Juliet* and *The Taming of the Shrew*.

125. Mr. Phillips is creating a unit to study *To Kill a Mockingbird* and wants to familiarize his high school freshmen with the attitudes and issues of the historical period. Which activity would familiarize students with the attitudes and issues of the Depression-era South? (Skill 16.7, Rigorous)

   A. Create a detailed timeline of 15-20 social, cultural, and political events that focus on race relations in the 1930s.

   B. Research and report on the life of its author Harper Lee. Compare her background with the events in the book.

   C. Watch the movie version and note language and dress.

   D. Write a research report on the stock market crash of 1929 and its effects.

Section III: Answer Key

#	Ans	#	Ans	#	Ans	#	Ans	#	Ans
1	C	26	A	51	C	76	D	101	D
2	D	27	A	52	B	77	A	102	A
3	C	28	A	53	C	78	D	103	C
4	C	29	C	54	D	79	C	104	C
5	C	30	D	55	D	80	D	105	A
6	A	31	D	56	B	81	C	106	A
7	D	32	A	57	D	82	D	107	D
8	B	33	A	58	A	83	D	108	B
9	D	34	B	59	A	84	C	109	D
10	A	35	B	60	D	85	A	110	C
11	B	36	C	61	B	86	D	111	C
12	D	37	D	62	D	87	D	112	A
13	B	38	D	63	C	88	D	113	A
14	D	39	A	64	C	89	A	114	D
15	B	40	D	65	C	90	A	115	B
16	A	41	B	66	A	91	B	116	D
17	C	42	C	67	C	92	B	117	B
18	A	43	A	68	A	93	C	118	A
19	D	44	A	69	D	94	B	119	D
20	A	45	B	70	C	95	D	120	C
21	C	46	A	71	A	96	D	121	C
22	B	47	D	72	B	97	C	122	B
23	D	48	B	73	B	98	A	123	A
24	A	49	A	74	C	99	C	124	D
25	C	50	D	75	A	100	A	125	A

Rigor Table

	Easy 20%	Average Rigor 40%	Rigorous 40%
Question #	1, 2, 11, 12, 25, 30, 39, 42, 47, 48, 49, 50, 52, 59, 61, 63, 67, 69, 76, 81, 82, 85, 86, 111, 122	3, 4, 5, 6, 13, 14, 15, 16, 21, 22, 23, 26, 27, 29, 32, 36, 37, 38, 40, 41, 43, 44, 46, 53, 55, 57, 58, 60, 68, 73, 74, 77, 78, 79, 87, 88, 89, 90, 91, 92, 99, 100, 101, 102, 103, 115, 116, 117, 123, 124	7, 8, 9, 10, 17, 18, 19, 20, 24, 28, 31, 33, 34, 35, 45, 51, 54, 56, 62, 64, 65, 66, 70, 71, 72, 75, 80, 83, 84, 93, 94, 95, 96, 97, 98, 104, 105, 106, 107, 108, 109, 110, 112, 113, 114, 118, 119, 120, 121, 125

Explanation of Rigor

Easy: The majority of test takers would get this question correct. It is a simple understanding of the facts and/or the subject matter is part of the basics of an education for teaching English.

Average Rigor: This question represents a test item that most people would pass. It requires a level of analysis or reasoning and/or the subject matter exceeds the basics of an education for teaching English.

Rigorous: The majority of test takers would have difficulty answering this question. It involves critical thinking skills such as a very high level of abstract thought, analysis or reasoning, and it would require a very deep and broad education for teaching English.

Rationales with Sample Questions

Part A

Each underlined portion of sentences 1-10 contains one or more errors in grammar, usage, mechanics, or sentence structure. Circle the choice which best corrects the error without changing the meaning of the original sentence.

1. Joe didn't hardly know his cousin Fred who'd had a rhinoplasty. (Skill 7.4, Easy)

    A. hardly did know his cousin Fred

    B. didn't know his cousin Fred hardly

    C. hardly knew his cousin Fred

    D. didn't know his cousin Fred

    E. didn't hardly know his cousin Fred

The correct answer is C: using the adverb "hardly" to modify the verb creates a negative, and adding "not" creates the dreaded double negative.

2. There were <u>fewer pieces</u> of evidence presented during the second trial (Skill 7.4, Easy)

    A. fewer peaces

    B. less peaces

    C. less pieces

    D. fewer pieces

The correct answer is D. Use "fewer" for countable items; use "less" for amounts and quantities, such as fewer minutes but less time. "Peace" is the opposite of war, not a "piece" of evidence.

3. **Mixing the batter for cookies**, the cat licked the Crisco from the cookie sheet. (Skill 7.4, Average Rigor)

    A. While mixing the batter for cookies

    B. While the batter for cookies was mixing

    C. While I mixed the batter for cookies

    D. While I mixed the cookies

    E. Mixing the batter for cookies

The correct answer is C. Answers A and E give the impression that the cat was mixing the batter (it is a dangling modifier.), Answer B that the batter was mixing itself, and Answer D lacks precision: it is the batter that was being mixed, not the cookies themselves.

4. Mr. Smith **respectfully submitted his resignation and had** a new job. (Skill 7.4, Average Rigor)

    A. respectfully submitted his resignation and has

    B. respectfully submitted his resignation before accepting

    C. respectfully submitted his resignation because of

    D. respectfully submitted his resignation and had

The correct answer is C. Answer A eliminates any relationship of causality between submitting the resignation and having the new job. Answer B just changes the sentence and, by omission, does not indicate the fact that Mr. Smith had a new job before submitting his resignation. Answer D means that Mr. Smith first submitted his resignation, and then got a new job.

5. The teacher **implied** from our angry words that there was conflict **between you and me**. (Skill 7.4, Average Rigor)

   A. Implied… between you and I

   B. Inferred… between you and I

   C. Inferred… between you and me

   D. Implied… between you and me

The correct answer is C: the difference between the verb "to imply" and the verb "to infer" is that implying is directing an interpretation toward other people; to infer is to deduce an interpretation from someone else's discourse. Moreover, "between you and I" is grammatically incorrect: after the preposition "between," the object (or 'disjunctive' with this particular preposition) pronoun form, "me," is needed.

6. Wally **groaned, "Why** do I have to do an oral interpretation **of "The Raven."** (Skill 7.4, Average Rigor)

   A. groaned "Why… of 'The Raven'?"

   B. groaned "Why… of "The Raven"?

   C. groaned ", Why… of "The Raven?"

   D. groaned, "Why… of "The Raven."

The correct answer is A. The question mark in a quotation that is an interrogation should be within the quotation marks. Also, when quoting a work of literature within another quotation, one should use single quotation marks ('…') for the title of this work, and they should close before the final quotation mark.

7. **The coach offered her assistance but the athletes** wanted to practice on their own. (Skill 7.4, Rigorous)

   A. The coach offered her assistance, however, the athletes wanted to practice on their own.

   B. The coach offered her assistance: furthermore, the athletes wanted to practice on their own.

   C. Having offered her assistance, the athletes wanted to practice on their own.

   D. The coach offered her assistance; however, the athletes wanted to practice on their own.

   E. The coach offered her assistance, and the athletes wanted to practice on their own.

The correct answer is D. A semicolon precedes a transitional adverb that introduces an independent clause. Answer A is a comma splice. In Answer B, the colon is used incorrectly since the second clause does not explain the first. In Answer C, the opening clause confuses the meaning of the sentence. In Answer E, the conjunction "and" is weak since the two ideas show contrast rather than an additional thought.

8. **Walt Whitman was famous for his composition, Leaves of Grass, serving as a nurse during the Civil War, and a devoted son (Skill 7.4, Rigorous)**

    A. *Leaves of Grass*, his service as a nurse during the Civil War, and a devoted son

    B. composing *Leaves of Grass*, serving as a nurse during the Civil War, and being a devoted son

    C. his composition, *Leaves of Grass*, his nursing during the Civil War, and his devotion as a son

    D. his composition *Leaves of Grass*, serving as a nurse during the Civil War and a devoted son

    E. his composition *Leaves of Grass*, serving as a nurse during the Civil War. and a devoted son

The correct answer is B: In order to be parallel, the sentence needs three gerunds. The other sentences use both gerunds and nouns, which is a lack of parallelism.

9. **A teacher must know not only her subject matter but also the strategies of content teaching. (Skill 7.4, Rigorous)**

    A. must not only know her subject matter but also the strategies of content teaching

    B. not only must know her subject matter but also the strategies of content teaching

    C. must not know only her subject matter but also the strategies of content teaching

    D. must know not only her subject matter but also the strategies of content teaching

The correct answer is D: the correlative conjunction "not only" must come directly after "know" because the intent is to create the clearest meaning link with the "but also" predicate section later in the sentence.

10. **The Taj Mahal has been designated one of the Seven Wonders of the World, and people know it for its unique architecture. (Skill 7.4, Rigorous)**

    A. The Taj Mahal has been designated one of the Seven Wonders of the World, and it is known for its unique architecture.

    B. People know the Taj Mahal for its unique architecture, and it has been designated one of the Seven Wonders of the World.

    C. People have known the Taj Mahal for its unique architecture, and it has been designated of the Seven Wonders of the World.

    D. The Taj Mahal has designated itself one of the Seven Wonders of the World.

The correct answer is A. In the original sentence, the first clause is passive voice and the second clause is active voice, causing a voice shift. B merely switches the clauses but does not correct the voice shift. In C, only the verb tense in the first clause has been changed but it still active voice. Sentence D changes the meaning. In A, both clauses are passive voice.

Part B

Directions: Select the best answer in each group of multiple choices.

11. **The literary device of personification is used in which example below? (Skill 1.2, Easy)**

    A. "Beg me no beggary by soul or parents, whining dog!"

    B. "Happiness sped through the halls cajoling as it went."

    C. "O wind thy horn, thou proud fellow."

    D. "And that one talent which is death to hide."

The correct answer is B. "Happiness," an abstract concept, is described as if it were a person with the words "sped" and "cajoling."

12. **The Elizabethans wrote in (Skill 1.3 Easy)**

    A. Celtic

    B. Old English

    C. Middle English

    D. Modern English

The correct answer is D. There is no document written in Celtic in England, and a work such as Beowulf is representative of Old English in the eighth century. It is also the earliest Teutonic written document. Before the fourteenth century, little literature is known to have appeared in Middle English, which had absorbed many words from the Norman French spoken by the ruling class, but at the end of the fourteenth century there appeared the works of Chaucer, John Gower, and the novel *Sir Gawain and the Green Knight*. The Elizabethans wrote in modern English and their legacy is very important: they imported the Petrarchan, or Italian, sonnet, which Sir Thomas Wyatt and Sir Philip Sydney illustrated in their works. Sir Edmund Spencer invented his own version of the Italian sonnet and wrote *The Faerie Queene*. Other literature of the time includes the hugely important works of Shakespeare and Marlowe.

13. **The synonyms *gyro, hero,* and *submarine* reflect which influence on language usage? (Skill 1.3, Average Rigor)**

    A. Social

    B. Geographical

    C. Historical

    D. Personal

The correct answer is B. They are interchangeable but their use depends on the region of the United States, not on the social class of the speaker. Nor is there any historical context around any of them. The usage can be personal but will most often vary with the region.

14. **Middle and high school students are more receptive to studying grammar and syntax (Skill 1.3, Average Rigor)**

    A. through worksheets and end of lessons practices in textbooks.

    B. through independent, homework assignment.

    C. through analytical examination of the writings of famous authors.

    D. through application to their own writing.

The correct answer is D. At this age, students learn grammatical concepts best through practical application in their own writing.

15. **Which event triggered the beginning of Modern English? (Skill 1.3, Average Rigor)**

    A. Conquest of England by the Normans in 1066

    B. Introduction of the printing press to the British Isles

    C. Publication of Samuel Johnson's lexicon.

    D. American Revolution

The correct answer is B. With the arrival of the written word, reading matter became mass-produced, so the public tended to adopt the speech and writing habits printed in books and the language became more stable.

16. **Which of the following is not true about the English language? (Skill 1.3, Average Rigor)**

    A. English is the easiest language to learn.

    B. English is the least inflected language.

    C. English has the most extensive vocabulary of any language.

    D. English originated as a Germanic tongue.

The correct answer is A. Just like any other language, English has inherent difficulties which make it difficult to learn, even though English has no declensions such as those found in Latin, Greek, or contemporary Russian, or a tonal system such Chinese.

TEACHER CERTIFICATION STUDY GUIDE

17. **What was responsible for the standardizing of dialects across America in the 20th century? (Skill 1.3, Rigorous)**

    A. With the immigrant influx, American became a melting pot of languages and cultures.

    B. Trains enabled people to meet other people of different languages and cultures.

    C. Radio, and later, television, used actors and announcers who spoke without pronounced dialects.

    D. Newspapers and libraries developed programs to teach people to speak English with an agreed-upon common dialect.

The correct answer is C. The growth of immigration in the early part of the 20th century created pockets of language throughout the country. Coupled with regional differences already in place, the number of dialects grew. Transportation enabled people to move to different regions where languages and dialects continued to merge. With the growth of radio and television, however, people were introduced to a standardized dialect through actors and announcers who spoke so that anyone across American could understand them. Newspapers and libraries never developed programs to standardize spoken English.

18. **Latin words that entered the English language during the Elizabethan age include (Skill 1.3, Rigorous)**

    A. allusion, education, and esteem

    B. vogue and mustache

    C. canoe and cannibal

    D. alligator, cocoa, and armadillo

The correct answer is A. These words reflect the Renaissance interest in the classical world and the study of ideas. The words in Answer B are French derivation, and the words in Answers C and D are more modern with younger etymologies.

19. The most significant drawback to applying learning theory research to classroom practice is that (Skill 1.3, Rigorous)

   A. today's students do not acquire reading skills with the same alacrity as when greater emphasis was placed on reading classical literature.

   B. development rates are complicated by geographical and cultural In analyzing literature and in looking for ways to bring a work to life for an audience, the use of comparable themes and ideas from other pieces of literature and from one's own life experiences, including from reading the daily newspaper, is very important and useful.

   C. homogeneous grouping has contributed to faster development of some age groups.

   D. social and environmental conditions have contributed to an escalated maturity level than research done twenty of more years ago would seem to indicate.

The correct answer is D. Because of the rapid social changes, topics that were not interesting to younger readers are now topics of books for even younger readers. Many books dealing with difficult topics, and it is difficult for the teacher to steer students toward books that they are ready for and to try to keep them away from books whose content, although well written, are not yet appropriate for their level of cognitive and social development. There is a fine line between this and censorship.

20. Which aspect of language is innate? (Skill 1.3, Rigorous)

   A. Biological capability to articulate sounds understood by other humans

   B. Cognitive ability to create syntactical structures

   C. Capacity for using semantics to convey meaning in a social environment

   D. Ability to vary inflections and accents

The correct answer is A. Language ability is innate and the biological capability to produce sounds lets children learn semantics and syntactical structures through trial and error. Linguists agree that language is first a vocal system of word symbols that enable a human to communicate his/her feelings, thoughts, and desires to other human beings.

21. **The English department is developing strategies to encourage all students to become a community of readers. From the list of suggestions below, which would be the least effective way for teachers to foster independent reading? (Skill 1.4, Average Rigor)**

   A. Each teacher will set aside a weekly 30-minute in-class reading session during which the teacher and students read a magazine or book for enjoyment.

   B. Teacher and students develop a list of favorite books to share with each other.

   C. The teacher assigns at least one book report each grading period to ensure that students are reading from the established class list.

   D. The students gather books for a classroom library so that books may be shared with each other.

The correct answer is C. Teacher-directed assignments such as book reports appear routine and unexciting. Students will be more excited about reading when they can actively participate. In Answer A, the teacher is modeling reading behavior and providing students with a dedicated time during which time they can read independently and still be surrounded by a community of readers. In Answers B and D, students share and make available their reading choices.

22. **Modeling is a practice that requires students to (Skill 1.7, Average Rigor)**

   A. create a style unique to their own language capabilities.

   B. emulate the writing of professionals.

   C. paraphrase passages from good literature.

   D. peer evaluate the writings of other students.

The correct answer is B. Modeling has students analyze the writing of a professional writer and try to reach the same level of syntactical, grammatical and stylistic mastery as the author whom they are studying.

23. Which of the following reading strategies calls for higher order cognitive skills? (Skill 1.8, Average Rigor)

    A. Making predictions

    B. Summarizing

    C. Monitoring

    D. Making inferences

The correct answer is D. Making inferences from a reading text involves using other reading skills such as making predictions, skimming, scanning, summarizing, then coming to conclusions or making inferences which are not directly stated in the text.

24. Before reading a passage, a teacher gives her students an anticipation guide with a list of statements related to the topic they are about to cover in the reading material. She asks the students to indicate their agreement or disagreement with each statement on the guide. This activity is intended to (Skill 1.8, Rigorous)

    A. elicit students' prior knowledge of the topic and set a purpose for reading.

    B. help students to identify the main ideas and supporting details in the text.

    C. help students to synthesize information from the text.

    D. help students to visualize the concepts and terms in the text.

The correct answer is A. Establishing a purpose for reading, the foundation for a reading unit or activity, is intimately connected to activating the students' prior knowledge in strategic ways. When the reason for reading is developed in the context of the students' experiences, they are far better prepared to succeed because they can make connections from a base they thoroughly understand. This influences motivation, and with proper motivation, students are more enthused and put forward more effort to understand the text. The other choices are only indirectly supported by this activity and are more specific in focus.

25. Among junior-high school students of low-to-average readability levels, which work would most likely stir reading interest? (Skill 2.1, Easy)

   A. *Elmer Gantry*, Sinclair Lewis

   B. *Smiley's People*, John Le Carre

   C. *The Outsiders*, S.E. Hinton

   D. *And Then There Were None*, Agatha Christie.

The correct answer is C. The students can easily identify with the characters and the gangs in the book. S.E. Hinton has actually said about this book: "*The Outsiders* is definitely my best-selling book; but what I like most about it is how it has taught a lot of kids to enjoy reading." The other three novels have more mature subject matter, more complex characters, and higher reading levels. Lewis' novel satirizes hypocrisy in the character of a debauched evangelist. Le Carre's novel is the third part of a spy novel trilogy. Christie's mystery has a wide cast of characters who are murdered one by one.

26. Which of the following would be the most significant factor in teaching Homer's *Iliad* and *Odyssey* to any particular group of students? (Skill 2.3, Average Rigor)

   A. Identifying a translation on the appropriate reading level

   B. Determining the students' interest level

   C. Selecting an appropriate evaluative technique

   D. Determining the scope and delivery methods of background study

The correct answer is A. Students will learn the importance of these two works if the translation reflects both the vocabulary that they know and their reading level. Greece will always be foremost in literary assessments due to Homer's works. Homer is the most often cited author, next to Shakespeare. Greece is the cradle of both democracy and literature. This is why it is so crucial that Homer be included in the works assigned.

27. **Which of the following is a formal reading-level assessment? (Skill 2.5, Average Rigor)**

    A. A standardized reading test

    B. A teacher-made reading test

    C. An interview

    D. A reading diary

The correct answer is A. If assessment is standardized, it has to be objective whereas Answers B, C and D are all subjective assessments.

28. **Read the following passage and identify the main idea. (Skill 2.5, Rigorous)**

    Sometimes too much of a good thing can become a very bad thing indeed. In an earnest attempt to consume a healthy diet, dietary supplement enthusiasts have been known to overdose. Vitamin C, for example, long thought to help people ward off cold viruses, is currently being studied for its possible role in warding off cancer and other disease that cases tissue degeneration. Unfortunately, an overdose of vitamin C—more than 10,000 mg—on a daily basis can cause nausea and diarrhea. Calcium supplements, commonly taken by women, are helpful in warding off osteoporosis. More than just a few grams a day, however, can lead to stomach upset and even kidney and bladder stones. Niacin, proven useful in reducing cholesterol levels, can be dangerous in large doses to those who suffer from heart problems, asthma or ulcers.

    A. Supplements taken in excess can be a bad thing indeed.

    B. Dietary supplement enthusiasts have been known to overdose.

    C. Vitamins can cause nausea, diarrhea, and kidney or bladder stones.

    D. People who take supplements are preoccupied with their health.

The correct answer is A. It is a paraphrase of the first sentence and provides a general framework for the rest of the paragraph: Excess supplement intake is bad. The rest of the paragraph discusses the consequences of taking too many vitamins. Options B and C refer to major details, and Option D introduces the idea of preoccupation, which is not included in this paragraph.

TEACHER CERTIFICATION STUDY GUIDE

29. Which teaching method would best engage underachievers in the required senior English class? (Skill 2.8, Average Rigor)

   A. Assign use of glossary work and extensively footnoted excerpts of great works.

   B. Have students take turns reading aloud the anthology selection

   C. Let students choose which readings they'll study and write about.

   D. Use a chronologically arranged, traditional text, but assigning group work, panel presentations, and portfolio management

The correct answer is C. It will encourage students to react honestly to literature. Students should take notes on what they're reading so they will be able to discuss the material. They should not only react to literature, but also experience it. Small-group work is a good way to encourage them. The other answers are not fit for junior-high or high school students. They should be encouraged, however, to read critics of works in order to understand criteria work.

30. To understand the origins of a word, one must study the (Skill 3.1, Easy)

   A. synonyms

   B. inflections

   C. phonetics

   D. etymology

The correct answer is D. Etymology is the study of word origins. A synonym is an equivalent of another word and can substitute for it in certain contexts. Inflection is a modification of words according to their grammatical functions, usually by employing variant word-endings to indicate such qualities as tense, gender, case, and number. Phonetics is the science devoted to the physical analysis of the sounds of human speech, including their production, transmission, and perception.

31. Which word in the following sentence is a bound morpheme: "The quick brown fox jumped over the lazy dog"? (Skill 3.1, Rigorous)

    A. The

    B. fox

    C. lazy

    D. jumped

The correct answer is D. The suffix "-ed" is an affix that cannot stand alone as a unit of meaning. Thus it is bound to the free morpheme "jump." "The" is always an unbound morpheme since no suffix or prefix can alter its meaning. As written, "fox" and "lazy" are unbound but their meaning is changed with affixes, such as "foxes" or "laziness."

32. If a student has a poor vocabulary, the teacher should recommend first that (Skill 3.4 Average Rigor)

    A. the student read newspapers, magazines and books on a regular basis.

    B. the student enroll in a Latin class.

    C. the student write the words repetitively after looking them up in the dictionary.

    D. the student use a thesaurus to locate synonyms and incorporate them into his/her vocabulary

The correct answer is A. The teacher can personally influence what the student chooses as reading material, but the student must be able to choose independently where to search for the reading pleasure indispensable for enriching vocabulary.

33. In a class of non-native speakers of English, which type of activity will help students the most? (Skill 4.1, Rigorous)

   A. Have students make oral presentations so that they can develop a phonological awareness of sounds.

   B. Provide students more writing opportunities to develop their written communication skills.

   C. Encourage students to listen to the new language on television and radio.

   D. Provide a variety of methods to develop speaking, writing, and reading skills.

The correct answer is A. Research indicates that non-native speakers of English develop stronger second language skills by understanding the phonological differences in spoken words.

34. Regularly requiring students to practice reading short, instructional-level texts at least three times to a peer and to give and receive peer feedback about these readings mainly addresses which reading skill? (Skill 4.4, Rigorous)

   A. Comprehension

   B. Fluency

   C. Evaluation

   D. Word-solving

The correct answer is B. Fluency is the ability to read text quickly with accuracy, phrasing, and expression. Fluency develops over time and requires substantial reading practice. This activity provides just this sort of practice. The peer feedback portion does address comprehension, evaluation, and some word-solving, but the main thrust is on fluency development.

35. To determine the credibility of information, researchers should do all of the following except (Skill 4.6, Rigorous)

    A. establish the authority of the document.

    B. disregard documents with bias.

    C. evaluate the currency and reputation of the source.

    D. use a variety of research sources and methods.

The correct answer is B. Keep an open mind. Researchers should examine the assertions, facts, and reliability of the information.

36. Which of the following is the least preferable strategy for teaching literature? (Skill 5.1, Average Rigor)

    A. teacher-guided total class discussion

    B. small group discussion

    C. teacher lecture

    D. dramatization of literature selections

The correct answer is C. In order to engage students' interest, it is necessary that they be involved whether through discussion or dramatization. A lecture is a much too passive technique to involve students of this age.

37. Sometimes readers can be asked to demonstrate their understanding of a text. This might include all of the following except (Skill 5.1, Average Rigor)

    A. role playing.

    B. paraphrasing.

    C. storyboarding a part of the story with dialogue bubbles.

    D. reading the story aloud

The correct answer is D. Reading the text aloud may help readers understand the text but it won't demonstrate their understanding of it. By role playing, paraphrasing, or storyboarding, they will convey their understanding of the purpose and main ideas of the text.

38. The students in Mrs. Cline's seventh grade language arts class were invited to attend a performance of Romeo and Juliet presented by the drama class at the high school. To best prepare, they should (Skill 5.4, Average Rigor)

    A. read the play as a homework exercise.

    B. read a synopsis of the plot and a biographical sketch of the author.

    C. examine a few main selections from the play to become familiar with the language and style of the author.

    D. read a condensed version of the story and practice attentive listening skills.

The correct answer is D. By reading a condensed version of the story, students will know the plot and therefore be able to follow the play on stage. It is also important for them to practice listening techniques such as one one-to-one tutoring and peer-assisted reading.

39. In writing a report, Hector has to explain where acid rain comes from and what it has done to the environment. What is the most likely form of organizational structure? (Skill 5.6, Easy)

   A. Cause and effect

   B. Problem and solution

   C. Exposition

   D. Definition

The correct answer is A. This report would discuss what has caused acid rain and what effects acid rain has had on the environment. Although it could offer a solution, the report questions do not focus on that. Most report writing is expository because it provided information and an explanation. While a definition might be an important detail, it would not be the major organizational structure.

40. Students returning from a field trip to the local newspaper want to thank their hosts for the guided tour. As their teacher, what form of communication should you encourage them to use? (Skill 6.1, Average Rigor)

   A. Each student will send an email expressing his or her appreciation.

   B. As a class, students will create a blog, and each student will write about what they learned.

   C. Each student will write a thank you letter that the teacher will fax to the newspaper.

   D. Each student will write a thank you note that the teacher will mail to the newspaper.

The correct answer is D. Courtesy requires a hand-written message that is brief and specific. While using technology such as emails, blogs, and faxes are quicker, they are less personal.

41. Which of the following is the least effective procedure for promoting consciousness of audience? (Skill 6.1, Average Rigor)

   A. Pairing students during the writing process

   B. Reading all rough drafts before the students write the final copies

   C. Having students compose stories or articles for publication in school literary magazines or newspapers

   D. Writing letters to friends or relatives

The correct answer is B. Reading all rough drafts will not encourage the students to take control of their text and might even inhibit their creativity. On the contrary, pairing students will foster their sense of responsibility, and having them compose stories for literary magazines will boost their self-esteem as well as their organization skills.

42. In "inverted triangle" introductory paragraphs, the thesis sentence occurs (Skill 6.2, Easy)

   A. at the beginning of the paragraph.

   B. in the middle of the paragraph.

   C. at the end of the paragraph.

   D. in the second paragraph.

The correct answer is C. The introduction to an essay should begin with a broad general statement, followed by one or more sentences adding interest and information to the topic. The thesis should be written at the end of the introduction.

43. What is the main form of discourse in this passage? (Skill 6.2, Average Rigor)

   It would have been hard to find a passer-by more wretched in appearance. He was a man of middle height, stout and hardy, in the strength of maturity; he might have been forty-six or seven. A slouched leather cap hid half his face, bronzed by the sun and wind, and dripping with sweat.

   A. Description

   B. Narration

   C. Exposition

   D. Persuasion

The correct answer is A. A description presents a thing or a person in detail, and tells the reader about the appearance of whatever it is presenting. Narration relates a sequence of events (the story) told through a process of narration (discourse), in which events are recounted in a certain order (the plot). Exposition is an explanation or an argument within the narration. It can also be the introduction to a play or a story. Persuasion strives to convince either a character in the story or the reader.

44. **Regarding the study of poetry, select the answer which is least applicable to all types of poetry. (Skill 6.2, Average Rigor)**

   A. Setting and audience

   B. Theme and tone

   C. Pattern and diction

   D. Diction and rhyme scheme

The correct answer is A. Setting and audience are important elements of narrative but there are many poems where the setting and audience are unimportant.

45. **Which sentence below best minimizes the impact of bad news? (Skill 6.2, Rigorous)**

   A. We have denied you permission to attend the event.

   B. Although permission to attend the event cannot be given, you are encouraged to buy the video.

   C. Although you cannot attend the event, we encourage you to buy the video.

   D. Although attending the event is not possible, watching the video is an option.

The correct answer is B. Subordinating the bad news and using passive voice minimizes the impact of the bad news. In Answer A, the sentence is active voice and thus too direct. The word *denied* sets a negative tone. In Answer C, the bad news is subordinated but it is still active voice with negative wording. In Answer D, the sentence is too unclear.

46. **The new teaching intern is developing a unit on creative writing and is trying to encourage her students to write poetry. Which of the following would not be an effective technique? (Skill 6.2, Average Rigor)**

    A. In groups, students will draw pictures to illustrate "The Love Song of J. Alfred Prufrock" by T.S. Eliot.

    B. Either individually or in groups, students will compose a song, writing lyrics that try to use poetic devices.

    C. Students will bring to class the lyrics of a popular song and discuss the imagery and figurative language.

    D. Students will read aloud their favorite poems and share their opinions of and responses to the poems.

The correct answer is A. While drawing is creative, it will not accomplish as much as the other activities to encourage students to write their own poetry. Furthermore, "The Love Song of J. Alfred Prufrock" is not an at-level poem. The other activities involve students in music and their own favorites, which will be more appealing.

47. **Writing ideas quickly without interruption of the flow of thoughts or attention to conventions is called (Skill 6.3, Easy)**

    A. brainstorming.

    B. mapping.

    C. listing.

    D. free writing.

The correct answer is D. Free writing for ten or fifteen minutes allows students to write out their thoughts about a subject. This technique allows the students to develop ideas that they are conscious of, but it also helps them to develop ideas that are lurking in the subconscious. It is important to let the flow of ideas run through the hand. If the students get stuck, they can write the last sentence over again until inspiration returns.

48. Which of the following is most true of expository writing? (Skill 6.5, Easy)

   A. It is mutually exclusive of other forms of discourse.

   B. It can incorporate other forms of discourse in the process of providing supporting details.

   C. It should never employ informal expression.

   D. It should only be scored with a summative evaluation.

The correct answer is B. Expository writing sets forth an explanation or an argument about any subject and can use distinct or combined forms of discourse, a sign of academic literacy. This directly contradicts Answer A. Writing can use formal and informal language and can be evaluated in many subjective and objective ways.

49. Explanatory or informative discourse is (Skill 6.5, Easy)

   A. exposition.

   B. narration.

   C. persuasion.

   D. description.

The correct answer is A. Exposition sets forth a systematic explanation of any subject. It can also introduce the characters of a literary work, and their situations in the story. Narration relates a sequence of events (the story) told through a process of narration (discourse), in which events are recounted in a certain order (the plot). Persuasion strives to convince either a character in the story or the reader.

TEACHER CERTIFICATION STUDY GUIDE

50. Which of the following is not a technique of prewriting? (Skill 7.1, Easy)

    A. Clustering

    B. Listing

    C. Brainstorming

    D. Proofreading

The correct answer is D. Proofreading cannot be a method of prewriting, since it is done on already written texts only. Clustering, listing, and brainstorming are all prewriting strategies.

51. In the following excerpt from "Civil Disobedience," what type of reasoning does Henry David Thoreau use? (Skill 7.1, Rigorous)

    Unjust laws exist; shall we be content to obey them, or shall we endeavor to amend them, and obey them until we have succeeded, or shall we transgress them at once? Men generally, under such a government as this, think that they ought to wait until they have persuaded the majority to alter them. They think that, if they should resist, the remedy would be worse than the evil. But it is the fault of the government itself that the remedy *is* worse than the evil. ... Why does it always crucify Christ, and excommunicate Copernicus and Luther, and pronounce Washington and Franklin rebels?
    --"Civil Disobedience" by Henry David Thoreau

    A. Ethical reasoning

    B. Inductive reasoning

    C. Deductive reasoning

    D. Intellectual reasoning

The correct answer is C. Deductive reasoning begins with a general statement that leads to the particulars. In this essay, Thoreau begins with the general question about what should be done about unjust laws. His argument leads to the government's role in suppressing dissent.

ENGLISH LANGUAGE ARTS

52. Which of the following sentences is properly punctuated? (Skill 7.4, Easy)

   A. The more you eat; the more you want.

   B. The authors—John Steinbeck, Ernest Hemingway, and William Faulkner—are staples of modern writing in American literature textbooks.

   C. Handling a wild horse, takes a great deal of skill and patience.

   D. The man, who replaced our teacher, is a comedian.

The correct answer is B. Dashes should be used instead of commas when commas are used elsewhere in the sentence for amplification or explanation — here within the dashes.

53. Which of the following sentences contains a subject-verb agreement error? (Skill 7.4, Average Rigor)

   A. Both mother and her two sisters were married in a triple ceremony.

   B. Neither the hen nor the rooster is likely to be served for dinner.

   C. My boss, as well as the company's two personnel directors, have been to Spain.

   D. Amanda and the twins are late again.

The correct answer is C. The reason for this is that the true subject of the verb is "My boss," not "two personnel directors."

54. In general, the most serious drawback of using a computer in writing is that (Skill 7.7, Rigorous)

    A. the copy looks so good that students tend to overlook major mistakes.

    B. the spell check and grammar programs discourage students from learning proper spelling and mechanics.

    C. the speed with which corrections can be made detracts from the exploration and contemplation of composing.

    D. the writer loses focus by concentrating on the final product rather than the details.

The correct answer is C. Because the process of revising is very quick with the computer, it can discourage contemplation, exploring, and examination, which are very important in the process of writing.

55. Which transition word would show contrast between these two ideas? (Skill 8.1, Average Rigor)

    We are confident in our skills to teach English. We welcome new ideas on this subject.

    A. We are confident in our skills to teach English, and we welcome new ideas on this subject.

    B. Because we are confident in our skills to teach English, we welcome new ideas on the subject.

    C. When we are confident in our skills to teach English, we welcome new ideas on the subject.

    D. We are confident in our skills to teach English; however, we welcome new ideas on the subject.

The answer is D. Transitional words, phrases and sentences help clarify meanings. In A, the transition word *and* introduces another equal idea. In B, the transition word *because* indicates cause and effect. In C, the transition word *when* indicates order or chronology. In D, *however,* shows that these two ideas contrast with each other.

56. Which of the following should students use to improve coherence of ideas within an argument? (Skill 8.2, Rigorous)

A. Transitional words or phrases to show relationship of ideas.

B. Conjunctions like "and" to join ideas together.

C. Direct quotes to improve credibility.

D. Adjectives and adverbs to provide stronger detail.

The correct answer is B. Transitional words and phrases are two-way indicators that connect the previous idea to the following idea. Sophisticated writers use transitional devices to clarify text (for example), to show contrast (despite), to show sequence (first, next), to show cause (because, since).

57. In preparing your high school freshmen to write a research paper about a social problem, what recommendation can you make so they can determine the credibility of their information? (Skill 9.2, Average Rigor)

A. Assure them that information on the Internet has been peer-reviewed and verified for accuracy.

B. Find one solid source and use that exclusively.

C. Use only primary sources.

D. Cross check your information with another credible source.

The correct answer is D. When researchers find the same information in multiple reputable sources, the information is considered credible. Using the Internet for research requires strong critical evaluation of the source. Nothing from the Internet should be taken without careful scrutiny of the source. To rely on only one source is dangerous and short-sighted. Most high school freshmen would have limited skills to conduct primary research for a paper about a social problem.

58. Which of the following are secondary research materials? (Skill 9.2, Average Rigor)

   A. The conclusions and inferences of other historians.

   B. Literature and nonverbal materials, novels, stories, poetry and essays from the period, as well as coins, archaeological artifacts, and art produced during the period.

   C. Interviews and surveys conducted by the researcher.

   D. Statistics gathered as the result of the research's experiments.

The correct answer is A. Secondary sources are works written significantly after the period being studied and based upon primary sources. In this case, historians have studied artifacts of the time and drawn their conclusion and inferences. Primary sources are the basic materials that provide raw data and information. Students or researchers may use literature and other data they have collected to draw their own conclusions or inferences.

59. Which of the following is not correct? (Skill 9.4, Easy)

   A. Because most students have wide access to media, teachers should refrain from using it in their classrooms to diminish the overload.

   B. Students can use CD-ROMs to explore information using a virtual reality experience.

   C. Teacher can make their instruction more powerful by using educational media.

   D. The Internet enables students to connect with people across cultures and to share interests.

The correct answer is A. Teachers can use media in productive ways to enrich instruction. Rather than ignoring it, educators should use a wide assortment of media for the benefit of their students.

60. Which of the following statements indicates an instructional goal for using multimedia in the classroom? (Skill 9.4 Average Rigor)

A. Audio messages invite the listener to form mental images consistent with the topic of the audio.

B. Print messages appeal almost exclusively to the mind and push students to read with more thought.

C. Listening to an audio message is more passive than reading a print message.

D. Teachers who develop activities to foster a critical perspective on audiovisual presentation will decrease passivity.

The correct answer is D. Each of the statements is true but only the last one establishes a goal for using multimedia in the classroom.

61. Which of the following should not be included in the opening paragraph of an informative essay? (Skill 10.2, Easy)

A. Thesis sentence

B. Details and examples supporting the main idea

C. Broad general introduction to the topic

D. A style and tone that grabs the reader's attention

The correct answer is B. The introductory paragraph should introduce the topic, capture the reader's interest, state the thesis and prepare the reader for the main points in the essay. Details and examples, however, should be given in the second part of the essay, so as to help develop the thesis presented at the end of the introductory paragraph, following the inverted triangle method consisting of a broad general statement followed by some information, and then the thesis at the end of the paragraph.

62. For their research paper on the effects of the Civil War on American literature, students have brainstormed a list of potential online sources and are seeking your authorization. Which of these represent the strongest source? (Skill 10.1, Rigorous)

   A. http://www.wikipedia.org/

   B. http://www.google.com

   C. http://www.nytimes.com

   D. http://docsouth.unc.edu/southlit/civilwar.html

The answer is D. Sites with an "edu" domain are associated with educational institutions and tend to be more trustworthy for research information. Wikipedia has an "org" domain, which means it is a nonprofit. While Wikipedia may be appropriate for background reading, its credibility as a research site is questionable. Both Google and the New York Times are "com" sites, which are for profit. Even though this does not discredit their information, each site is problematic for researchers. With Google, students will get overwhelmed with hits and may not choose the most reputable sites for their information. As a newspaper, the New York Times would not be a strong source for historical information.

TEACHER CERTIFICATION STUDY GUIDE

63. **In the paragraph below, which sentence does not contribute to the overall task of supporting the main idea? (Skill 10.2 Easy)**

    1) The Springfield City Council met Friday to discuss new zoning restrictions for the land to be developed south of the city. 2) Residents who opposed the new restrictions were granted 15 minutes to present their case. 3) Their argument focused on the dangers that increased traffic would bring to the area. 4) It seemed to me that the Mayor Simpson listened intently. 5) The council agreed to table the new zoning until studies would be performed.

    A. Sentence 2

    B. Sentence 3

    C. Sentence 4

    D. Sentence 5

The correct answer is C. The other sentences provide detail to the main idea of the new zoning restrictions. Because sentence 4 provides no example or relevant detail, it should be omitted.

64. **In this paragraph from a student essay, identify the sentence that provides a detail. (Skill 10.2 Rigorous)**

    (1) The poem concerns two different personality types and the human relation between them. (2) Their approach to life is totally different. (3) The neighbor is a very conservative person who follows routines. (4) He follows the traditional wisdom of his father and his father's father. (5) The purpose in fixing the wall and keeping their relationship separate is only because it is all he knows.

    A. Sentence 1

    B. Sentence 3

    C. Sentence 4

    D. Sentence 5

The correct answer is C. Sentence 4 provides a detail to sentence 3 by explaining how the neighbor follows routine. Sentence 1 is the thesis sentence, which is the main idea of the paragraph. Sentence 3 provides an example to develop that thesis. Sentence 4 is a reason that explains why.

65. Which part of a classical argument is illustrated in this excerpt from the essay "What Should Be Done About Rock Lyrics?" (Skill 10.3, Rigorous)

> But violence against women is greeted by silence. It shouldn't be.
>
> This does not mean censorship, or book (or record) burning. In a society that protects free expression, we understand a lot of stuff will float up out of the sewer. Usually, we recognize the ugly stuff that advocates violence against any group as the garbage it is, and we consider its purveyors as moral lepers. We hold our nose and tolerate it, but we speak out against the values it proffers.
> --"What Should Be Done About Rock Lyrics?" Caryl Rivers

A. Narration

B. Confirmation

C. Refutation and concession

D. Summation

The correct answer is C. The author acknowledges refutes the idea of censorship and concedes that society tolerates offensive lyrics as part of our freedom of speech. Narration provides background material to produce an argument. In confirmation, the author details the argument with claims that support the thesis. In summation, the author concludes the argument by offering the strongest solution.

66. Which of the following situations is not an ethical violation of intellectual property? (Skill 10.5, Rigorous)

   A. A student visits ten different websites and writes a report to compare the costs of downloading music. He uses the names of the websites without their permission.

   B. A student copies and pastes a chart verbatim from the Internet but does not document it because it is available on a public site.

   C. From an online article found in a subscription database, a student paraphrases a section on the problems of music piracy. She includes the source in her Works Cited but does not provide an in-text citation.

   D. A student uses a comment from M. Night Shyamalan without attribution claiming the information is common knowledge.

The correct answer is A. In this scenario, the student is conducting primary research by gathering the data and using it for his own purposes. He is not violating any principle by using the names of the websites. In Answer B, students who copy and paste from the Internet without documenting the sources of their information are committing plagiarism, a serious violation of intellectual property. Even when a student puts information in her own words by paraphrasing or summarizing as in Answer C, the information is still secondary and must be documented. While dedicated movie buffs might consider anything that M. Night Shyamalan says to be common knowledge in Answer D, his comments are not necessarily known in numerous places or known by a lot of people.

67. Which of the following would not be a major concern in an oral presentation? (Skill 11.1, Easy)

    A. Establishing the purpose of the presentation

    B. Evaluating the audience's demographics and psychographics.

    C. Creating a PowerPoint slide for each point.

    D. Developing the content to fit the occasion.

The correct answer is C. PowerPoint slides should be kept to a minimum of one slide per minute and should not overwhelm the presentation. The slides should be a supplement so that the speaker can accomplish the purpose. To reach that goal, the speaker should understand the makeup of the audience: demographics, such as age, education level or other quantifiable characteristic; and, psychographics, such as attitudes or values. Knowing the purpose and the audience will enable the speaker to develop the content to fit the occasion.

68. If students use slang and expletives, what is the best course of action to take in order to improve their formal communication skills? (Skill 11.5, Average Rigor)

    A. Ask the students to paraphrase their writing, that is, translate it into language appropriate for the school principal to read.

    B. Refuse to read the students' papers until they conform to a more literate style.

    C. Ask the students to read their work aloud to the class for peer evaluation.

    D. Rewrite the flagrant passages to show the students the right form of expression.

The correct answer is A. Asking the students to write for a specific audience will help them become more involved in their writing. If they continue writing to the same audience—the teacher—they will continue seeing writing as just another assignment, and they will not apply grammar, vocabulary and syntax the way they should be. By rephrasing their own writing, they will learn to write for a different public.

69. **Oral debate is most closely associated with which form of discourse? (Skill 11.6, Easy)**

    A. Description

    B. Exposition

    C. Narration

    D. Persuasion

The correct answer is D. It is extremely important to be convincing while having an oral debate. This is why persuasion is so important, because this is the way that you can influence your audience.

70. **In presenting a report to peers about the effects of Hurricane Katrina on New Orleans, the students wanted to use various media in their argument to persuade their peers that more needed to be done. Which of these would be the most effective? (Skill 11.7, Rigorous)**

    A. A PowerPoint presentation showing the blueprints of the levees before the flood and redesigned now for current construction..

    B. A collection of music clips made by the street performers in the French Quarter before and after the flood.

    C. A recent video showing the areas devastated by the floods and the current state of rebuilding.

    D. A collection of recordings of interviews made by the various government officials and local citizens affected by the flooding.

The correct answer is C. For maximum impact, a video would offer dramatic scenes of the devastated areas. A video by its very nature is more dynamic than a static PowerPoint presentation. Further, the condition of the levees would not provide as much impetus for change as seeing the devastated areas. Oral messages such as music clips and interviews provide another way of supplementing the message but, again, they are not as dynamic as video.

71. In preparing a speech for a contest, your student has encountered problems with gender specific language. Not wishing to offend either women or men, she seeks your guidance. Which of the following is not an effective strategy? (Skill 11.9, Rigorous)

    A. Use the generic "he" and explain that people will understand and accept the male pronoun as all-inclusive.

    B. Switch to plural nouns and use "they" as the gender-neutral pronoun.

    C. Use passive voice so that the subject is not required.

    D. Use male pronouns for one part of the speech and then use female pronouns for the other part of the speech.

The correct answer is A. No longer is the male pronoun considered the universal pronoun. Speakers and writers should choose gender-neutral words and avoid nouns and pronouns that inaccurately exclude one gender or another.

72. Mr. Ledbetter has instructed his students to prepare a slide presentation that illustrates an event in history. Students are to include pictures, graphics, media clips and links to resources. What competencies will students exhibit at the completion of this project? (Skill 11.11, Rigorous)

    A. Analyze the impact of society on media.

    B. Recognize the media's strategies to inform and persuade.

    C. Demonstrate strategies and creative techniques to prepare presentations using a variety of media.

    D. Identify the aesthetic effects of a media presentation.

The correct answer is B. Students will have learned how to use various media to convey a unified message.

73. **Students have been asked to evaluate the message in several television commercials for credit cards. Which type of listening skill would be most appropriate? (Skill 12.2, Average Rigor)**

    A. Informative listening

    B. Critical listening

    C. Appreciative listening

    D. Relationship listening

The correct answer is B. By listening critically, students will examine the message to identify the strategies of the appeals and to evaluate the substance of the claims. In informative listening, the students will merely identify the main ideas. In appreciative listening, the students pay attention to the message for the enjoyment it brings them. In relationship listening, the students would try to establish a personal relationship.

74. **In literature, evoking feelings of pity or compassion is to create (Skill 12.2, Average Rigor)**

    A. colloquy.

    B. irony.

    C. pathos.

    D. paradox

The correct answer is C. A very well known example of pathos is Desdemona's death in *Othello*, but there are many other examples of pathos. In *King Lear*, Cordelia accepts defeat with this line: "We are not the first / Who with best meaning have incurred the worst." A colloquy is a formal conversation. Irony is a discrepancy between what is expected and what occurs. A paradox is a contradictory statement.

75. **Identify the type of appeal used by Molly Ivins's in this excerpt from her essay "Get a Knife, Get a Dog, But Get Rid of Guns." (Skill 12.3, Rigorous)**

> As a civil libertarian, I, of course, support the Second Amendment. And I believe it means exactly what it says:
> *A well regulated militia being necessary to the security of a free state, the right of the people to keep and bear arms shall not be infringed.*

A. Ethical

B. Emotional

C. Rational

D. Literary

The correct answer is A. An ethical appeal is using the credentials of a reliable and trustworthy authority. In this case, Ivins cites the Constitution. Pathos is an emotional appeal and logos is a rational appeal. Literature might appeal to you but it's not a rhetorical appeal.

76. **What is not one of the advantages of collaborative or cooperative learning? (Skill 13.4, Easy)**

A. Students that work together in groups or teams develop their skills in organizing, leadership, research, communication, and problem solving.

B. Working in teams can help students overcome anxiety in distance learning courses and contribute a sense of community and belonging for the students.

C. Students tend to learn more material being taught and retain the information longer than when the same information is taught using different methods.

D. Teachers reduce their workload and the time spent on individuals the assignments, and grading.

The correct answer is D. Teacher continue to expend time in planning, monitoring and evaluating the students, their groups, and their activities.

77. Overcrowded classes prevent the individual attention needed to facilitate language development. This drawback can be best overcome by (Skill 13.4, Average Rigor)

   A. dividing the class into independent study groups.

   B. assigning more study time at home.

   C. using more drill practice in class.

   D. Team teaching.

The correct answer is A. Dividing a class into small groups fosters peer enthusiasm and evaluation, and sets an atmosphere of warmth and enthusiasm. It is much preferable to divide the class into smaller study groups than to lecture, which will bore students and therefore fail to facilitate curricular goals. Also, it is preferable to do this than to engage the whole class in a general teacher-led discussion because such discussion favors the loquacious and inhibits the shy.

78. In preparing students for their oral presentations, the instructor provided all of these guidelines, except one. Which is not an effective guideline? (Skill 13.6, Average Rigor)

   A. Even if you are using a lectern, feel free to move about. This will connect you to the audience.

   B. Your posture should be natural, not stiff. Keep your shoulders toward the audience.

   C. Gestures can help communicate as long as you don't overuse them or make them distracting.

   D. You can avoid eye contact if you focus on your notes. This will make you appear more knowledgeable.

The correct answer is D. Although many people are nervous about making eye contact, they should focus on two or three people at a time. Body language, such as movement, posture, and gestures, helps the speaker connect to the audience.

79. **Which of the following is not an advantage of oral communication over written communication? (Skill 13.9, Average Rigor)**

    A. Oral communication provides immediate feedback.

    B. Oral communication relies on non-verbal clues to express meaning.

    C. Oral communication is carefully prepared and presented.

    D. Oral communication is more social than written communication.

The correct answer is C. Unless you are making a speech that has been prepared and practiced, you will not always control your oral communication. You cannot easily edit as you speak; distractions and interruptions will change the track of the conversation. What you meant to say is not always what you say.

80. **The arrangement and relationship of words in sentences or sentence structures best describes (Skill 13.9, Rigorous)**

    A. style.

    B. discourse.

    C. thesis.

    D. syntax.

The correct answer is D. Syntax is the grammatical structure of sentences. Style is the manner of expression of writing or speaking. Discourse is an extended expression of thought through either oral or written communication. A thesis is the unifying main idea that can be either explicit or implicit.

81. A traditional, anonymous story, ostensibly having a historical basis, usually explaining some phenomenon of nature or aspect of creation, defines a/an (Skill 14.1, Easy)

    A. proverb.

    B. idyll.

    C. myth.

    D. epic.

The correct answer is C. A myth is usually traditional and anonymous and explains natural and supernatural phenomena. Myths are usually about creation, divinity, the significance of life and death, and natural phenomena. A proverb is a saying or adage. An idyll is a short, pastoral poem. In its simplest form, an epic is a narrative poem.

82. Which of the following is not a characteristic of a fable? (Skill 14.1, Easy)

    A. Animals that feel and talk like humans.

    B. Happy solutions to human dilemmas.

    C. Teaches a moral or standard for behavior.

    D. Illustrates specific people or groups without directly naming them.

The correct answer is D. A fable is a short tale with animals, humans, gods, or even inanimate objects as characters. Fables often conclude with a moral, delivered in the form of an epigram (a short, witty, and ingenious statement in verse). Fables are among the oldest forms of writing in human history: it appears in Egyptian papyri of c 1500 BC. The most famous fables are those of Aesop, a Greek slave living in about 600 BC. In India, the *Pantchatantra* appeared in the third century. The most famous modern fables are those of seventeenth century French poet Jean de La Fontaine.

83. **The following lines from Robert Browning's poem "My Last Duchess" come from an example of what form of dramatic literature? (Skill 14.1, Rigorous)**

   That's my last Duchess painted on the wall,
   Looking as if she were alive. I call
   That piece a wonder
   now: Frà Pandolf's hands
   Worked busily a day
   and there she stands.
   Will 't please you sit and look at her?

   A. Tragedy

   B. Comic opera

   C. Dramatis personae

   D. Dramatic monologue

The correct answer is D. A dramatic monologue is a speech given by a character or narrator that reveals characteristics of the character or narrator. This form was first made popular by Robert Browning, a Victorian poet. Tragedy is a form of literature in which the protagonist is overwhelmed by opposing forces. Comic opera is a form of sung music based on a light or happy plot. *Dramatis personae* is the Latin phrase for the cast of a play.

84. **Hoping to take advantage of the popularity of the Harry Potter series, a teacher develops a unit on mythology comparing the story and characters of Greek and Roman myths with the story and characters of the Harry Potter books. Which of these is a commonality that would link classical literature to popular fiction? (Skill 14.2, Rigorous)**

    A. The characters are gods in human form with human-like characteristics.

    B. The settings are realistic places in the world where the characters interact as humans would.

    C. The themes center on the universal truths of love and hate and fear.

    D. The heroes in the stories are young males and only they can overcome the opposing forces.

The correct answer is C. Although the gods in Greek and Roman myths take human form, they are immortal as gods must be. The characters in Harry Potter may be wizards, but they are not immortal. Although the settings in these stories have familiar associations, their worlds are vastly different from those inhabited by mortals and Muggles. While male heroes may dominate the action, the females (Hera, Dianna, Hermione) are powerful as well.

85. **Charles Dickens, Robert Browning, and Robert Louis Stevenson were (Skill 14.4, Easy)**

    A. Victorians.

    B. Medievalists.

    C. Elizabethans.

    D. Absurdists.

The correct answer is A. The Victorian Period is remarkable for the diversity and quality of its literature. Robert Browning wrote chilling monologues such as "My Last Duchess," and long poetic narratives such as *The Pied Piper of Hamlin*. Robert Louis Stevenson wrote his works partly for young adults, whose imaginations were quite taken by his *Treasure Island* and *The Case of Dr. Jekyll and Mr. Hyde*. Charles Dickens tells of the misery of the time and the complexities of Victorian society in novels such as *Oliver Twist* or *Great Expectations*.

86. What is considered the first work of English literature because it was written in the vernacular of the day? (Skill 14.4, Easy)

   A. *Beowulf*

   B. *Le Morte d'Arthur*

   C. *The Faerie Queene*

   D. *Canterbury Tales*

The correct answer is D. Chaucer wrote the *Canterbury Tales* in the street language of medieval England. *Beowulf* was written during the Anglo-Saxon period and is a Teutonic saga. *Le Morte d'Arthur*, by Thomas Malory was written after Chaucer. Sir Edmund Spencer's *The Faerie Queene* was written during the Renaissance under the reign of Queen Elizabeth I.

87. Considered one of the first feminist plays, this Ibsen drama ends with a door slamming symbolizing the lead character's emancipation from traditional societal norms. (Skill 14.4, Average Rigor)

   A. *The Wild Duck*

   B. *Hedda Gabler*

   C. *Ghosts*

   D. *The Doll's House*

The correct answer is D. Nora in *The Doll's House* leaves her husband and her children when she realizes her husband is not the man she thought he was. Hedda Gabler, another feminist icon, shoots herself. *The Wild Duck* deals with the conflict between idealism and family secrets. *Ghosts,* considered one of Ibsen's most controversial plays, deals with many social ills, some of which include alcoholism, incest, and religious hypocrisy.

88. American colonial writers were primarily (Skill 14.4, Average Rigor)

   A. Romanticists.

   B. Naturalists.

   C. Realists.

   D. Neo-classicists.

The correct answer is D. The early colonists had been schooled in England, and even though their writing became quite American in content, their emphasis on clarity and balance in their language remained British. This literature reflects the lives of the early colonists, such as William Bradford's excerpts from "The Mayflower Compact," Anne Bradstreet's poetry and William Byrd's journal, *A History of the Dividing Line*.

89. Arthur Miller wrote *The Crucible* as a parallel to what twentieth century event? (Skill 14.4, Average Rigor)

   A. Sen. McCarthy's House un-American Activities Committee Hearing

   B. The Cold War

   C. The fall of the Berlin wall

   D. The Persian Gulf War

The correct answer is A. The episode of the seventeenth century witch-hunt in Salem, Mass., gave Miller a storyline that was very comparable to what was happening to persons suspected of communist beliefs in the 1950s.

90. **Which of the writers below is a renowned Black poet? (Skill 14.4, Average Rigor)**

    A. Maya Angelou

    B. Sandra Cisneros

    C. Richard Wilbur

    D. Richard Wright

The correct answer is A. Among her most famous work are *I Know Why the Caged Bird Sings* (1970), *And Still I Rise* (1978), and *All God's Children Need Traveling Shoes* (1986). Richard Wilbur is a poet and a translator of French dramatists Racine and Moliere, but he is not African American. Richard Wright is a very important African American author of novels such as *Native Son* and *Black Boy*. However, he was not a poet. Sandra Cisneros is a Latina author who is very important in developing Latina Women's literature.

91. **Which of the following is not a theme of Native American writing? (Skill 14.4, Average Rigor)**

    A. Emphasis on the hardiness of the human body and soul

    B. The strength of multi-cultural assimilation

    C. Contrition for the genocide of native peoples

    D. Remorse for the love of the Indian way of life

The correct answer is B. Native American literature was first a vast body of oral traditions from as early as before the fifteenth century. The characteristics include reverence for and awe of nature and the interconnectedness of the elements in the life cycle. The themes often reflect the hardiness of body and soul, remorse for the destruction of the Native American way of life, and the genocide of many tribes by the encroaching settlements of European Americans. These themes are still present in today's contemporary Native American literature, such as in the works of Duane Niatum, Gunn Allen, Louise Erdrich and N. Scott Momaday.

92. The writing of Russian naturalists is (Skill 14.4, Average Rigor)

   A. optimistic.

   B. pessimistic.

   C. satirical.

   D. whimsical.

The correct answer is B. Although the movement, which originated with the critic Vissarion Belinsky, was particularly strong in the 1840's, it can be said that the works of Dostoevsky, Tolstoy, Chekov, Turgenev and Pushkin owe much to it. These authors' works are among the best in international literature, yet are shrouded in stark pessimism. Tolstoy's *Anna Karenina* or Dostoevsky's *Crime and Punishment* are good examples of this dark outlook.

93. In the following poem, what literary movement is reflected? (Skill 14.4, Rigorous)

"My Heart Leaps Up" by William Wordsworth

My heart leaps up when I behold
  A rainbow in the sky:
So was it when my life began;
So is it now I am a man;
So be it when I shall grow old,
  Or let me die!
The Child is father of the Man;
And I could wish my days to be
Bound each to each by natural piety

A. Neo-classicism

B. Victorian literature

C. Romanticism

D. Naturalism

The correct answer is C. The Romantic period of the 19th century is known for its emphasis on feelings, emotions, and passions. William Wordsworth and William Blake were two notable poets from this period. In the neoclassicism of the previous period, the literature echoed the classical ideals of proportion, common sense, and reason over raw emotion and imagination, and the purpose was more didactic than celebratory. The Victorian period of the late 19th century exerted more restraint on emotions and feelings. In naturalistic writing, authors depict the world more harshly and more objectively.

TEACHER CERTIFICATION STUDY GUIDE

94. "Every one must pass through Vanity Fair to get to the celestial city" is an allusion from a (Skill 14.4, Rigorous)

    A. Chinese folk tale.

    B. British allegory.

    C. Norse sage.

    D. German fairy tale.

The correct answer is B. This is a reference to John Bunyan's *Pilgrim's Progress* from *This World to That Which Is to Come* (Part I, 1678; Part II, 1684), in which the hero, Christian, flees the City of Destruction and must undergo different trials and tests to get to the Celestial City.

95. Which author did not write satire? (Skill 14.4, Rigorous)

    A. Joseph Addison

    B. Richard Steele

    C. Alexander Pope

    D. John Bunyan

The correct answer is D. John Bunyan was a religious writer, known for his autobiography, *Grace Abounding to the Chief of Sinners,* as well as other books, all religious in their inspiration, such as *The Holy City, or the New Jerusalem* (1665), *A Confession of My Faith,* and *A Reason of My Practice* (1672), or *The Holy War* (1682).

96. What were two major characteristics of the first American literature? (Skill 14.4, Rigorous)

   A. Vengefulness and arrogance

   B. Bellicosity and derision

   C. Oral delivery and reverence for the land

   D. Maudlin and self-pitying egocentricism

The correct answer is D. This characteristic can be seen in Captain John Smith's work, as well as William Bradford's and Michael Wigglesworth's works.

97. Which of the following is the best definition of existentialism? (Skill 14.4, Rigorous)

   A. The philosophical doctrine that matter is the only reality and that everything in the world, including thought, will and feeling, can be explained only in terms of matter.

   B. Philosophy that views things as they should be or as one would wish them to be.

   C. A philosophical and literary movement, variously religious and atheistic, stemming from Kierkegaard and represented by Sartre.

   D. The belief that all events are determined by fate and are hence inevitable.

The correct answer is C. Even though there are other very important thinkers in the movement known as Existentialism, such as Camus and Merleau-Ponty, Sartre remains the main figure in this movement.

98. Which sonnet form describes the following? (Skill 14.4, Rigorous)

    My galley charg'd with forgetfulness,
    Through sharp seas, in winter night doth pass
    'Tween rock and rock; and eke mine enemy, alas,
    That is my lord steereth with, cruelness.
    And every oar a thought with readiness,
    As though that death were light in such a case.
    An endless wind doth tear the sail apace
    Or forc'ed sighs and trusty fearfulness.
    A rain of tears, a cloud of dark disdain,
    Hath done the wearied cords great hinderance,
    Wreathed with error and eke with ignorance.
    The stars be hid that led me to this pain
    Drowned is reason that should me consort,
    And I remain despairing of the poet

    A. Petrarchan or Italian sonnet

    B. Shakespearian or Elizabethan sonnet

    C. Romantic sonnet

    D. Spenserian sonnet

The correct answer is A. The Petrarchan sonnet, also known as Italian sonnet, is named after the Italian poet Petrarch (1304-74). It is divided into an octave rhyming abbaabba and a sestet normally rhyming cdecde.

99. Which is the least true statement concerning an author's literary tone? (Skill 15.2, Average Rigor)

    A. Tone is partly revealed through the selection of details.

    B. Tone is the expression of the author's attitude towards his/her subject.

    C. Tone in literature is usually satiric or angry.

    D. Tone in literature corresponds to the tone of voice a speaker uses.

The correct answer is C. Tone in literature conveys a mood and can be as varied as the tone of voice of a speaker (see D), e.g. sad, nostalgic, whimsical, angry, formal, intimate, satirical, sentimental, etc.

100. In the following quotation, addressing the dead body of Caesar as though he were still a living being is to employ an (Skill 15.2, Average Rigor)

    O, pardon me, though
    Bleeding piece of earth
    That I am meek and gentle with
    These butchers.
        -Marc Antony from *Julius Caesar*

    A. apostrophe

    B. allusion

    C. antithesis

    D. anachronism

The correct answer is A. This rhetorical figure addresses personified things, absent people or gods. An allusion, on the other hand, is a quick reference to a character or event known to the public. An antithesis is a contrast between two opposing viewpoints, ideas, or presentation of characters. An anachronism is the placing of an object or person out of its time with the time of the text. The best-known example is the clock in Shakespeare's *Julius Caesar*.

101. An extended metaphor comparing two very dissimilar things (one lofty one lowly) is a definition of a/an (Skill 15.2, Average Rigor)

    A. antithesis.

    B. aphorism.

    C. apostrophe.

    D. conceit.

The correct answer is D. A conceit is an unusually far-fetched metaphor in which an object, person or situation is presented in a parallel and simpler analogue between two apparently very different things or feelings, one very sophisticated and one very ordinary, usually taken either from nature or a well known every day concept, familiar to both reader and author alike. The conceit was first developed by Petrarch and spread to England in the sixteenth century.

102. Which of the following is a characteristic of blank verse? (Skill 15.2, Average Rigor)

    A. Meter in iambic pentameter

    B. Clearly specified rhyme scheme

    C. Lack of figurative language

    D. Unspecified rhythm

The correct answer is A. An iamb is a metrical unit of verse having one unstressed syllable followed by one stressed syllable. This is the most commonly used metrical verse in English and American poetry. An iambic pentameter is a ten-syllable verse made of five of these metrical units, either rhymed as in sonnets, or unrhymed as in free, or blank, verse.

103. **Which is the best definition of free verse, or *vers libre*? (Skill 15.2, Average Rigor)**

    A. Poetry, which consists of an unaccented syllable followed by an unaccented sound.

    B. Short lyrical poetry written to entertain but with an instructive purpose.

    C. Poetry, which does not have a uniform pattern of rhythm.

    D. A poem which tells the story and has a plot

The correct answer is C. Free verse has lines of irregular length (but it does not run on like prose).

104. **Which level of meaning is the hardest aspect of a language to master? (Skill 15.2, Rigorous)**

    A. Denotation

    B. Jargon

    C. Connotation

    D. Slang

The correct answer is C. Connotation refers to the meanings suggested by a word, rather than the dictionary definition. For example, the word "slim" means thin, and it is usually used with a positive connotation, to compliment of admire someone's figure. The word "skinny" also means thin, but its connotations are not as flattering as those of the word "slim." The connotative aspect of language is more difficult to master than the denotation (dictionary definition), as the former requires a mastery of the social aspect of language, not just the linguistic rules.

105. Which of the following would not help students understand the concept of connotation and its impact of conveying tone? (Skill 13.2, Rigorous)

   A. A world atlas

   B. The poems of Robert Frost

   C. A dictionary of synonyms and antonyms

   D. Real estate advertisements

The correct answer is A. Connotation is the emotional attachment of words. Denotation is the literal meanings of words. In the poems of Robert Frost, students would study the poet's diction and its relationship to the themes. A dictionary of synonyms and antonyms would enable students to evaluate word choices for their impact. By studying real estate ads, students would learn to understand the emotional impact of words. A world atlas is a collection of maps. Any text in an atlas would be denotative, fact-based with literal meanings.

106. Which choice below best defines naturalism? (Skill 15.2, Rigorous)

   A. A belief that the writer or artist should apply scientific objectivity in his/her observation and treatment of life without imposing value judgments.

   B. The doctrine that teaches that the existing world is the best to be hoped for.

   C. The doctrine that teaches that God is not a personality, but that all laws, forces and manifestations of the universe are God-related.

   D. A philosophical doctrine that professes that the truth of all knowledge must always be in question.

The correct answer is A. Naturalism is a movement that was started by French writers Jules and Edmond de Goncourt with their novel *Germinie Lacerteux* (1865), but its real leader is Emile Zola, who wanted to bring "a slice of life" to his readers. His saga, *Les Rougon Macquart,* consists in twenty-two novels depicting various aspects of social life. English writing authors representative of this movement include George Moore and George Gissing in England, but the most important naturalist novel in English is Theodore Dreiser's *Sister Carrie.*

107. **Which term best describes the form of the following poetic excerpt? (Skill 15.2, Rigorous)**

> And more to lulle him in his slumber soft,
> A trickling streake from high rock tumbling downe,
> And ever-drizzling raine upon the loft.
> Mixt with a murmuring winde, much like a swowne
> No other noyse, nor peoples troubles cryes.
> As still we wont t'annoy the walle'd towne,
> Might there be heard: but careless Quiet lyes,
> Wrapt in eternall silence farre from enemyes.

A. Ballad

B. Elegy

C. Spenserian stanza

D. *Octava rima*

The correct answer is D. The *octava rima* is a specific eight-line stanza whose rhyme scheme is abababcc. A ballad is a narrative poem. An elegy is a form of lyric poetry typically used to mourn someone who has died. A form of the English sonnet created by Edmond Spenser combines the English form and the Italian. The Spenserian sonnet follows the English quatrain and couplet pattern but resembles the Italian in its rhyme scheme, which is linked: abab bcbc cdcd ee.

108. In the phrase "The Cabinet conferred with the President," Cabinet is an example of a/an (Skill 15.2, Rigorous)

    A. metonym

    B. synecdoche

    C. metaphor

    D. allusion

The correct answer is B. In a synecdoche, a whole is referred to by naming a part of it. Also, a synecdoche can stand for a whole of which it is a part: for example, the Cabinet for the Government. Metonymy is the substitution of a word for a related word. For example, "hit the books" means "to study." A metaphor is a comparison such as "a cat burglar." An allusion is a reference to someone or something in history. To say that 'she met her Waterloo and was fired" alludes to Napoleon's defeat.

109. What syntactic device is most evident from Abraham Lincoln's "Gettysburg Address"? (Skill 15.2, Rigorous)

    It is rather for us to be here dedicated to the great task remaining before us -- that from these honored dead we take increased devotion to that cause for which they gave the last full measure of devotion—that we here highly resolve that these dead shall not have died in vain -- that this nation, under God, shall have a new birth of freedom—and that government of the people, by the people, for the people, shall not perish from the earth.

    A. Affective connotation

    B. Informative denotations

    C. Allusion

    D. Parallelism

The correct answer is D. Parallelism is the repetition of grammatical structure. In speeches such as this as well as speeches of Martin Luther King, Jr., parallel structure creates a rhythm and balance of related ideas. Lincoln's repetition of clauses beginning with "that" ties four examples back "to the great task." Connotation is the emotional attachment of words; denotation is the literal meaning of words. Allusion is a reference to a historic event, person, or place.

110. What is the salient literary feature of this excerpt from an epic? (Skill 15.2, Rigorous)

  Hither the heroes and the nymphs resorts,
To taste awhile the pleasures of a court;
In various talk th'instructive hours they passed,
Who gave the ball, or paid the visit last;
One speaks the glory of the English Queen,
And another describes a charming Indian screen;
A third interprets motion, looks, and eyes;
At every word a reputation dies.

 A. Sprung rhythm

 B. Onomatopoeia

 C. Heroic couplets

 D. Motif

The correct answer is C. A couplet is a pair of rhyming verse lines, usually of the same length. It is one of the most widely used verse-forms in European poetry. Chaucer established the use of couplets in English, notably in the *Canterbury Tales*, using rhymed iambic pentameters (a metrical unit of verse having one unstressed syllable followed by one stressed syllable) later known as heroic couplets. Other authors who used heroic couplets include Ben Jonson, Dryden, and especially Alexander Pope, who became the master of them.

111. The following passage is written from which point of view? (Skill 15.3, Easy)

> As she mused the pitiful vision of her mother's life laid its spell on the very quick of her being —that life of commonplace sacrifices closing in final craziness. She trembled as she heard again her mother's voice saying constantly with foolish insistence: *Dearevaun Seraun! Dearevaun Seraun!**

* "The end of pleasure is pain!" (Gaelic)

A. First person, narrator

B. Second person, direct address

C. Third person, omniscient

D. First person, omniscient

The correct answer is C. The passage is clearly in the third person (the subject is "she"), and it is omniscient since it gives the characters' inner thoughts.

112. Which of the following is not a fallacy in logic? (Skill 16.3, Rigorous)

A. All students in Ms. Suarez's fourth period class are bilingual.
Beth is in Ms. Suarez's fourth period.
Beth is bilingual.

B. All bilingual students are in Ms. Suarez's class.
Beth is in Ms. Suarez's fourth period.
Beth is bilingual.

C. Beth is bilingual.
Beth is in Ms. Suarez's fourth period.
All students in Ms. Suarez's fourth period are bilingual.

D. If Beth is bilingual, then she speaks Spanish.
Beth speaks French.
Beth is not bilingual.

The correct answer is A. The second statement, or premise, is tested against the first premise. Both premises are valid and the conclusion is logical. In Answer B, the conclusion is invalid because the first premise does not exclude other students. In Answer C, the conclusion cannot be logically drawn from the preceding premises—you cannot conclude that all students are bilingual based on one example. In Answer D, the conclusion is invalid because the first premise is faulty.

113. Which of the following is an example of the post hoc fallacy? (Skill 16.3, Rigorous)

A. When the new principal was hired, student-reading scores improved; therefore, the principal caused the increase in scores.

B. Why are we spending money on the space program when our students don't have current textbooks?

C. You can't give your class a 10-minute break. Once you do that, we'll all have to give our students a 10-minute break.

D. You can never believe anything he says because he's not from the same country as we are.

The correct answer is A. A post hoc fallacy assumes that because one event preceded another, the first event caused the second event. In this case, student scores could have increased for other reasons. Answer B is a red herring fallacy in which one raises an irrelevant topic to side track from the first topic. In this case, the space budget and the textbook budget have little effect on each other. Answer C is an example of a slippery slope, in which one event is followed precipitously by another event. Answer D is an ad hominem ("to the man") fallacy in which a person is attacked rather than the concept or interpretation.

114. **Based on the excerpt below from Kate Chopin's short story "The Story of an Hour," what can students infer about the main character? (Skill 16.3, Rigorous)**

> She did not stop to ask if it were or were not a monstrous joy that held her. A clear and exalted perception enabled her to dismiss the suggestion as trivial. She knew that she would weep again when she saw the kind, tender hands folded in death; the face that had never looked save with love upon her, fixed and gray and dead. But she saw beyond that bitter moment a long procession of years to come that would belong to her absolutely. And she opened and spread her arms out to them in welcome.

   A. She dreaded her life as a widow.

   B. Although she loved her husband, she was glad that he was dead for he had never loved her.

   C. She worried that she was too indifferent to her husband's death.

   D. Although they had both loved each other, she was beginning to appreciate that opportunities had opened because of his death.

The correct answer is D. Dismissing her feeling of "monstrous joy" as insignificant, the young woman realizes that she will mourn her husband who had been good to her and had loved her. But that "long procession of years" does not frighten her; instead she recognizes that this new life belongs to her alone and she welcomes it with open arms.

115. **Written on the sixth grade reading level, most of S. E. Hinton's novels (for instance, *The Outsiders*) have the greatest reader appeal with (Skill 16.4, Average Rigor)**

   A. sixth graders.

   B. ninth graders.

   C. twelfth graders.

   D. adults.

The correct answer is B. Adolescents are concerned with their changing bodies, their relationships with each other and adults, and their place in society. Reading *The Outsiders* makes them confront different problems that they are only now beginning to experience as teenagers, such as gangs and social identity. The book is universal in its appeal to adolescents.

116. **What is the best course of action when a child refuses to complete a reading/ literature assignment on the grounds that it is morally objectionable? (Skill 16.4, Average Rigor)**

   A. Speak with the parents and explain the necessity of studying this work

   B. Encourage the child to sample some of the text before making a judgment

   C. Place the child in another teacher's class where they are studying an acceptable work

   D. Provide the student with alternative selections that cover the same performance standards that the rest of the class is learning.

The correct answer is D. In the case of a student finding a reading offensive, it is the responsibility of the teacher to assign another title. As a general rule, it is always advisable to notify parents if a particularly sensitive piece is to be studied.

117. **Which of the following responses to literature typically give middle school students the most problems? (Skill 16.4, Average Rigor)**

   A. Interpretive

   B. Evaluative

   C. Critical

   D. Emotional

The correct answer is B. Middle school readers will exhibit both emotional and interpretive responses. In middle/junior high school, organized study models enable students to identify main ideas and supporting details, to recognize sequential order, to distinguish fact from opinion, and to determine cause/effect relationships. Also, a child's being able to say why a particular book was boring or why a particular poem made him/her sad evidences critical reactions on a fundamental level. It is a bit early for evaluative responses, however. These depend on the reader's consideration of how the piece represents its genre, how well it reflects the social/ethical mores of a given society, and how well the author has approached the subject for freshness and slant. Evaluative responses are made only by a few advanced high school students.

118. How will literature help students in a science class able understand the following passage? (Skill 16.4, Rigorous)

> Just as was the case more than three decades ago, we are still sailing between the Scylla of deferring surgery for too long and risking irreversible left ventricular damage and sudden death, and the Charibdas of operating too early and subjecting the patient to the early risks of operation and the later risks resulting from prosthetic valves.
> --E. Braunwald, *European Heart Journal,* July 2000

A. They will recognize the allusion to Scylla and Charibdas from Greek mythology and understand that the medical community has to select one of two unfavorable choices.

B. They will recognize the allusion to sailing and understand its analogy to doctors as sailors navigating unknown waters.

C. They will recognize that the allusion to Scylla and Charibdas refers to the two islands in Norse mythology where sailors would find themselves shipwrecked and understand how the doctors feel isolated by their choices.

D. They will recognize the metaphor of the heart and relate it to Eros, the character in Greek mythology who represents love. Eros was the love child of Scylla and Charibdas.

The correct answer is A. Scylla and Charibdas were two sea monsters guarding a narrow channel of water. Sailors trying to elude one side would face danger by sailing too close to the other side. The allusion indicates two equally undesirable choices.

119. In preparing a report about William Shakespeare, students are asked to develop a set of interpretive questions to guide their research. Which of the following would not be classified as an interpretive question? (Skill 3.1, Rigorous)

   A. What would be different today if Shakespeare had not written his plays?

   B. How will the plays of Shakespeare affect future generations?

   C. How does the Shakespeare view nature in *A Midsummer's Night Dream* and *Much Ado About Nothing*?

   D. During the Elizabethan age, what roles did young boys take in dramatizing Shakespeare's plays?

The answer is D. This question requires research into the historical facts; *Shakespeare in Love* notwithstanding, women did not act In Shakespeare's plays, and their parts were taken by young boys. Answers A and B are hypothetical questions requiring students to provide original thinking and interpretation. Answer C requires comparison and contrast, which are interpretive skills.

120. Which is not a Biblical allusion? (Skill 16.4, Rigorous)

   A. The patience of Job

   B. Thirty pieces of silver

   C. "Man proposes; God disposes"

   D. "Suffer not yourself to be betrayed by a kiss"

The correct answer is C. This saying is attributed to Thomas à Kempis (1379-1471) in his *Imitation of Christ,* Book 1, chapter 19. Anyone who exhibits the patience of Job is being compared to the Old Testament biblical figure who retained his faith despite being beset by a series of misfortunes. "Thirty pieces of silver" refers to the amount of money paid to Judas to identify Jesus. Used by Patrick Henry, the quote in D is a biblical reference to Judas' betrayal of Judas by a kiss.

121. Recognizing empathy in literature is mostly a/an (Skill 16.4, Rigorous)

    A. emotional response.

    B. interpretive response.

    C. critical response.

    D. evaluative response.

The correct answer is C. In critical responses, students make value judgments about the quality and atmosphere of a text. Through class discussion and written assignments, students react to and assimilate a writer's style and language.

122. The tendency to emphasize and value the qualities and peculiarities of life in a particular geographic area exemplifies (Skill 16.5, Easy)

    A. pragmatism.

    B. regionalism.

    C. pantheism.

    D. abstractionism.

The correct answer is B. Pragmatism is a philosophical doctrine according to which there is no absolute truth. All truths change their trueness as their practical utility increases or decreases. The main representative of this movement is William James who in 1907 published *Pragmatism: A New Way for Some Old Ways of Thinking*. Pantheism is a philosophy according to which God is omnipresent in the world, everything is God and God is everything. The great representative of this sensibility is Spinoza. Also, the works of writers such as Wordsworth, Shelly and Emerson illustrate this doctrine. Abstract Expressionism is one of the most important movements in American art. It began in the 1940's with artists such as Willem de Kooning, Mark Rothko and Arshile Gorky. The paintings are usually large and non-representational.

123. **In preparing a unit on 20th century immigration you prepare a list of books for students to read. Which book would not be appropriate for this topic? (Skill 16.7, Average Rigor)**

    A. *The Things They Carried* by Tim O'Brien

    B. *Exodus* by Leon Uris

    C. *The Joy Luck Club* by Amy Tan

    D. *Tortilla Flats* by John Steinbeck

The correct answer is A. O'Brien's book centers on American soldiers serving in Viet Nam. Uris' book details the founding of Israel after World War II. Tan's novel contrasts her family's life in China and in the United States. Steinbeck's novel illustrates the plight of Mexican migrant workers.

124. **To explore the relationship of literature to modern life, which of these activities would not enable students to explore comparable themes? (Skill 16.7, Average Rigor)**

    A. After studying various world events, such as the Palestinian-Israeli conflict, students write an updated version of *Romeo and Juliet* using modern characters and settings.

    B. Before studying *Romeo and Juliet,* students watch *West Side Story*.

    C. Students research the major themes of *Romeo and Juliet* by studying news stories and finding modern counterparts for the story.

    D. Students would explore compare the romantic themes of *Romeo and Juliet* and *The Taming of the Shrew*.

The correct answer is D. By comparing the two plays by Shakespeare, students will be focusing on the culture of the period in which the plays were written. In Answer A, students should be able to recognize modern parallels with current culture clashes. By comparing the *Romeo and Juliet* to the 1950's update of *West Side Story,* students can study how themes are similar in two completely different historical periods. In Answer C, students can study local, national, and international news for comparable stories and themes.

125. Mr. Phillips is creating a unit to study *To Kill a Mockingbird* and wants to familiarize his high school freshmen with the attitudes and issues of the historical period. Which activity would familiarize students with the attitudes and issues of the Depression-era South? (Skill 16.7, Rigorous)

   A. Create a detailed timeline of 15-20 social, cultural, and political events that focus on race relations in the 1930s.

   B. Research and report on the life of its author Harper Lee. Compare her background with the events in the book.

   C. Watch the movie version and note language and dress.

   D. Write a research report on the stock market crash of 1929 and its effects.

The correct answer is A. By identifying the social, cultural, and political events of the 1930s, students will better understand the attitudes and values of America during the time of the novel. While researching the author's life could add depth to their understanding of the novel, it is unnecessary to the appreciation of the novel by itself. The movie version is an accurate depiction of the novel's setting but it focuses on the events in the novel, not the external factors that fostered the conflict. The stock market crash and the subsequent Great Depression would be important to note on the timeline but students would be distracted from themes of the book by narrowing their focus to only these two events.